D1423697

Principles of
Literary Criticism

'To us Richards was infinitely more than a brilliantly new literary critic: he was our guide, our evangelist, who revealed to us, in a succession of astounding lightning flashes, the entire expanse of the Modern World.'

Christopher Isherwood

'*Principles of Literary Criticism* is an important contribution to the rehabilitation of English criticism – perhaps because of its sustained nature, the most important contribution yet made. Mr Richards begins with an account of the present chaos of critical theories and follows with an analysis of the fallacy in modern aesthetics.'

Herbert Read, The Criterion

'Richards is simply the most influential theorist of the century.'

George Watson, The Literary Critics

I. A.
Richards

Principles of
Literary Criticism

London and New York

First published 1924
by Routledge & Kegan Paul
Second edition (with two new appendices) 1926

First published in Routledge Classics 2001
by Routledge
11 New Fetter Lane, London EC4P 4EE
29 West 35th Street, New York, NY 10001

Reprinted 2002

Routledge is an imprint of the Taylor & Francis Group

Typeset in Joanna by RefineCatch Limited, Bungay, Suffolk
Printed and bound in Great Britain by
TJ International Ltd, Padstow, Cornwall

All rights reserved. No part of this book may be reprinted
or reproduced or utilised in any form or by any electronic,
mechanical, or other means, now known or hereafter
invented, including photocopying and recording, or in
any information storage or retrieval system, without
permission in writing from the publishers.

British Library Cataloguing in Publication Data
A catalogue record for this book is available from the British Library

Library of Congress Cataloging in Publication Data
A catalog record for this book has been applied for

ISBN 0–415–25402–7

CONTENTS

PREFACE

A book is a machine to think with, but it need not, therefore, usurp the functions either of the bellows or the locomotive. This book might better be compared to a loom on which it is supposed to re-weave some ravelled parts of our civilization. What is most important about it, the interconnection of its several points of view, might have been exhibited, though not with equal clarity, in a pamphlet or in a two-volume work. Few of the separate items are original. One does not expect novel cards when playing so traditional a game; it is the hand which matters. I have chosen to present it here on the smallest scale which would allow me to fit together the various positions adopted into a whole of some firmness. The elaborations and expansions which suggest themselves have been constantly cut short at the point at which I thought that the reader would be able to see for himself how they would continue. The danger of this procedure, which otherwise has great advantages both for him and for me, is that the different parts of a connected account such as this mutually illumine one another. The writer, who has, or should have, the whole position in his mind throughout, may overlook sources of obscurity for the reader, due to the serial form of the exposition. This I have endeavoured to prevent by means of numerous cross-references, forwards and backwards.

But some further explanation of the structure of the book is due to the reader. At sundry points – notably in Chapters Six, Seven, and Eleven to Fifteen – its progress appears to be interrupted by lengthy excursions into theory of value, or into general psychology. These I would have omitted if it had seemed in any way possible to develop the argument of the rest strongly and clearly in their absence. Criticism, as I understand it, is the endeavour to discriminate between experiences and to evaluate them. We cannot do this without some understanding of the nature of experience, or without theories of valuation and communication. Such principles as apply in criticism must be taken from these more fundamental studies. All other critical principles are arbitrary, and the history of the subject is a record of their obstructive influence. The view of value implied throughout is one which must be held in some form by very many persons. Yet I have been unable to discover anywhere any statement of it to which I might satisfactorily refer the reader. I had to make a fairly full statement with applications and illustrations myself. And I had to put in the forefront of the book where, to the more exclusively literary reader, it will appear a dry and uninviting tract to be crossed for problematical advantages. The same remarks apply to the second theoretical expansion, the psychological chapters; they are to the value chapters, I fear, as a Sahara to a Gobi. No other choice seemed open if I did not wish any later, critical, sections to be misunderstood, than to include as a preliminary what amounts to a concise treatise on psychology. For nearly all the topics of psychology are raised at one point or another by criticism, but raised from an angle which ordinary text-books do not contemplate.

These two deserts passed, the rest of the book accords, I

believe, much more closely with what may be expected of an essay in criticism, although the language in which some of the more obvious remarks are couched may seem unnecessarily repellant. The explanation of much of the turgid uncouthness of its terminology is the desire to link even the commonplaces of criticism to a systematic exposition of psychology. The reader who appreciates the advantages so gained will be forgiving.

I have carefully remembered throughout that I am not writing for specialists alone. The omissions, particularly as to qualifications and reservations, which this fact entails, should in fairness to myself be mentioned.

My book, I fear, will seem to many sadly lacking in the condiments which have come to be expected in writings upon literature. Critics and even theorists in criticism currently assume that their first duty is to be moving, to excite in the mind emotions appropriate to their august subject-matter. This endeavour I have declined. I have used, I believe, few words which I could not define in the actual use which I have made of them, and necesarily such words have little or no emotive power. I have comforted myself with the reflection that there is perhaps something debilitated about a taste for speculation which requires a flavouring of the eternal and the ultimate or even of the literary spices, mystery and profundity. Mixed modes of writing which enlist the reader's feeling as well as his thinking are becoming dangerous to the modern consciousness with its increasing awareness of the distinction. Thought and feeling are able to mislead one another at present in ways which were hardly possible six centuries ago. We need a spell of purer science and purer poetry before the two can again be mixed, if indeed this will ever become once more desirable. In the Second Edition I added a note on Mr. Eliot's poetry which will elucidate what I mean here by purity, and some supplementary remarks upon Value; in the Third, a few minor improvements have been made.

It should be borne in mind that the knowledge which the

men of A.D. 3000 will possess, if all goes well, may make all our aesthetics, all our psychology, all our modern theory of value, look pitiful. Poor indeed would be the prospect if this were not so. The thought, 'What shall we do with the powers, which we are so rapidly developing, and what will happen to us if we cannot learn to guide them in time?' already marks for many people the chief interest of existence. The controversies which the world has known in the past are as nothing to those which are ahead. I would wish this book to be regarded as a contribution towards these choices of the future.

Between the possession of ideas and their application there is a gulf. Every teacher winces when he remembers this. As an attempt to attack this difficulty, I am preparing a companion volume, *Practical Criticism*. Extremely good and extremely bad poems were put *unsigned* before a large and able audience. The comments they wrote at leisure give, as it were, a stereoscopic view of the poem and of possible opinion on it. This material when systematically analysed, provides, not only an interesting commentary upon the state of contemporary culture, but a new and powerful educational instrument.

I. A. R.
Cambridge, May 1928.

.

1

THE CHAOS OF CRITICAL THEORIES

O monstrous! but one half-pennyworth of bread to this
intolerable deal of sack!

The First Part of King Henry the Fourth

The literature of Criticism is not small or negligible, and its chief
figures, from Aristotle onwards, have often been among the first
intellects of their age. Yet the modern student, surveying the field
and noting the simplicity of the task attempted and the fragments of work achieved, may reasonably wonder what has been
and is amiss. For the experiences with which criticism is concerned are exceptionally accessible, we have only to open the
book, stand before the picture, have the music played, spread out
the rug, pour out the wine, and the material upon which the
critic works is presently before us. Even too abundantly, in
too great fullness perhaps: 'More warmth than Adam needs'
the critic may complain, echoing Milton's complaint against the
climate of the Garden of Eden; but he is fortunate not to be

starved of matter like the investigator of psychoplasm. And the questions which the critic seeks to answer, intricate though they are, do not seem to be extraordinarily difficult. What gives the experience of reading a certain poem its value? How is this experience better than another? Why prefer this picture to that? In which ways should we listen to music so as to receive the most valuable moments? Why is one opinion about works of art not as good as another? These are the fundamental questions which criticism is required to answer, together with such preliminary questions – What is a picture, a poem, a piece of music? How can experiences be compared? What is value? – as may be required in order to approach these questions.

But if we now turn to consider what are the results yielded by the best minds pondering these questions in the light of the eminently accessible experiences provided by the Arts, we discover an almost empty garner. A few conjectures, a supply of admonitions, many acute isolated observations, some brilliant guesses, much oratory and applied poetry, inexhaustible confusion, a sufficiency of dogma, no small stock of prejudices, whimsies and crotchets, a profusion of mysticism, a little genuine speculation, sundry stray inspirations, pregnant hints and random aperçus; of such as these, it may be said without exaggeration, is extant critical theory composed.

A few specimens of the most famous utterances of Aristotle, Longinus, Horace, Boileau, Dryden, Addison, Wordsworth, Coleridge, Carlyle, Matthew Arnold and some more modern authors, will justify this assertion. 'All men naturally receive pleasure from imitation.' 'Poetry is chiefly conversant about general truth.' 'It demands an enthusiasm allied to madness; transported out of ourselves we become what we imagine.' 'Beautiful words are the very and peculiar light of the mind.' 'Let the work be what you like, provided it has simplicity and unity.' 'De Gustibus. . . .' 'Of writing well right thinking is the beginning and the fount.' 'We must never separate ourselves from

Nature.' 'Delight is the chief, if not the only end; instruction can be admitted but in the second place.' 'The pleasures of Fancy are more conducive to health than those of the understandiing.' 'The spontaneous overflow of powerful feeling.' 'The best words in the best order.' 'The whole soul of man in activity.' 'Unity in variety.' 'The synthetic and magical power of the imagination.' 'The eye on the object.' 'The disimprsionment of the soul of fact.' 'The identification of content and form.' 'A criticism of Life.' 'Empathy favourable to our existence.' 'Significant form.' 'The expression of impressions,' etc. etc.

Such are the pinnacles, the *apices* of critical theory, the heights gained in the past by the best thinkers in their attempt to reach explanations of the value of the arts. Some of them, many of them indeed, are profitable starting-points for reflection, but neither together, nor singly, nor in any combination do they give what is required. Above them and below them, around and about them can be found other things of value, of service for the appreciation of particular poems and works of art; comment, elucidation, appraisal, much that is fit occupation for the con-templative mind. But apart from hints such *as* have been cited, no explanations. The central question, What is the value of the arts, why are they worth the devotion of the keenest hours of the best minds, and what is their place in the system of human endeavours? is left almost untouched, although without some clear view it would seem that even the most judicious critic must often lose his sense of position.

But perhaps the literature of Criticism is the wrong place in which to expect such an inquiry. Philosophers, Moralists and Aestheticians are perhaps the competent authorities? There is certainly no lack of treatises upon the Good and the Beautiful, upon Value and upon the Aesthetic State, and the treasures of earnest endeavour lavished upon these topics have not been in vain. Those investigators who have relied upon Reason, upon the

Select Intuition and the Ineluctable Argument, who have sat down without the necessary facts to think the matter out, have at least thoroughly discredited a method which apart from their labours would hardly have been suspected of the barrenness it has shown. And those who, following Fechner, have turned instead to the collection and analysis of concrete, particular facts and to empirical research into aesthetics have supplied a host of details to psychology. In recent years especially, much useful information upon the process which make up the appreciation of works of art has been skilfully elicited. But it is showing no ingratitude to these investigators if we point out certain defects of almost all experimental work on aesthetics, which make their results at best of only indirect service to our wider problems.

The most obvious of these concerns their inevitable choice of experiments. Only the simplest human activities are at present amenable to laboratory methods. Aestheticians have therefore been compelled to begin with as simple form of 'aesthetic choice' as can be devised. In practice, line-lengths and elementary forms, single notes and phrases, single colours and simple collocations, nonsense syllables, metronomic beats, skeleton rhythms and metres and similar simplifications have alone been open to investigation. Such more complex objects as have been examined have yielded very uncertain results, for reasons which anyone who has ever both looked at a picture or read a poem and been inside a psychological laboratory or conversed with a representative psychologist will understand.

The generalizations to be drawn from these simple experiments are, if we do not expect too much, encouraging. Some light upon obscure processes, such as empathy, and upon the intervention of muscular imagery and tendencies to action into the apprehension of shapes and of sequences of sounds which had been supposed to be apprehended by visual or auditory apparatus alone, some interesting facts about the plasticity of rhythm, some approach towards a classification of the different ways in which colours may be regarded, increased recognition of the complexity of even the simplest activities, these and similar results have been well worth the trouble expended. But more important has been the revelation of the great variety in the responses which even the simplest stimuli elicit. Even so unambiguous an object as a plain colour, it has been found, can arouse in different persons and in the same person at different times extremely different states of mind. From this result it may seem no illegitimate step to conclude that highly complex objects, such as pictures, will arouse a still greater variety of responses, a conclusion very awkward for any theory of criticism, since it would appear to decide adversely the preliminary question: 'How may experiences be compared?' which any such theory must settle if the more fundamental questions of value are to be satisfactorily approached.

But just here a crucial point arises. 'There seems to be good reason to suppose that the more simple the object contemplated the more varied the responses will be which can be expected from it. For it is difficult, perhaps impossible, to contemplate a comparatively simple object by itself. Inevitably it is taken by the contemplator into some context, and made part of some larger whole, and under such experimental conditions as have yet been devised it seems not possible to guarantee the kind of context into which it is taken. A comparison with the case of words is instructive. A single word by itself, let us say 'night', will raise almost as many different thoughts and feelings as there are persons who hear it. The range of variety with a single word is very little restricted. But put it into a sentence and the variation is narrowed; put it into the context of a whole passage, and it is still further fixed; and let it occur in such an intricate whole as a poem and the responses of competent readers may have a similarity which only its occurrence in such a whole can secure. The point will arise for discussion when the problem of corroboration for critical judgements is dealt with later (cf. pp. 166, 178,

192). It had to be mentioned here in order to explain why the theory of criticism shows no great dependence upon experimental aesthetics, useful in many respects as these investigations are.

2

THE PHANTOM AESTHETIC STATE

None of his follies will he repent, none will he wish to repeat;
no happier lot can be assigned to man.

Wilhelm Meister

A more serious defect in aesthetics is the avoidance of considerations as to value. It is true that an ill-judged introduction of
value considerations usually leads to disaster, as in Tolstoy's case.
But the fact that some of the experiences to which the arts give
rise are valuable and take the form they do because of their value
is not irrelevant. Whether this fact is of service in analysis will
naturally depend upon the theory of value adopted. But to leave
it out of account altogether is to run the risk of missing the clue
to the whole matter. And the clue has in fact been missed.

All modern aesthetics rests upon an assumption which has
been strangely little discussed, the assumption that there is a
distinct *kind* of mental activity present in what are called aesthetic experiences. Ever since 'the first rational word concerning

beauty'[1] was spoken by Kant, the attempt to define the 'judge-ment of taste' as concerning pleasure which is disinterested, universal, unintellectual, and not to be confused with the pleas-ures of sense or of ordinary emotions, in short to make it a thing *sui generis*, has continued. Thus arises the phantom problem of the aesthetic mode or aesthetic state, a legacy from the days of abstract investigation into the Good, the Beautiful and the True.

The temptation to align this tripartite division with a similar division into Will, Feeling and Thought was irresistible. 'All the faculties of the Soul, or capacities, are reducible to three, which do not admit of any further derivation from a common ground: the *faculty of knowledge*, the *feeling of pleasure or displeasure*, and the *faculty of desire*'[2] said Kant. Legislative for each of these faculties stood Understanding, Judgement and Reason respectively. 'Between the faculties of knowledge and desire stands the feel-ing of pleasure, just as judgement is intermediate between understanding and reason.' And he went on to discuss aesthe-tics as appertaining to the province of judgement, the middle one of these three, the first and last having already occupied him in his two other Critiques of Pure and Practical Reason respectively. The effect was virtually to annex aesthetics to Idealism, in which fabric it has ever since continued to serve important purposes.

This accident of formal correspondence has had an influence upon speculation which would be ridiculous if it had not been so disastrous. It is difficult even now to get out of ruts which have been seen to lead nowhere. With the identification of the provinces of Truth and Thought no quarrel arises, and the Will and the Good are, as we shall see, intimately connected, but the attempts to fit Beauty into a neat pigeon-hole with Feeling have

---

[1] Hegel's dictum, *History of Philosophy*, iii, 543.
[2] *Critique of Judgment*, transl. by Meredith, p. 15. ·

led to calamitous distortions. It is now generally abandoned,[1] although echoes of it can be heard everywhere in critical writings. The peculiar use of 'emotion' by reviewers, and the prevalence of the phrase 'aesthetic emotion' is one of them. In view, then, of the objections to Feeling, something else, some special mode of mental activity, had to be found, to which Beauty could belong. Hence arose the aesthetic mode. Truth was the object of the inquiring activity, of the Intellectual or Theoretical part of the mind, and the Good that of the willing, desiring, practical part; what part could be found for the Beautiful? Some activity that was neither inquisitive nor practical, that did not question and did not seek to use. The result was the aesthetic, the contemplative, activity which is still defined, in most treatments,[2] by these negative conditions alone, as that mode of commerce with things which is neither intellectual inquiry into their nature, nor an attempt to make them satisfy our desire. The experiences which arise in contemplating objects of art were then discovered to be describable in some such terms, and system secured a temporary triumph.

It is true that many of these experiences do present peculiarities, both in the intellectual interest which is present and in the way in which the development of desires within them takes place, and these peculiarities – detachment, impersonality, serenity and so forth – are of great interest. They will have to be carefully examined in the sequel.

We shall find that two entirely different sets of characters are involved. They arise from quite different causes but are hard to distinguish introspectively. Taken as marking off a special province for inquiry they are most unsatisfactory. They would yield for our purposes, even if they were not so ambiguous, a diagonal or slant classification. Some of the experiences which most

---

[1] Dr. Bosanquet was one of the last adherents. See his *Three Lectures on Æsthetics*.
[2] E.g. Vernon Lee, *The Beautiful*.

require to be considered would be left out and many which arc without importance brought in. To choose the aesthetic state as the starting-point for an inquiry into the values of the arts is in fact somewhat like choosing 'rectangular, and red in parts' as a definition of a picture. We should find ourselves ultimately discussing a different collection of things from those we intended to discuss.

But the problem remains – Is there any such thing as the aesthetic state, or any asethetic character of experiences which is *sui generis*? Not many explicit arguments have ever been given for one. Vernon Lee, it is true, in *Beauty and Ugliness*, p. 10, argues that 'a relation entirely *sui generis* between visible and audible forms and ourselves' can be deduced from the fact 'that given proportions, shapes, patterns, compositions have a tendency to recur in art'. How this can be done it is hard to divine. Arsenic tends to recur in murder cases, and tennis in the summer, but no characters or relations *sui generis* anywhere are thereby proved. Obviously you can only tell whether anything is like or unlike other things by examining it and them, and to notice that one case of it is like another case of it, is not helpful. It may be suspected that where the argument is so confused, the original question was not very clear.

The question is whether a certain kind of experience is or is not *like* other kinds of experience. Plainly it is a question as to degree of likeness. Be it granted at once, to clear the air, that there are all sorts of experiences involved in the values of the arts, and that attributions of Beauty spring from all sorts of causes. Is there among these one kind of experience as different from experiences which don't so occur as, say envy is from remembering, or as mathematical calculation is from eating cherries? And what degree of difference would make it specific? Put this way it is plainly not an easy question to answer. These differences, none of them measurable, are of varying degree, and all are hard to estimate. Yet the vast majority of post-Kantian writers, and many before him, have unhesitatingly replied, 'Yes! the aesthetic experience is peculiar and specific.' And their grounds, when not merely verbal, have usually been those of direct inspection.

It requires some audacity to run counter to such a tradition, and I do not do so without reflection. Yet, after all, the matter is one of classification, and when so many other divisions in psychology are being questioned and reorganized, this also may be re-examined.

The case for a distinct aesthetic species of experience can take two forms. It may be held that there is some unique kind of mental element which enters into aesthetic experiences and into no others. Thus Mr. Clive Bell used to maintain the existence of a unique emotion 'aesthetic emotion' as the *differentia*. But psychology has no place for such an entity. What other will be suggested? Empathy, for example, as Vernon Lee herself insists, enters into innumerable other experiences as well as into aesthetic experiences. I do not think any will be proposed.

Alternatively, the aesthetic experience may contain no unique constituent, and be of the usual stuff but with a special form. This is what it is commonly supposed to be. Now the special form as it is usually described – in terms of disinterestedness, detachment, distance, impersonality, subjective universality, and so forth – this form, I shall try to show later, is sometimes no more than a consequence of the incidence of the experience, a condition or an effect of communication. But sometimes a structure which can be described in the same terms is an essential feature of the experience, the feature in fact upon which its value depends. In other words, at least two different sets of characters, due to different causes, are, in current usage, ambiguously covered by the term 'aesthetic.' It is very necessary to distinguish the sense in which merely putting something in a frame or writing it in verse gives it an 'aesthetic character', from a sense in which value is implied. This confusion, together with other confusions,[1] has made the term nearly useless.

The aesthetic mode is generally supposed to be a peculiar way of regarding things which can be exercised, whether the resulting experiences are valuable, disvaluable or indifferent. It is intended to cover the experience of ugliness as well as that of beauty, and also intermediate experiences. What I wish to maintain is that there is no such mode, that the experience of ugliness has nothing in common with that of beauty, which both do not share with innumerable other experiences no one (except Croce; but this qualification is often required) would dream of calling aesthetic. But a narrower sense of aesthetic is also found in which it *is* confined to experiences of beauty and does imply value. And with regard to this, while admitting that such experiences can be distinguished, I shall be at pains to show that they are closely similar to many other experiences, that they differ chiefly in the connections between their constituents, and that they are only a further development, a finer organization of ordinary experiences, and not in the least a new and different kind of thing. When we look at a picture, or read a poem, or listen to music, we are not doing something quite unlike what we were doing on our way to the Gallery or when we dressed in the morning. The fashion in which the experience is caused in us is different, and as a rule the experience is more complex and, if we are successful, more unified. But our activity is not of a fundamentally different kind. To assume that it is, puts difficulties in the way of describing and explaining it, which are unnecessary and which no one has yet succeeded in overcoming.

The point here raised, and particularly the distinction between the two quite different sets of characters, on the ground of

---

[1] E.g. Any choice for which the chooser cannot give his reasons tends in the laboratory to be called an 'aesthetic choice'.

which an experience may be described as aesthetic or
impersonal and disinterested, will become clearer at a later
stage.[1]

A further objection to the assumption of a peculiar aesthetic
attitude is that it makes smooth the way for the idea of a peculiar
aesthetic value, a pure art value. Postulate a peculiar kind of
experience, aesthetic experience, and it is an easy step to the
postulation of a peculiar unique value, different in kind and cut
off from the other values of ordinary experiences. 'To appreciate
a work of art we need bring with us nothing from life, no knowledge of its ideas and affairs, no familiarity with its emotions.'[2] So
runs a recent extreme statement of the Aesthetic Hypothesis,
which has had much success. To quote another example less
drastic but also carrying with it the implication that aesthetic
experiences are sui generis, and their value is not of the same kind
as other values. 'Its nature is to be not part, nor yet a copy, of the
real world (as we commonly understand that phrase), but a
world in itself independent, complete, autonomous.'[3]

This view of the arts as providing a private heaven for aes-
thetes is, as will appear later, a great impediment to the investigation of their value. The effects upon the general attitudes of those
who accept it uncritically are also often regrettable; while the
effects upon literature and the arts have been noticeable, in a
narrowing and restriction of the interests active, in preciousness,
artificiality and spurious aloofness. Art envisaged as a mystic,
ineffable virtue is a close relative of the 'aesthetic mood', and
may easily be pernicious in its effects, through the habits of
mind which, as an idea, it fosters, and to which, as a mystery, it
appeals.

---

[1] Cf. Chapters Ten and Thirty-two, and Impersonality, Index.
[2] Clive Bell, Art, p. 25.
[3] A. C. Bradley, Oxford Lectures on Poetry, p. 5.

3

THE LANGUAGE OF CRITICISM

> . . . I too have seen
> My vision of the rainbow Aureoled face
> Of her whom men name Beauty: proud, austere:
> Divinely fugitive, that haunts the world . . . .
> *The Dominion of Dreams*

Whatever the disadvantages of modern aesthetics as a basis for a theory of Criticism, the great advance made upon prescientific speculation into the nature of Beauty must also be recognized. That paralysing apparition Beauty, the ineffable, ultimate, unanalysable, simple Idea, has at least been dismissed and with her have departed or will soon depart a flock of equally bogus entities. Poetry and inspiration together, it is true, still dignify respectable quarters with their presence.

'Poetry, like life, is one thing. . . . Essentially a continuous substance or energy, poetry is historically a connected movement, a series of successive integrated manifestations. Each poet, from Homer or the predecessors of Homer to our own day, has been, to some degree and at some point, the voice of the movement

THE LANGUAGE OF CRITICISM 15

and energy of poetry; in him, poetry has for the moment become visible, audible, incarnate; and his extant poems are the record left of that partial transitory incarnation. . . . The progress of poetry, with its vast power and exalted function, is immortal.'[1]

A diligent search will still find many other Mystic Beings, for the most part of a less august nature, sheltering in verbal thickets. Construction, Design, Form, Rhythm, Expression . . . are more often than not mere *vacua* in discourse, for which a theory of criticism should provide explainable substitutes.

While current attitudes to language persist, this difficulty of the linguistic phantom must still continue. It has to be recognized that all our natural turns of speech are misleading, especially those we use in discussing works of art. We become so accustomed to them that even when we are aware that they are ellipses, it is easy to forget the fact. And it has been extremely difficult in many cases to discover that any ellipsis is present. We are accustomed to say that a picture is beautiful, instead of saying that it causes an experience in us which is valuable in certain ways.[2] The discovery that the remark, 'This is beautiful,' must be turned round and expanded in this way before it is anything but

---

[1] G. W. Mackail, *Lectures on Poetry*. Introduction.

[2] We can diagrammatically represent the delusion as follows. What actually occurs is that A, a work of art, causes E an effect *in us*, which has the character b; A *causes* E. We *speak* as though we perceived that A has the quality B (Beauty); we are perceiving A; and if we are not careful we think so too. No one of our recent revolutions in thought is more important than this progressive rediscovery of what we are talking about. It is being inevitably followed by wide changes in our attitudes to the world and to fellow-creatures. One current in this change is towards tolerance, another towards scepticism, a third towards far more secure founding of our motives of action. The startling philosophical changes in the general outlook sometimes predicted for Relativity (or for popular ideas about it when once they become widespread) appear likely, if they occur at all, to be engulfed by these more unobtrusive but more domestic changes.

a mere noise signalling the fact that we approve of the picture, was a great and difficult achievement. Even today, such is the insidious power of grammatical forms, the belief that there is such a quality or attribute, namely Beauty, which attaches to the things which we rightly call beautiful, is probably inevitable for all reflective persons at a certain stage of their mental development.

Even among those who have escaped from this delusion and are well aware that we continually talk as though things possess qualities, when what we ought to say is that they cause effects in us of one kind or another, the fallacy of 'projecting' the effect and making it a quality of its cause tends to recur. When it does so it gives a peculiar obliquity to thought and although few competent persons are nowadays so deluded as actually to hold the mystical view that there is a quality Beauty which inheres or attaches to external objects, yet throughout all the discussion of works of art the drag exercised by language towards this view can be felt. It perceptibly increases the difficulty of innumerable problems and we shall have constantly to allow for it. Such terms as 'construction', 'form', 'balance', 'composition', 'design', 'unity', 'expression', for all the arts; as 'depth', 'movement' 'texture', 'solidity', in the criticism of painting; as 'rhythm', 'stress', 'plot', 'character', in literary criticism; as 'harmony', 'atmosphere', 'development', in music, are instances. All these terms are currently used as though they stood for qualities inherent in things outside the mind, as a painting, in the sense of an assemblage of pigments, is undoubtedly outside the mind. Even the difficulty of discovering, in the case of poetry, what thing other than print and paper is there for these alleged qualities to belong to, has not checked the tendency.

But indeed language has succeeded until recently in hiding from us almost all the things we talk about. Whether we are discussing music, poetry, painting, sculpture or architecture, we are forced to speak as though certain physical objects –

vibrations of strings and of columns of air, marks printed on paper, canvasses and pigments, masses of marble, fabrics of free stone, are what we are talking about. And yet the remarks we make as critics do not apply to such objects but to states of mind, to experiences.

A certain strangeness about this view is often felt but diminishes with reflection. If anyone says that 'The May Queen' is sentimental, it is not difficult to agree that he is referring to a state of mind. But if he declares that the masses in a Giotto exactly balance one another, this is less apparent, and, if he goes on to discuss time in music, form in visual art, plot in drama, the fact that he is all the while talking about mental happenings becomes concealed. The verbal apparatus comes between us and the things with which we are really dealing. Words which are useful, indeed invaluable, as handy stop-gaps and makeshifts in conversation, but which need elaborate expansions before they can be used with precision, are treated as simply as people's proper names. So it becomes natural to seek for the things these words appear to stand for, and thus arise innumerable subtle investigations, doomed *ab initio* as regards their main intent to failure.

We must be prepared then to translate, into phrases pedantic and uncouth, all the too simple utterances which the conversational decencies exact. We shall find later, in their peculiar emotive power, the main reason why, in spite of all manner of confusions and inconveniences, these current ways of speaking are retained. For emotive purposes they are indispensable, but for clarity, for the examination of what is actually happening, translations are equally a necessity.

Moet critical remarks state in an abbreviated form that an object causes certain experiences, and as a rule the form of the statement is such as to suggest that the object has been said to possess certain qualities. But often the critic goes further and affirms that the effect in his mind is due to special particular features of the object. In this case he is pointing out something about the object in addition to its effect upon him, and this fuller kind of criticism is what we desire. Before his insight can greatly benefit, however, a very clear demarcation between the object, with its features, and his experience, which is the effect of contemplating it, is necessary. The bulk of critical literature is unfortunately made up of examples of their confusion.

It will be convenient at this point to introduce two definitions. In a full critical statement which states not only that an experience is valuable in certain ways, but also that it is caused by certain features in a contemplated object, the part which describes the value of the experience we shall call the *critical* part. That which describes the object we shall call the *technical* part. Thus to say that we feel differently towards wooden crosses and stone crosses is a technical remark. And to say that metre is more suited to the tender passion than is prose would be, as it stands, a technical remark, but here it is evident that a critical part might easily be also present. All remarks as to the ways and means by which experiences arise or are brought about are technical, but critical remarks are about the values of experiences and the reasons for regarding them as valuable, or not valuable. We shall endeavour in what follows to show that critical remarks are merely a branch of psychological remarks, and that no special ethical or metaphysical ideas need be introduced to explain value.

The distinction between technical and critical remarks is of real importance. Confusion here is responsible for some most curious passages in the histories of the arts. A certain technique in certain cases produces admirable results; the obvious features of this technique come to be regarded at first as sure signs of excellence, and later as the excellence itself. For a while nothing, however admirable, which does not show these superficial marks, gets fair consideration. Thomas Rymer's denigration of

Shakespeare, Dr. Johnson's view of Milton's pauses, the aftermath of the triumph of Pope, archaistic sculpture, the Greek poses in the compositions of David, the imitations of Cézanne, are famous instances; they could be multiplied indefinitely. The converse case is equally common. An obvious technical blemish in a special case is recognized. It may be too many S's in a particular line, or the irregularity and rimelessness of a 'Pindaric' Ode; henceforth any line superficially similar.

The lustre of the long convolvulusses,

any unrhymed lyric, is regarded as defective.

This trick of judging the whole by the detail, instead of the other way about, of mistaking the means for the end, the technique for the value, is in fact much the most successful of the snares which waylay the critic. Only the teacher knows (and sometimes he is guilty himself) how great is the number of readers who think, for example, that a defective rime – bough's house, bush thrush, blood good – is sufficient ground for condemning a poem in the neglect of all other considerations. Such sticklers, like those with a scansion obsession (due as a rule to Exercises in Latin Verse), have little understanding of poetry. We pay attention to externals when we do not know what else to do with a poem.

4

COMMUNICATION AND
THE ARTIST

Poetry is the record of the best and happiest moments of the
happiest and best minds.

The Defence of Poetry

The two pillars upon which a theory of criticism must rest are an
account of value and an account of communication. We do not
sufficiently realize how great a part of our experience takes the
form it does, because we are social beings and accustomed to
communication from infancy. That we acquire many of our ways
of thinking and feeling from parents and others is, of course, a
commonplace. But the effects of communication go much
deeper than this. The very structure of our minds is largely
determined by the fact that man has been engaged in communi-
cating for so many hundreds of thousands of years, throughout
the course of his human development and beyond even that. A
large part of the distinctive features of the mind are due to its
being an instrument for communication. An experience has to

be formed, no doubt, before it is communicated, but it takes the form it does largely because it may have to be communicated. The emphasis which natural selection has put upon communicative ability is overwhelming.

There are very many problems of psychology, from those with which some of the exponents of *Gestalt theorie* are grappling to those by which psycho-analysts are bewildered, for which this neglected, this almost overlooked aspect of the mind may provide a key, but it is pre-eminently in regard to the arts that it is of service. For the arts are the supreme form of the communicative activity. As we shall see, most of the difficult and obscure points about the structures of the arts, for example the priority of formal elements to content,[1] or the impersonality and detachment so much stressed by aestheticians, become easily intelligible as soon as we consider them from this angle. But a possible misunderstanding must be guarded against. Although it is as a communicator that it is most profitable to consider the artist, it is by no means true that he commonly looks upon himself in this light. In the course of his work he is not as a rule deliberately and consciously engaged in a communicative endeavour. When asked, he is more likely than not to reply that communication is an irrelevant or at best a minor issue, and that what he is making is something which is beautiful in itself, or satisfying to him personally, or something expressive, in a more or less vague sense, of his emotions, or of himself, something personal and individual. That other people are going to study it, and to receive experiences from it may seem to him a merely accidental, inessential circumstance. More modestly still, he may say that when he works he is merely amusing himself.

That the artist is not as a rule consciously concerned with communication, but with getting the work, the poem or play or statue or painting or whatever it is, 'right', apparently regardless

[1] See Chapter Twenty-four.

of its communicative efficacy, is easily explained. To make the work 'embody', accord with, and represent the precise experience upon which its value depends is his major preoccupation, in difficult cases an overmastering preoccupation, and the dissipation of attention which would be involved if he considered the communicative side as a separate issue would be fatal in most serious work. He cannot stop to consider how the public or even how especially well qualified sections of the public may like it or respond to it. He is wise, therefore, to keep all such considerations out of mind altogether. Those artists and poets who can be suspected of close separate attention to the communicative aspect tend (there are exceptions to this, of which Shakespeare might be one) to fall into a subordinate rank.

But this conscious neglect of communication does not in the least diminish the importance of the communicative aspect. It would only do so if we were prepared to admit that only our conscious activities matter. The very process of getting the work 'right' has itself, so far as the artist is normal,[1] immense communicative consequences. Apart from certain special cases, to be discussed later, it will, when 'right', have much greater communicative power than it would have had if 'wrong'. The degree to which it accords with the relevant experience of the artist is a measure of the degree to which it will arouse similar experiences in others.

But more narrowly the reluctance of the artist to consider communication as one of his main aims, and his denial that he is at all influenced in his work by a desire to affect other people, is no evidence that communication is not actually his principal object. On a simple view of psychology, which overlooked unconscious motives, it would be, but not on any view of human behaviour which is in the least adequate. When we find the artist constantly struggling towards impersonality, towards a

[1] This point will be discussed in Chapter Twenty-four.

structure for his work which excludes his private, eccentric, momentary idiosyncrasies, and using always as its basis those elements which are most uniform in their effects upon impulses; when we find private works of art, works which satisfy the artist,[1] but are incomprehensible to everybody else, so rare, and the publicity of the work so constantly and so intimately bound up with its appeal to the artist himself, it is difficult to believe that efficacy for communication is not a main part of the 'right-ness'[2] which the artist may suppose to be something quite different.

How far desire actually to communicate, as distinguished from desire to produce something with communicative efficacy (however disguised), is an 'unconscious motive' in the artist is a question to which we need not hazard an answer. Doubtless individual artists vary enormously. To some the lure of 'immortality' of enduring fame, of a permanent place in the influences which govern the human mind, appears to be very strong. To others it is often negligible. The degree to which such notions are avowed certainly varies with current social and intel-lectual fashions. At present the appeal to posterity, the 'nurslings of immortality' attitude to works of art appears to be much out of favour. 'How do we know what posterity will be like? They may be awful people!' a contemporary is likely to remark, thus confusing the issue. For the appeal is not to posterity merely as living at a certain date, but as especially qualified to judge, a qualification most posterities have lacked.

What concerns criticism is not the avowed or unavowed motives of the artist, however interesting these may be to psych-ology, but the fact that his procedure does, in the majority of

---

[1] Again the normality of the artist has to be considered.

[2] As will be seen, I am not going to identify 'beauty' with 'communicative efficacy'. This is a trap which it is easy to fall into. A number of the exoteric followers of Croce may be found in it, though not Croce himself.

instances, make the communicative efficacy of his work correspond with his own satisfaction and sense of its rightness. This may be due merely to his normality, or it may be due to unavowed motives. The first suggestion is the more plausible. In any case it is certain that no mere careful study of communicative possibilities, together with any desire to communicate, however intense, is ever sufficient without close natural correspondence between the poet's impulses and possible impulses in his reader. All supremely successful communication involves this correspondence, and no planning can take its place. Nor is the deliberate conscious attempt directed to communication so successful as the unconscious indirect method.

Thus the artist is entirely justified in his apparent neglect of the main purpose of his work. And when in what follows he is alluded to without qualification as being primarily concerned with communication, the reservations here made should be recalled.

Since the poet's unconscious motives have been alluded to, it may be well at this point to make a few additional remarks. Whatever psycho-analysts may aver, the mental processes of the poet are not a very profitable field for investigation. They offer far too happy a hunting-ground for uncontrollable conjecture. Much that goes to produce a poem is, of course, unconscious. Very likely the unconscious processes are more important than the conscious, but even if we knew far more than we do about how the mind works, the attempt to display the inner working of the artist's mind by the evidence of his work alone must be subject to the gravest dangers. And to judge by the published work of Freud upon Leonardo da Vinci or of Jung upon Goethe (e.g. *The Psychology of the Unconscious*, p. 305), psycho-analysts tend to be peculiarly inept as critics.

The difficulty is that nearly all speculations as to what went on in the artist's mind are unverifiable, even more unverifiable than the similar speculations as to the dreamer's mind. The most plausible explanations are apt to depend upon features whose actual causation is otherwise. I do not know whether anyone but Mr. Graves has attempted to analyse *Kubla Khan*, a poem which by its mode of composition and by its subject suggests itself as well fitted for analysis. The reader acquainted with current methods of analysis can imagine the results of a thoroughgoing Freudian onslaught.

If he will then open *Paradise Lost*, Book IV, at line 223, and read onwards for sixty lines, he will encounter the actual sources of not a few of the images and phrases of the poem. In spite of —

> Southward through *Eden* went a River large,
> Nor changed his course, but through the shaggie hill
> Pass'd underneath ingulft . . .

in spite of —

> Rose a fresh Fountain, and with many a rill
> Watered the Garden; thence united fell
> Down the steep glade, and met the neather Flood . . .

in spite of —

> Rowling on Orient Pearl and sands of Gold
> With maize error under pendant shades
> Ran Nectar . . .

in spite of —

> Meanwhile murmuring waters fall
> Down the slope hills, disperst . . .

his doubts may still linger until he reaches

> Nor where *Abassin Kings* their issue Guard,
> Mount Amara.

and one of the most cryptic points in Coleridge's poem, the Abyssinian maid, singing of Mount Abora, finds its simple explanation. The closing line of the poem perhaps hardly needs this kind of derivation.

From one source or another almost all the matter of *Kubla Khan* came to Coleridge in a similar fashion. I do not know whether this particular indebtedness has been remarked before, but *Purchas his Pilgrimage*, Bartram's *Travels in North and South Carolina*, and Maurice's *History of Hindostan* are well-known sources, some of them indicated by Coleridge himself.

This very representative instance of the unconscious working of a poet's mind may serve as a not inapposite warning against one kind at least of possible applications of psychology in criticism.

The extent to which the arts and their place in the whole scheme of human affairs have been misunderstood, by Critics, Moralists, Educators, Aestheticians . . . is somewhat difficult to explain. Often those who most misunderstand have been perfect in their taste and ability to respond, Ruskin for example. Those who both knew what to do with a work of art and also understood what they were doing, have been for the most part artists and little inclined for, or capable of, the rather special task of explaining. It may have seemed to them too obvious to need explanation. Those who have tried have as a rule been foiled by language. For the difficulty which has always prevented the arts from being explained as well as 'enjoyed' (to use an inadequate word in default of an adequate) is language.

> 'Happy who can
> Appease this virtuous enemy of man!'

It was perhaps never so necessary as now that we should know why the arts are important and avoid inadequate answers. It will probably become increasingly more important in the future. Remarks such as these, it is true, are often uttered by enthusiastic persons, and are apt to be greeted with the same smile as the assertion that the future of England is bound Up with Hunting. Yet their full substantiation will be found to involve issues which are nowhere lightly regarded.

The arts are our storehouse of recorded values. They spring from and perpetuate hours in the lives of exceptional people, when their control and command of experience is at its highest, hours when the varying possibilities of existence are most clearly seen and the different activities which may arise are most exquisitely reconciled, hours when habitual narrowness of interests or confused bewilderment are replaced by an intricately wrought composure. Both in the genesis of a work of art, in the creative moment, and in its aspect as a vehicle of communication, reasons can be found for giving to the arts a very important place in the theory of Value. They record the most important judgements we possess as to the values of experience. They form a body of evidence which, for lack of a serviceable psychology by which to interpret it, and through the desiccating influence of abstract Ethics, has been left almost untouched by professed students of value. An odd omission, for without the assistance of the arts we could compare very few of our experiences, and without such comparison we could hardly hope to agree as to which are to be preferred. Very simple experiences – a cold bath in an enamelled tin, or running for a train – may to some extent be compared without elaborate vehicles; and friends exceptionally well acquainted with one another may manage some rough comparisons in ordinary conversation. But subtle or recondite experiences are for most men incommunicable and indescribable, though social conventions or terror of the loneliness of the human situation may make us pretend the contrary. In the arts we find the record in the only form in which these things can be recorded of the experiences which have seemed worth having to the most sensitive and discriminating persons. Through the obscure perception of this fact the poet has been regarded as a seer and the artist as a priest, suffering from usurpations. The arts, if rightly approached, supply the best data available for deciding what experiences are more valuable than others. The qualifying clause is all-important however. Happily there is no lack of glaring examples to remind us of the difficulty of approaching them rightly.

5

THE CRITICS' CONCERN WITH VALUE

What hinders? Are you beam-blind, yet to a fault
In a neighbour deft-handed? Are you that liar?
And cast by conscience out, spendsavour salt?
Gerrard Hopkins

Between the general inquiry into the nature of the good and the appreciation of particular works of art, they may seem to be a wide gap, and the discussion upon which we are about to embark may appear a roundabout way of approaching our subject. Morals have often been treated, especially in recent times, as a side-issue for criticism, from which the special concern of the critic must be carefully separated. His business, so it has been said, is with the work of art in itself, not with any consequences which lie outside it. These may be left, it has been supposed, to others for attention, to the clergy perhaps or to the police.

That these authorities are sadly incompetent is a minor disadvantage. Their blunderings are as a rule so ridiculous that the effects are brief. They often serve a useful purpose in calling attention to work which might be overlooked. What is more serious is that these indiscretions, vulgarities and absurdities encourage the view that morals have little or nothing to do with the arts, and the even more unfortunate opinion that the arts have no connection with morality. The ineptitudes of censors, their choice of censorable objects, ignoble blasphemy, such as that which declared *Esther Waters* an impure book, displays of such intelligence as considered *Madame Bovary* an apology for adulterous wrong, innumerable comic, stupefying, enraging interferences fully explain this attitude, but they do not justify it.

The common avoidance of all discussion of the wider social and moral aspects of the arts by people of steady judgement and strong heads is a misfortune, for it leaves the field free for folly, and cramps the scope of good critics unduly. So loath have they been to be thought at large with the wild asses that they have virtually shut themselves up in a paddock. If the competent are to refrain because of the antics of the unqualified, an evil and a loss which are neither temporary nor trivial increase continually. It is as though medical men were all to retire because of the impudence of quacks. For the critic is as closely occupied with the health of the mind as the doctor with the health of the body. In a different way, it is true, and with a wider and subtler definition of health, by which the healthiest mind is that capable of securing the greatest amount of value.

The critic cannot possibly avoid using some ideas about value. His whole occupation is an application and exercise of his ideas on the subject, and an avoidance of moral preoccupations on his part can only be either an abdication or a rejection under the title of 'morality' of what he considers to be mistaken or dishonest ideas and methods. The term has a dubious odour, it has been handled by many objectionable as well as admirable people, and we may agree to avoid it. But the errors exemplified by censorship exploits are too common, and misconceptions as to the nature of value too easy to fall into and too widespread, for useful criticism to remain without a general theory and an explicit set of principles.

What is needed is a defensible position for those who believe that the arts are of value. (Only a general theory of value which will show the place and function of the arts in the whole system of values will provide such a stronghold. At the same time we need weapons with which to repel and overthrow misconceptions. With the increase of population the problem presented by the gulf between what is preferred by the majority and what is accepted as excellent by the most qualified opinion bas become infinitely more serious and appears likely to become threatening in the near future. For many reasons standards are much more in need of defence than they used to be. It is perhaps premature to envisage a collapse of values, a transvaluation by which popular taste replaces trained discrimination. Yet commercialism has done stranger things: we have not yet fathomed the more sinister potentialities of the cinema and the loud-speaker, and there is some evidence uncertain and slight no doubt, that such things as 'best-sellers' (compare *Tarzan* with *She*), magazine verses, mantel-piece pottery, Academy picture, Music Hall songs, County Council buildings, War Memorials . . . are decreasing in merit. Notable exceptions, in which the multitude are better advised than the experts, of course occur sometimes, but not often.

To bridge the gulf, to bring the level of popular appreciation nearer to the consensus of best qualified opinion, and to defend this opinion against damaging attacks (Tolstoy's is a typical example), a much clearer account than has yet been produced, of why this opinion is right, is essential. These attacks are dangerous, because they appeal to a natural instinct, hatred of 'superior persons'. The expert in matters of taste is in an awkward position when he differs from the majority. He is forced to say in effect, 'I am better than you. My taste is more refined, my nature more cultured, you will do well to become more like me than you are.'. It is not his fault that he has to be so arrogant. He may, and usually does, disguise the fact as far as possible, but his claim to be heard as an expert depends upon the truth of these assumptions. He ought then to be ready with reasons of a clear and convincing kind as to why his preferences are worth attention, and until these reasons are forthcoming, the accusations that he is a charlatan and a prig are embarrassing. He may indeed point to years of preoccupation with his subject, he may remark like the wiseacre Longinus, sixteen hundred years ago, 'The judgement of literature is the final outcome of much endeavour,' but with him are many Professors to prove that years of endeavour may lead to nothing very remarkable in the end.

To habilitate the critic, to defend accepted standards against Tolstoyan attacks, to narrow the interval between these standards and popular taste, to protect the arts against the crude moralities of Puritans and perverts, a general theory of value, which will not leave the statement 'This is good, that bad,' either vague or arbitrary, must be provided. There is no alternative open. Nor is it such an excursus from the inquiry into the nature of the arts as may be supposed. For if a well-grounded theory of value is a necessity for criticism, it is no less true that an understanding of what happens in the arts is needed for the theory. The two problems 'What is good?' and 'What are the arts?' reflect light upon one another. Neither in fact can be fully answered without the other. To the unravelling of the first we may now proceed.

6

VALUE AS AN ULTIMATE IDEA

Some lovely glorious nothing I did see.
Aire and Angels

It has always been found far more easy to divide experiences[1] into good and bad, valuable and the reverse, than to discover what we are doing when we make the division. The history of opinions as to what constitutes value, as to why and when anything is rightly called good, shows a bewildering variety. But in modem times the controversy narrows itself down to two questions. The first of these is whether the difference between experiences which are valuable and those which are not can be fully described in psychological terms; whether some additional

---

[1] Throughout this discussion 'experience' will be used in a wide sense to stand for any occurrence in the mind. It is equivalent to 'mental state, or process'. The term has often unfortunate suggestions of passiveness and of consciousness, but many of the 'experiences' here referred to would ordinarily be called 'actions' and have parts which are not conscious and not accessible to introspection as important as those which are.

distinctive 'ethical' or 'moral' idea of a non-psychological nature is or is not required. The second question concerns the exact psychological analysis needed in order to explain value if no further 'ethical' idea is shown to be necessary.

The first question will not detain us long. It has been ably maintained[1] and widely accepted that when we say that an experience is good we are simply saying that it is endowed with a certain ethical property or attribute not to be reduced to any psychological properties or attributes such as being desired or approved, and that no further elucidation of this special ethical property by way of analysis is possible. 'Good' on this view is in no way a shorthand term for some more explicit account. The things which are good, it is held, are just good, possess a property which can be recognized by immediate intuition, and here, since good is unanalysable, the matter must rest. All that the study of value can do is to point out the things which possess this property, classify them, and remove certain confusions between ends which are good in themselves and means which are only called good, because they are instrumental in the attainment of intrinsically good ends. Usually those who maintain this view also hold that the only things which are good for their own sakes and not merely as a means are certain conscious experiences, for example, knowledge, admiring contemplation of beauty, and feelings of affection and veneration under some circumstances. Other things, such as mountains, books, railways, courageous actions, are good instrumentally because, and in so far as, they cause or make possible states of mind which are valuable intrinsically. Thus the occurrence of states of mind which are recognized as good is regarded as an isolated fact of experience, not capable of being accounted for, or linked up with the rest of human peculiarities as a product

[1] A chief advocate of this view is Dr. G. E. Moore, whose *Principia Ethica* and *Ethics* contain brilliant statements of the position.

of development in the way made familiar by the biological sciences.

The plausibility of this view derives principally from the metaphysical assumption that there are properties, in the sense of subsistent entities, which attach to existent particulars, but which might without absurdity be supposed to attach to nothing. These metaphysical entities, variously named Ideas, Notions, Concepts or Universals, may be divided into two kinds, sensuous and supersensuous.[1] The sensuous are those which may be apprehended by the senses, such as 'red', 'cold', 'round', 'swift', 'painful', and the supersensuous, those apprehended not in sensuous perception but otherwise. Logical relations, 'necessity' or 'impossibility', and such ideas as 'willing', 'end', 'cause', and 'being three in number', have in this way been supposed to be directly apprehensible by the mind. Amongst these supersensuous Ideas good is to be found.

Nothing could be simpler than such a view, and to many people the subsistence of such a property of goodness appears not surprising. But to others the suggestion seems merely a curious survival of abstractionism, if such a term may be defended by its close parallel with obstructionism. A blind man in a dark room chasing a black cat which is not there would seem to them well employed in comparison with a philosopher apprehending such 'Concepts'. While ready for convenience of discourse to talk and even to think as though Concepts and Particulars were separable and distinct kinds of entities, they refuse to believe that the structure of the world actually contains such a cleavage. The point is perhaps undiscussable, and is probably unimportant, except in so far as the habit of regarding the world as actually so cloven is a fruitful source of bogus entities, usually hypostatized words. The temptation to introduce premature ultimates – Beauty in Aesthetics, the Mind and its faculties in psychology,

[1] Cf. F. Brentano, *The Origin of the Knowledge of Right and Wrong*, pp. 12, 46.

Life in physiology, are representative examples – is especially great for believers in Abstract Entities. The objection to such ultimates is that they bring an investigation to a dead end too suddenly. An ultimate Good is, in this instance, just such an arbitrary full stop.

It will be agreed that a less cryptic account of good, if one can be given, which is in accordance with verifiable facts, would be preferable, even though no means were available for refuting the simpler theory. Upholders of this theory, however, have produced certain arguments to show that no other view of good is possible, and these must first be briefly examined. They provide, in addition, an excellent example of the misuse of psychological assumptions in research, for although a psychological approach is often of the utmost service, it can also be a source of obscurantism and over-confidence. The arguments against any naturalistic account depend upon the alleged results of directly inspecting what is before our minds when we judge that anything is good. If we substitute, it is maintained, any account of good whatever for 'good' in the assertion, 'This is good' – for example, 'This is desired' or 'This is approved' – we can detect that what is substituted is different from 'good', and that we are not then making the same judgement. The result, it is claimed, is confirmed by the fact that we can always ask, 'Is what is desired, or what is approved, good?' however we may elaborate the account provided, and that this is always a genuine question which would be impossible were the substituted account actually the analysis of good.

The persuasiveness of this refutation is found to vary enormously from individual to individual, for the results of the experiments upon which it relies differ. Those who have accustomed themselves to the belief that good is a supersensuous simple Idea readily discover the fraudulent character of any offered substitute, while those who hold some psychological theory of value, with equal ease identify their account with 'good'. The further question, 'When and under what conditions can judgements be distinguished?' arises, a question so difficult to answer that any argument becomes suspect which depends upon assuming that they can be infallibly recognized as different. If for any reason we wish to distinguish two judgements, we can persuade ourselves, in any case in which they are differently formulated, that they are different. Thus it has been thought that 'a exceeds b' and 'a is greater than b' are distinguishable, the first being supposed to state simply that a has the relation 'exceeds' to b, while the second is supposed to state that a has the relation 'is', to greater which again has the relation 'than' to b.[1] The conclusion to be drawn from the application of such methods to the problem of the meaning of Good would seem to be that they are not competent to decide anything about it – by no means a valueless result.

Since nothing can be concluded from a comparison of 'This is good' with, let us say, 'This is sought by an impulse belonging to a dominant group', let us see whether light can be gained by considering analogous instances in which special distinct ideas have for a time been thought indispensable only to yield later to analysis and substitution. The case of Beauty is perhaps too closely related to that of Good for our purpose. Those who can persuade themselves that Good is an unique irreducible entity might believe the same of Beauty. An episode in the theory of the tides is more instructive. It was once thought that the moon

[1] Cf. Russell, *The Principles of Mathematics*, p. 100. 'On this principle, from which I can see no escape, that every genuine word must have some meaning, the *is* and *than* must form part of 'a is greater than b', which thus contains more than two terms and a relation. The *is* seems to state that a has to *greater* the relation of referent, while the *than* states similarly that b has to *greater* the relation of relatum. But 'a exceeds b' may be held to express solely the relations of a to b, without including any of the implications of further relations On the introspective comparison of judgements *The Meaning of Meaning*, by C. K. Ogden and the writer, may be consulted.

must have a peculiar Affinity with water. When the moon is full the tides are higher. Clearly the seas swell in sympathy with the increase of the moon. The history of science is full of mysterious unique entities which have gradually evaporated as explanation advanced.

The struggles of economists with 'utility', of mathematical philosophers with 'points' and 'instants', of biologists with 'entelechies', 'and the adventures of psycho-analysts with 'the libido' and 'the collective unconscious' are instances in point. At present theoretical psychology in particular is largely made up of the manipulation of similar suspects. The Act of Judgement, the relation of Presentation, Immediate Awareness, Direct Inspection, the Will, Feeling, Assumption, Acceptance, are only a few of the provisional ultimates introduced for convenience of discussion. Some of them may in the end prove to be indispensable, but meanwhile they are not, to prudent people, more than symbolic conveniences; theories dependent upon them must not be allowed to shut off from investigation fields which may be fruitful.

7

A PSYCHOLOGICAL THEORY
OF VALUE

Hands that can grasp, eyes
that can dilate, hair that can rise
    if it must, these things are important not because a high-
sounding interpretation can be put upon them, but because
they are useful.

                                                    Marianne Moore

The method then by which any attempt to analyse 'good' has
been condemned is itself objectionable, and yields no sound
reason why a purely psychological account of the differences
between good, bad, and indifferent experiences should not be
given. The data for the inquiry are in part supplied by anthro-
pology. It has become clear that the disparity among the states of
mind recognized as good by persons of different races, habits
and civilizations is overwhelming. Any observant child, it is true,
might discover in the home circle how widely people disagree,
but the effect of education is to suppress these scientific efforts. It
has needed the vast accumulations of anthropological evidence

now available to establish the fact that as the organization of life and affairs alters very different experiences are perceived to be good or bad, are favoured or condemned. The Bakairi of Central Brazil and the Tahitians, among others, are reported, for example, to look upon eating with the same feelings which we reserve for quite different physiological performances, and to regard the public consumption of food as a grave breach of decency. In many parts of the world feelings of forgiveness towards enemies, for example, are looked upon as low and ignoble. The experiences which one person values are thought vicious by another. We must allow, it is true, for widespread confusion between intrinsic and instrumental values, and for the difficulty of identifying experiences. Many states of mind in other people which we judge to be bad or indifferent are no doubt unlike what we imagine them to be, or contain elements which we overlook, so that with fuller knowledge we might discover them to be good. In this manner it may be possible to reduce the reported disparity of value intuitions, but few people acquainted with the varying moral judgements of mankind will doubt that circumstances and necessities, present and past, explain our approval and disapproval. We start, then, with a hearty scepticism of all immediate intuitions, and inquire how it is that individuals in different conditions, and at different stages of their development, esteem things so differently.

With the exception of some parents and nursemaids we have lately all been aghast at revelations of the value judgements of infants. Their impulses, their desires, their preferences, the things which they esteem, as displayed by the psycho-analysts, strike even those whose attitude towards humanity is not ideal-istic with some dismay. Even when the stories are duly dis-counted, enough which is verifiable remains for *infans polypervers* to present a truly impressive figure dominating all future psychological inquiry into value.

There is no need here to examine in detail how these early

impulses are diverted and disguised by social pressures. The rough outlines are familiar of the ways in which by growth, by the appearance of fresh instinctive tendencies, by increase of knowledge and of command over the world, under the control of custom, magical beliefs, public opinion, inculcation and example, the primitive new-born animal may be gradually transformed into a bishop. At every stage in the astonishing metamorphosis, the impulses, desires, and propensities of the individual take on a new form, or, it may be, a further degree of systematization. This systematization is never complete. Always some impulse, or set of impulses, can be found which in one way or another interferes, or conflicts, with others. It may do so in two ways, directly or indirectly. Some impulses are in themselves psychologically incompatible, some are incompatible only indirectly, through producing contrary effects in the world outside. The difficulty some people have in smoking and writing at the same time is a typical instance of the first kind of incompatibility; the two activities get in each other's way by a psychological accident as it were. Interference of this kind can be overcome by practice to an unexpected degree, as the feats of jugglers show; some, however, are insurmountable; and these incompatibilities are often, as we shall see, of supreme consequence in moral development. Indirect incompatibilities arising through the consequences of our acts are more easy to find. Our whole existence is one long study of them, from the infant's first choice whether he shall use his mouth for screaming or for sucking, to the last codicil to his Will.

These are simple instances, but the conduct of life is throughout an attempt to organize impulses so that success is obtained for the greater number or mass of them, for the most important and the weightiest set. And here we come face to face again with the problem of value. How shall we decide which among these are more important than others, and how shall we distinguish different organizations as yielding more or less value one than another? At this point we need to be on our guard not to smuggle in any peculiar ethical, non-psychological, idea under some disguise, under 'important' or 'fundamental', for example.

Among those who reject any metaphysical view of value it has become usual to define value as capacity for satisfying feeling and desire in various intricate ways.[1] For the purpose of tracing in detail the very subtle and varied modes in which people actually value things, a highly intricate treatment is indispensable, but here a simpler definition will suffice.

We may start from the fact that impulses may be divided into appetencies and aversions, and begin by saying that anything is valuable which satisfies an appetency or 'seeking after'. The term 'desire' would do as well if we could avoid the implication of accompanying conscious beliefs as to what is sought and a further restriction to felt and recognized longings. The term 'want' used so much by economists has the same disadvantages. Appetencies may be, and for the most part are, unconscious, and to leave out those which we cannot discover by introspection would involve extensive errors. For the same reason it is wiser not to start from feeling. Appetencies then, rather than felt appetencies or desires, shall be our starting-point.

The next step is to agree that apart from consequences anyone will *actually prefer* to satisfy a greater number of equal appetencies rather than a less. Observation of people's behaviour, including our own, is probably sufficient to establish this agreement. If now we look to see what consequences can intervene to upset this simple principle, we shall find that only interferences, immediate or remote, direct or indirect, with other appetencies,

---

[1] E.g., 'The value of the object is its capacity of becoming the object of feeling and desire through actualization of dispositional tendencies by acts of presumption, judgement, and assumption.' Urban, *Valuation*, p. 53.

need to be considered. The only *psychological* restraints upon appetencies are other appetencies.[1]

We can now extend our definition. Anything is valuable which will satisfy an appetency without involving the frustration of some equal or *more important* appetency; in other words, the only reason which can be given for not satisfying a desire is that more important desires will thereby be thwarted. Thus morals become purely prudential, and ethical codes merely the expression of the most general scheme of expediency[2] to which an individual or a race has attained. But we have still to say what 'important' stands for in this formulation. (Cf. p. 46.)

There are certain evident priorities among impulses, some of which have been studied in various ways by economists under the headings of primary wants and secondary wants. Some needs or impulses must be satisfied in order that others may be possible. We must eat, drink, sleep, breathe, protect ourselves and carry on an immense physiological business as a condition for any further activities. Some of these impulses, breathing, for example, can be satisfied directly, but most of them involve us in complicated cycles of instrumental labour. Man for the most part must exert himself half his life to satisfy even the primitive

---

[1] Or, of course, aversions. In what follows we shall take no further note of aversions. To do so would introduce inessential complications. The omission in no way affects the argument, since for our present purposes they may be counted in with appetencies.

[2] This view plainly has close connections with Utilitarianism. In fact if Bentham's editor is to be trusted in his interpretation of his master's doctrine, it would be what Bentham intended to teach. 'The term nearest to being synonymous with pleasure is *volition*: what it pleases a man to do is simply what he wills to do. . . . What a man wills to do, or what he pleases to do, may be far from giving him enjoyment; yet shall we say that in doing it, he is not following his own pleasure? . . . A native of Japan, when he is offended, stabs himself to prove the intensity of his feelings. It is difficult to prove enjoyment in this case: yet the man obeyed his impulses.' John Hill Burton, *Jeremy Bentham's Works*, vol. 1, p. 22.

needs, and these activities, failing other means of reaching the same ends, share their priority. In their turn they involve as conditions a group of impulses, whose satisfaction becomes only second in importance to physiological necessities, those, namely, upon which communication and the ability to co-operate depend. But these, since man is a social creature, also become more directly necessary to his well-being. The very impulses which enable him to co-operate in gaining his dinner would themselves, if not satisfied, wreck by their mere frustration all his activities. This happens all through the hierarchy. Impulses, whose exercise may have been originally only important as means, and which might once have been replaced by quite different sets, become in time necessary conditions for innumerable quite different performances. Objects, again, originally valued because they satisfy one need, are found later to be also capable of satisfying others. Dress, for example, appears to have originated in magical, 'lifegiving', ornaments,[1] but so many other interests derive satisfaction from it that controversy can still arise as to its primitive uses.

The instances of priorities given must only be taken as examples. It is hardly necessary to remind the reader that for a civilized man, activities originally valuable as means only, often become so important through their connections with the rest of his activities, that life without them is regarded as intolerable. Thus acts which will debar him from his normal relations with his fellows are often avoided, even at the cost of death. Total cessation of all activities is preferred to the dreadful thwarting and privation which would ensue. The case of the soldier, or of the conscientious objector, is thus no exception to the principle. Life deprived of all but the barest physiological necessities, for example, prison life, is for many people worse than non-existence. Those who even so incur it in defence of some 'moral

---

[1] Cf. W. J. Perry, *The Origin of Magic and Religion*, p. 15.

ideal' do so because they are so organized, either permanently or temporarily, that only in this way can their dominant impulses secure satisfaction. The self-regarding impulses form only a part of the total activities of social man, and the impulse of the martyr to bear witness at any cost to what he regards as truth, is only one extreme instance of the degree to which other impulses often assume supremacy.

For another reason any priorities mentioned must be taken only as illustrations. We do not know enough yet about the precedences, the hierarchies, the modes of systematization, actual and possible, in that unimaginable organization, the mind, to say what order in any case actually exists, or between what the order holds. We only know that a growing order is the principle of the mind, that its function is to co-ordinate, and we can detect that in some of its forms the precedence is different from that in others. This we could do by observation, by comparing the drunken man with the sober, but from our own experience of our own activity we can go much further. We can feel differences between clear coherent thinking and confusion or stupidity, between free, controlled emotional response and dull or clogged impassivity, between moments when we do with our bodies more delicate and dexterous things than seem possible, and moments of clumsiness, when we are 'all thumbs', have no 'balance' or 'timing', and nothing 'comes off'. These differences are differences in momentary organization, differences in precedence between rival possible systematizations. The more permanent and more specifically 'moral' differences between individuals grow out of differences such as these and correspond to similar precedences between larger systems.

The complications possible in the systematization of impulses might be illustrated indefinitely. The plasticity of special appetencies and activities varies enormously. Some impulses can be diverted more easily than others. Sex has a wider range of satisfactions than hunger, for example; some are weaker than others;

some (not the same necessarily) can be suppressed in the long run with less difficulty. Some can be modified; some obey the 'all or none' rule – they must either be satisfied specifically or completely inhibited – well-established habits may have this peculiarity. In judging the importance of any impulse all these considerations must be taken into account. The affiliations of impulses, at present often inexplicable, need especially to be considered. Within the whole partially systematized organization, numerous sub-systems can be found, and what would be expected to be quite trivial impulses are often discovered to be important, because they belong to powerful groups. Thus there are reasonable persons who, without a high polish on their shoes, are almost incapacitated.

The importance of an impulse, it will be seen, can be defined for our purposes as *the extent of the disturbance of other impulses in the individual's activities which the thwarting of the impulse involves*. A vague definition, it is true, but therefore suitable to our at present incomplete and hazy knowledge of how impulses are related. It will be observed that no special ethical idea is introduced. We can now take our next step forward and inquire into the relative merits of different systematizations.

No individual can live one minute without a very intricate and, so far as it goes, very perfect co-ordination of impulses. It is only when we pass from the activities which from second to second maintain life to those which from hour to hour determine what kind of life it shall be, that we find wide differences. Fortunately for psychology we can each find wide enough differences in ourselves from hour to hour. Most people in the same day are Bonaparte and Oblomov by turns. Before breakfast Diogenes, after dinner Petronius or Bishop Usher. But throughout these mutations certain dispositions usually remain much the same, those which govern public behaviour in a limited number of affairs varying very greatly from one society or civilization to another. Every systematization in the degree to which it is stable involves a degree of sacrifice, but for some the price to be paid in opportunities forgone is greater than for others. By the extent of the loss, the range of impulses thwarted or starved, and their degree of importance, the merit of a systematization is judged. That organization which is least wasteful of human possibilities is, in short, the best. Some individuals, hag-ridden by their vices, or their virtues, to a point at which the law of diminishing returns has deprived even these of their appropriate satisfactions, are still unable to reorganize; they go through life incapacitated for most of its possible enjoyments.[1] Others, paralysed with their conflicts, are unable to do anything freely; whatever they attempt some implicated but baffled impulse is still fitfully and fretfully stirring. The debauchee and the victim of conscience alike have achieved organizations whose price in sacrifice is excessive. Both their individual satisfactions, and those for which they are dependent upon sympathetic relations with their fellows, an almost equal group, are unduly restricted. Upon grounds of prudence alone they have been injudicious, and they may be condemned without any appeal to peculiarly 'ethical' standards. The muddle in which they are forced to live is itself sufficient ground for reprobation.

At the other extreme are those fortunate people who have achieved an ordered life, whose systems have developed clearing-houses by which the varying claims of different impulses are adjusted. Their free, untrammelled activity gains for them a maximum of varied satisfactions and involves a minimum of suppression and sacrifice. Particularly is this so with regard to those satisfactions which require humane, sympathetic, and friendly relations between individuals. The charge of egoism, or

---

[1] Both 'enjoyment' and 'satisfaction' are unsuitable terms in this connection. An unfortunate linguistic gap must be recognized. The full exercise of an activity is commonly its own 'satisfaction', and, as we shall see later, what pleasure may accompany it is derivative and incidental.

'Beatitudo non est virtutis præmium, sed ipsa virtus.'

selfishness, can be brought against a naturalistic or utilitarian morality such as this only by overlooking the importance of these satisfactions in any well-balanced life. Unfair or aggressive behaviour, and preoccupation with self-regarding interests to the exclusion of due sensitiveness to the reciprocal claims of human intercourse, lead to a form of organization which deprives the person so organized of whole ranges of important values. No mere loss of social pleasures is in question, but a twist or restriction of impulses, whose normal satisfaction is involved in almost all the greatest goods of life. The two senses in which a man may 'take advantage' of his fellows can be observed in practice to conflict. Swindling and bullying, whether in business matters or in personal relations, have their cost; which the best judges agree to be excessive. And the greater part of the cost lies not in the consequences of being found out, in the loss of social esteem and so forth, but in actual systematic disability to attain important values.

Although the person who habitually disregards the claims of his fellows to fair treatment and sympathetic understanding may be condemned, in most cases, upon the ground of his own actual loss of values in such behaviour, this of course is not the reason for the steps which may have to be taken against him. It may very well be the case that a person's own interests are such that, if he understood them, were well organized in other words, he would be a useful and charming member of his community; but, so long as people are about who are not well organized, communities must protect themselves. They can defend their action on the ground that the general loss of value which would follow if they did not protect themselves far outweighs such losses as are incurred by the people whom they suppress or deport.

To extend this individual morality to communal affairs is not difficult. Probably the best brief statement upon the point is the following note by Bentham, if we interpret 'happiness' in his formula not as pleasure but as the satisfaction of impulses.

June 29, 1827.

1   Constantly actual end of action on the part of every indi-
    vidual at the moment of action, his greatest happiness,
    according to his view of it at that moment.
2   Constantly proper end of action on the part of every indi-
    vidual at the moment of action, his real greatest happiness
    from that moment to the end of life.
3   Constantly proper end of action on the part of every indi-
    vidual considered as trustee for the community, of which
    he is considered as a member, the greatest happiness of
    that same community, in so far as it depends upon the
    interest which forms the bond of union between its
    members.[1]

But communities, as is well known, tend to behave in the
same way to people who are better organized as well as to people
who are worse organized than the standard of the group. They
deal with Socrates or Bruno as severely as with Turpin or
Bottomley. Thus mere interference with ordinary activities is not
by itself a sufficient justification for excluding from the group
people who are different and therefore nuisances. The precise
nature of the difference must be considered, and whether and to
what degree it is the group, not the exceptional member, which
ought to be condemned. The extent to which alteration is prac-
ticable is also relevant, and the problem in particular cases
becomes very intricate.

But the final court of appeal concerns itself in such cases with
questions, not of the wishes of majorities, but of the actual range
and degree of satisfaction which different possible systematizations of impulse yield. Resentment at interference and gratitude
for support and assistance are to be distinguished from disapproval and approval. The esteem and respect accorded to persons

[1] *Works*, Vol. X, p. 560.

with the social[1] virtues well developed is only in a small degree due to the use which we find we can make of them. It is much more a sense that their lives are rich and full.

When any desire is denied for the sake of another, the approved and accepted activity takes on additional value; it is coveted and pursued all the more for what it has cost. Thus the spectacle of other people enjoying both activities without difficulty, thanks to some not very obvious adjustment, is peculiarly distressing, and such people are usually regarded as especially depraved. In different circumstances this view may or may not be justified. The element of sacrifice exacted by any stable system explains to a large extent the tenacity with which custom is clung to, the intolerance directed against innovations, the fanaticism of converts, the hypocrisy of teachers, and many other lamentable phenomena of the moral attitudes. However much an individual may privately find his personality varying from hour to hour, he is compelled to join in maintaining a public façade of some rigidity and buttressed with every contrivance which can be invented. The Wills of Gods, the Conscience, the Catechism, Taboos, Immediate Intuitions, Penal Laws, Public Opinion, Good Form, are all more or less ingenious and efficient devices with the same aim – to secure the uniformity which social life requires. By their means and by Custom, Convention, and Superstition, the underlying basis of morality, the effort to attain maximum satisfaction through coherent systematization, is veiled and disguised to an extraordinary degree. Whence arise great difficulties and many disasters. It is so necessary and so difficult to secure a stable and general system of public behaviour that any means whatever are justifiable, failing the discovery of better. All societies hitherto achieved, however, involve waste and misery of appalling extent.

[1] Not necessarily 'social workers'. Only personal communication can show who have the virtues here referred to.

Any public code of behaviour must, it is generally agreed, represent a cruder and more costly systematization than those attained to by many of the individuals who live under the code, a point obviously to be remembered in connection with censorship problems. Customs change more slowly than conditions, and every change in conditions brings with it new possibilities of systematization. None of the afflictions of humanity are worse than its obsolete moral principles. Consider the effects of the obsolete virtues of nationalism under modern conditions, or the absurdity of the religious attitude to birth control. The present lack of plasticity in such things involves a growing danger. Human conditions and possibilities have altered more in a hundred years than they had in the previous ten thousand, and the next fifty may overwhelm us, unless we can devise a more adaptable morality. The view that what we need in this tempestuous turmoil of change is a Rock to shelter under or to cling to, rather than an efficient aeroplane in which to ride it, is comprehensible but mistaken.

To guard against a possible misunderstanding it may be added that the organization and systematization of which I have been speaking in this chapter are not primarily an affair of conscious planning or arrangement, as this is understood, for example, by a great business house or by a railway. (Cf. p. 188.) We pass as a rule from a chaotic to a better organized state by ways which we know nothing about. Typically through the influence of other minds. Literature and the arts are the chief means by which these influences are diffused. It should be unnecessary to insist upon the degree to which high civilization, in other words, free, varied and unwasteful life, depends upon them in a numerous society.

8

ART AND MORALS

Com, no more,
This is meer moral babble, and direct
Against the canon laws of our foundations.
Comus

From this excursus let us return to our proper task, the attempt to outline a morality which will change its values as circumstances alter, a morality free from occultism, absolutes and arbitrariness, a morality which will explain, as no morality has yet explained, the place and value of the arts in human affairs. What is good or valuable, we have said, is the exercise of impulses and the satisfaction of their appetencies. When we say that anything is good we mean that it satisfies, and by a good experience we mean one in which the impulses which make it are fulfilled and successful, adding as the necessary qualification that their exercise and satisfaction shall not interfere in any way with more important impulses. Importance we have seen to be a complicated matter, and which impulses are more important than others can only be discovered by an extensive inquiry into what actually happens. The problem of morality then, the problem of how we are to obtain the greatest possible value from life, becomes a problem of organization, both in the individual life and in the adjustment of individual lives to one another, and is delivered from all non-psychological ideas, from absolute goods and immediate convictions, which incidentally help greatly to give unnecessary stiffness and fixity to obsolescent codes. Without system, needless to say, value vanishes, since in a state of chaos important and trivial impulses alike are frustrated.

A minor problem may occur here to the reader. It concerns the choice between a 'crowded hour' and 'an age without a name', and the place of the time factor in valuation. There are many very valuable states which cannot last very long in the nature of the case, and some of these seem to have disabling consequences. But, to take merely the most interesting instance, if we knew more about the nervous constitution of genius we might discover that the instability from which so many people suffer who are at times best able to actualize the possibilities of life is merely a consequence of their plasticity; not in the least a price which they pay for such 'high moments', but rather a result in system of great delicacy of wear and tear at lower levels of adjustment. It is generally those who have the least refined views of value who most readily believe that highly valuable hours must be paid for afterwards. Their conception of a 'hectic time' as the summit of human possibilities explains the opinion. For those who find that the most valuable experiences are those which are also most fruitful of further valuable experiences no problem arises. To the query whether they prefer a long life to a joyous one, they will reply that they find very satisfactory a life which is both

The most valuable states of mind then are those which involve the widest and most comprehensive co-ordination of activities and the least curtailment, conflict, starvation and restriction. States of mind in general are valuable in the degree in which they tend to reduce waste and frustration. We must be careful in considering this formulation to remember how varied human activities are and avoid, for example, undue admiration for practical efficient persons whose emotional life is suppressed. But, thanks to the psycho-analysts, we are hardly likely at the moment to overlook the consequences of suppressions.

It is plain that no one systematization can claim a supreme position. Men are naturally different and in any society specialization is inevitable. There are evidently a great number of good systematizations and what is good for one person will not be good for another. A sailor, a doctor, a mathematician and a poet can hardly have the same organization throughout. With different conditions different values necessarily arise. Doubtless conditions may be, and too often are, such that no life of high value is possible. With a naturalistic morality the reasons for altering them and the way to do so both become clearer. But even with our present resources and command over nature, it is universally agreed that intelligence and goodwill could contrive that no man should be so situated as to be deprived of all the generally accessible values. The clearing away from moral questions of an ethical lumber and superstitious interpolations is a step long overdue in this undertaking. But until it has been carried further, so it is often thought, to be busied with such apparently 'unpractical' activities as art or criticism is to behave too much like a passenger on a short-handed ship. This is true enough doubtless of some who so busy themselves. But it is not true that criticism is a luxury trade. The rear-guard of society cannot be extricated until the vanguard has gone further. Goodwill and intelligence are still too little available. The critic, we have said, is as much concerned with the health of the mind as any doctor with the health of the body. To set up as a critic is to set up as a judge of values. What are the other qualifications required we shall see later. For the arts are inevitably and quite apart from any intentions of the artist an appraisal of existence. Matthew Arnold when he said that poetry is a criticism of life was saying something so obvious that it is constantly overlooked. The artist is concerned with the record and perpetuation of the experiences which seem to him most worth having. For reasons which we shall consider in Chapter Twenty-two, he is also the man who is most likely to have experiences of value to record. He is the point at which the growth of the mind shows itself. His experiences, those at least which give value to his work, represent conciliations of impulses which in most minds are still confused, intertrammelled and conflicting. His work is the ordering of what in most minds is disordered. That his *failures* to bring order out of chaos are often more conspicuous than those of other men is due in part at least to his greater audacity; it is a penalty of ambition and a consequence of his greater plasticity. But when he succeeds, the value of what he has accomplished is found always in a more perfect organization which makes more of the possibilities of response and activity available.

What value is and which experiences are most valuable will never be understood so long as we think in terms of those large abstractions, the virtues and the vices. 'You do invert the covenants of her trust,' said Comus, that disreputable advocate of Utilitarianism, to the Lady, that enemy of Nature. Instead of recognizing that value lies in the 'minute particulars' of response and attitude, we have tried to find it in conformity to abstract prescriptions and general rules of conduct. The artist is an expert in the 'minute particulars' and *qua* artist pays little or no attention to generalizations which he finds in actual practice are too crude to discriminate between what is valuable and the reverse. For this reason the moralist has always tended to distrust or to ignore him. Yet since the fine conduct of life springs only from fine ordering of responses far too subtle to be touched by any general ethical maxims, this neglect of art by the moralist has been tantamount to a disqualification. The basis of morality, as Shelley insisted, is laid not by preachers but by poets. Bad taste and crude responses are not mere flaws in an otherwise admir-able person. They are actually a root evil from which other defects follow. No life can be excellent in which the elementary responses are disorganized and confused.

9

ACTUAL AND POSSIBLE MISAPPREHENSIONS

> Who
> Saith that? It is not written so on high!
> *Cain*

Every true view, perhaps, has its crude analogues, due sometimes to a confused perception of the real state of affairs, sometimes to faulty statement. Often these clumsy or mistaken off-shoots are responsible for the difficulty with which the true view gains acceptance. Like shadows, reflections, or echoes, they obscure and baffle apprehension. Nowhere are they more convenient than in the problem of the moral function of art. A consideration of some instances will help to make clearer what has been said, to distinguish the view recommended from its disreputable relatives and to remove possible misapprehensions.

Allusion has several times been made to Tolstoy, and nothing in the recent history of aesthetic opinion is so remarkable as the onslaught made by that great artist against all the arts. No better example could be found of how not to introduce moral preoccupations into the judgement of values. Blinded by the light of a retarded conversion, knowing, as an artist, the extreme importance of the arts, but forgetting in the fierceness of his new convictions all the experiences that had in earlier years made up his own creations, he flung himself, a Principle in each hand, upon the whole host of European masterpieces and left as he believed hardly a survivor standing.

He begins by emphasizing the enormous output of energy which is devoted to Art in civilized countries. He then very rightly asserts that it is of great importance to know what this activity is about; and he devotes thirty pages to the various definitions which have been attempted of Art and Beauty. He concludes, after ransacking the somewhat uncritical compilations of Schasler and Knight, that aesthetics have been hitherto an idle amalgam of reverie and phantasy, from which no definition of Art emerges. Partly he traces this result to the use in aesthetics of notions of beauty; partly to an anxiety in the critics to justify the existent forms of Art. They are, he insists, less concerned to discover what Art is, than to show that those things which are currently termed Art must in fact be Art. To these sections of *What is Art?* assent may be accorded. He then sets out his own definition. 'To evoke in oneself a sensation which one has experienced before, and having evoked it in oneself, to communicate this sensation in such a way that others may experience the same sensation . . . so that other men are infected by these sensations and pass through them; in this does the activity of Art consist.'[1] So far excellent; if we translate 'sensation', the current aesthetico-psychological jargon of the art schools in Tolstoy's day, by some more general term such as experience. But this is only a first stage of the definition; there are additions to be made. Any Art which is infective, as he uses that word in the quotation

[1] *What is art?* Section V.

above, is pure Art as opposed to modern or adulterated Art; but in deciding the full value of any work of Art we have to consider the nature of its contents, the nature, that is, of the experiences communicated. The value of art contents is judged, according to Tolstoy, by the religious consciousness of the age. For Tolstoy the religious consciousness is the higher comprehension of the meaning of life, and this, according to him, is the universal union of men with God and with one another.

When Tolstoy applies his criterion to the judgement of particular works of art, he is able to deduce striking results: 'Christian Art, that is, the Art of our time, must be catholic in the direct sense of that word – that is, universal – and so must unite all men. There are but two kinds of sensations which unite all men – the sensations which arise from the recognition of man's filial relation to God and of the brotherhood of men, and the simplest vital sensations which are accessible to all men without exception, such as the sensations of joy, meekness of spirit, alacrity, calm, etc. It is only these two kinds of sensations that form the subject of the Art of our time, which is good according to its contents.' Tolstoy in fact denied the value of all human endeavours except those which tend directly to the union of men. It may be suspected that his religious enthusiasm was due to his belief that Religion had this tendency. He distinguished, it will be remembered, very sharply between Religion and religions; a distinction with which many besides Tolstoy have consoled themselves. But his essential aim, his single value, was the union of men. All other things are of value only in so far as they tend to promote this, and art shares the general subordination. Even a joke, for Tolstoy, is only a joke so long as all men may share in it, a truly revolutionary amendment. The sharing is more important than the merriment. On these principles he surveys European Art and Literature. With magnificent defiance of accepted values, and the hardness of heart of a supreme doctrinaire, one after another of the unassailables is toppled from its eminence.

Shakespeare, Dante, Goethe, etc., are rejected; Wagner in especial is the object of a critical *tour de force*. In their place are set *A Tale of Two Cities, The Chimes, Adam Bede, Les Miserables* (almost the only thing in French literature of which Tolstoy could approve), and *Uncle Tom's Cabin*.[1] All art which does not directly urge the union of men, or whose appeal is suspected to be limited to cultured and aristocratic circles, is condemned. 'All who are not hand in hand with me are against me,' thought Tolstoy, under the urgency of his sense of human misery. Any diversion of art from a single narrow channel seemed to him an irreparable waste. Remembering no doubt how deeply he had been affected and influenced in the past by the things which he now deplored, he came in the end to assign unlimited powers to art when rightly directed. But, if we think of the other things which he also invoked to the same end, there is a ring of despair in his final cry: 'Art must remove violence, only Art can do this.'

We may compare with this a famous utterance of another aristocrat, equally a supreme artist, equally in rebellion against the whole fabric of conventional civilization, whose 'passion for reforming the world' was not less than Tolstoy's, but who differed from him in the possession of a wider and more complete sense of values and a mind not riven and distorted by a late conversion.

'The whole objection of the immorality of poetry rests upon a misconception of the manner in which poetry acts to produce the moral improvement of man. Ethical science arranges the elements which poetry has created, and propounds schemes and proposes examples of civil and domestic life: nor is it for want of admirable doctrines that men hate, and despise, and censure, and deceive and subjugate one another.

'But poetry acts in a diviner manner. It awakens and enlarges the mind itself by rendering it the receptacle of a thousand

---

[1] *What is Art?* Section XVI.

unapprehended combinations of thought. Whatever strengthens and purifies the affections, enlarges the imagination, and adds spirit to sense, is useful. It exceeds all imagination to conceive what would have been the moral condition of the world if neither Dante, Petrarch, Boccaccio, Chaucer, Shakespeare, Calderon, Lord Bacon, nor Milton, had ever existed.'

It is curious how the insertion of particular names here seems to weaken the argument. The world we feel fairly certain, would be on the whole much the same even if there had been no Boccaccio and no Lord Bacon. Things would not be very different, some people will think, even if none of these authors had ever bestirred themselves to write. Shakespeare, as so often, would perhaps be counted an exception. But this sense that there are, after all, very few poets who individually make much difference is not in the least an objection to Shelley's main thesis. We could bale a vast amount of water out of the sea without making any apparent difference to it, but this would not prove that it does not consist of water. Even if the removal of the influence of all the poets whose names we know made no appreciable difference in human affairs, it would still be true that the enlargement of the mind, the widening of the sphere of human sensibility, is brought about through poetry.

A too narrow view of values, or a too simple conception of morality is usually the cause of these misunderstandings of the arts. The agelong controversy as to whether the business of poetry is to please or to instruct shows this well. 'Poets wish either to instruct or to delight or to combine the two,' said the cautious Horace. 'Join the solid and useful with the agreeable.' 'It is only for the purpose of being useful that Poetry ought to be agreeable; pleasure is only a means which she uses for the end of profit.' So thought Boileau and Rapin. Dryden, modest and penetrating in his fashion, was 'satisfied if it cause delight: for delight is the chief, if not the only, end of poetry: instruction can be admitted but in the second place; for poesy only instructs as it delights.' But he does not further specify the nature of the delight or the instruction, an omission in which most critics except Shelley agree. Our view on the point entirely depends upon this. If we set the sugar-coated-pill view aside as beneath serious consideration, there still remains a problem. A reviewer of the recent performance of the *Cenci* will state it excellently for us.

'It had been better had Shelley's *Cenci* remained for ever banned. It represents three hours of unrelieved, agonizing misery. . . . What excuse is there for the depicting of horrors such as these? There must be some, for a house packed with literary celebrities fiercely applauded. If the function of the theatre is to amuse, then in the presentation of the *Cenci* it has missed its aim. If it is to instruct, what moral can be pointed for the better conduct of our lives by a tragedy such as this? If Art be the answer, then Art may well be sacrificed.'

No doubt the literary celebrities, with their applause, were to blame, in part, for this. Our relic of the Age of Good Sense made a just reaction. He accurately registered the effect to which bad acting and inept production[1] gave rise. But it is with his argument not with his reaction that we are concerned. The celebrities, if they had not been too busy giving vent (though in a mistaken form) to their loyalty to the memory of Shelley, and to their sense of triumph over the Censor, might have told him that neither amusement nor instruction is what the judicious seek from Tragedy, and referred him to Aristotle. Neither term, unless we wrench it right out of its usual setting is appropriate to the greater forms of art. The experiences which they occasion are

[1] 'This story of the Cenci is indeed eminently fearful and monstrous: anything like a dry exhibition of it on the stage would be insupportable. The person who would treat such a subject must increase the ideal, and diminish the actual horror of the events.' From Shelley's preface. The producers, however, were of the contrary opinion.

too full, too varied, too whole, too subtly balanced upon oppos-
ing impulses, whether of pity and terror or of joy and despair, to
be so easily described. Tragedy –

> beneath whose sable roof
> Of boughs as if for festal purpose decked
> With unrejoicing berries – ghostly shapes
> May meet at noontide; Fear and Trembling Hope,
> Silence and Foresight, Death the Skeleton
> And Time the Shadow,

is still the form under which the mind may most clearly and
freely contemplate the human situation, its issues unclouded, its
possibilities revealed. To this its value is due and the supreme
position among the arts which it has occupied in historical times
and still occupies; what will happen in the future we can only
conjecture. Tragedy is too great an exercise of the spirit to be
classed among amusements or even delights, or to be regarded
as a vehicle for the inculcation of such crude valuations as may
be codified in a moral. But the fuller discussion of Tragedy we
must defer.

   These remarks seemed necessary in order to avoid the impression, which our theory of value might have given, that the arts
are merely concerned with happy solutions and ingenious
reconciliations of diverse gratifications, 'a box where sweets
compacted lie'. It is not so. Only a crude psychology, as we shall
see, would identify the satisfaction of an impulse with a pleasure.
No hedonic theory of value will fit the facts over even a small
part of the field, since it must take what is a concomitant merely
of a phase in the process of satisfaction as the mainspring of the
whole. Pleasure, however, has its place in the whole account of
values, and an important place, as we shall see later. But it must
not be allowed to encroach on ground to which it has no right.

10

POETRY FOR POETRY'S SAKE

On passe plus facilement d'un extrême à un autre
que d'une nuance à une autre nuance.
Attirance de la Mort

Another possible misapprehension which cannot be left unmentioned arises in connection with the doctrine 'Art for Art's sake', a doctrine definitely and detrimentally dated; it concerns the place of what are called ulterior effects in the valuing of a work of art. It has been very fashionable to turn up the nose at any attempt to apply, as it is said, 'external canons' to art. But it may be recalled that of all the great critical doctrines, the 'moral', theory of art (it would be better to call it the 'ordinary values' theory) has the most great minds behind it. Until Whistler came to start the critical movements of the last half-century, few poets, artists or critics had ever doubted that the value of art experiences was to be judged as other values are. Plato, Aristotle, Horace, Dante, Spenser, Milton, the Eighteenth Century, Coleridge, Shelley, Matthew Arnold and Pater, to name only the most prominent, all with varying degrees of refinement, held the same view.[1] The last is a somewhat unexpected adherent.

'Given the conditions I have tried to explain as constituting good art, then if it be devoted further to the increase of men's happiness, to the redemption of the oppressed, or to the enlargement of our sympathies with each other, or to such presentment of new and old truth about ourselves and our relation to the world as may fortify us in our sojourn here . . . it will also be great art; if, over and above those qualities which I have summed up . . . it has something of the soul of humanity in it, and finds its logical, its architectural place, in the great structure of human life."[2] No better brief emotive account of the conditions under which an experience has value could be desired.

Against all these weighty opinions, the view – supported largely by a distinction between Form and Content, Subject and Handling, which will be examined elsewhere,[3] and relying upon the doctrine of intrinsic, supersensible, ultimate Goods discussed above – that the values of art are unique, or capable of being considered in isolation from all others, has held sway for some thirty years in many most reputable quarters. The reasons for this attempted severance have already been touched upon;

---

[1] It is true that in mechanics one might draw up a formidable list of names and say 'Opposed to all these appeared a certain Einstein', but the cases are not parallel. A scientific advance is different from a change of fashion, and no new facts nor any new hypothesis – no Michelson-Morley experiment, nor any widened purview – led up to the separate value theory of art. Although historians of aesthetics are sometimes pleased to present their facts as though they represented a progress from cruder to more refined opinion, from ignorance to wisdom, there is no sound basis for the procedure. Aristotle was at least as clearly and fully aware of the relevant facts and as adequate in his explanations as any later inquirers. Aesthetics in fact has hardly yet reached the scientific stage, in which succeeding investigators can start where their predecessors left off.

[2] *An Essay on Style*. The final paragraph.

[3] See Chapters Sixteen, Eighteen and Twenty-one.

they are of all sorts. Partly it may be due to the influence of Whistler and Pater, and of those still more influential disciples who spread their doctrines. Partly it may be due to a massed reaction against Ruskin. Partly again we may suspect the influence, rather suddenly encountered, of Continental and German aesthetics upon the English mind. Almost from the beginning of scientific aesthetics, the insistence upon the aesthetic experience as an experience, peculiar, complete, and capable of being studied in isolation, has received prominence. Often it is no more than an extension into this field of a part of scientific method – the method of considering, whenever possible, one thing at a time. When critics in England, not very long ago, heard that there was something connected with art and poetry – namely, the aesthetic experience – which could be considered and examined in isolation by the methods of introspection, they not unnaturally leapt to the conclusion that its value also could be isolated and described without reference to other things. In some hands the further conclusions drawn were too queer to outlive their hour of fashion. They amounted often to the postulation of a 'specific thrill' yielded by works of art and nothing else, unlike and unconnected with all other experiences. 'No queerer,' it was said, 'than anything else in this incredibly queer universe.'[1] But the queerness of the universe is of a different and a more interesting sort. It may be a curiosity shop but it nowhere seems to be a chaos.

For our present purposes we need only consider the view as it is put forward by its ablest exponent, a critic who by his own explanations of this formula goes very far towards meeting the objection we urge.

'What then does the formula "Poetry for Poetry's sake" tell us about this experience? It says, as I understand it, these things. First, this experience is an end in itself, is worth having on its

[1] Clive Bell, *Art*, p. 49.

own account, has an intrinsic value. Next, its *poetic* value is this intrinsic worth alone. Poetry may have also an ulterior value as a means to culture or religion; because it conveys instruction or softens the passions, or furthers a good cause; because it brings the poet fame, or money, or a quiet conscience. So much the better: let it be valued for these reasons too. But its ulterior worth neither is nor can directly determine its poetic worth as a satisfying imaginative experience; and this is to be judged entirely from within. . . . The consideration of ulterior ends whether by the poet in the act of composing or by the reader in the act of experiencing, tends to lower poetic value. It does so because it tends to change the nature of poetry by taking it out of its own atmosphere. For its nature is to be not a part, nor yet a copy of the real world (as we commonly understand that phrase) but to be a world by itself, independent, complete, autonomous.'[1]

There seem four points well worth close consideration here. The first is that the things mentioned as possible ulterior values in Dr. Bradley's list – culture, religion, instruction, softening of the passions, furtherance of good causes, the poet's fame, or money, or quiet conscience – these things are plainly upon quite different levels. He says of all of them that they cannot possibly determine the poetic worth of an aesthetic experience; that whether or not any poetic experience is *poetically* valuable cannot depend upon any of these ulterior values. But it is certain that some of these stand in a quite different relation to the poetic experience than do others. Culture, religion, instruction in some special senses, softening of the passions, and the furtherance of good causes may be directly concerned in our judgements of the *poetic* values of experiences. Otherwise, as we shall see, the word 'poetic' becomes a useless sound. On the other hand, the poet's fame, his reward, or his conscience, seem plainly to be irrelevant. That is the first point.

---

[1] A. C. Bradley, *Oxford Lectures on Poetry*, p. 5.

The second point is that what Dr. Bradley says as to the imaginative experience – that it is to be judged entirely from within – is misleading. In most cases we do not judge it from within. Our judgement as to its value is no part of it. In rare instances such a judgement may be part of it, but this is exceptional. As a rule we have to come out of it in order to judge it, and we judge it by memory or by other residual effects which we learn to be good indices to its value. If by judging it in the experience we mean merely while these residual effects are fresh, we may agree. In so judging it, however, its 'place in the great structure of human life' cannot possibly be ignored. The value which it has is dependent upon this, and we cannot judge that value without taking this place, and with it innumerable ulterior worths, into account. It is not that we shall evaluate it wrongly if we neglect them, but that evaluation is just this taking account of everything, and of the way things hang together.

The third point arises with regard to Dr. Bradley's third position, that the consideration of ulterior ends, whether by the poet in the act of composing, or by the reader in the act of experiencing, tends to lower poetic value. Here all depends upon *which are the ulterior ends in question*, and what the kind of poetry. It will not be denied that for some kinds of poetry the intrusion of certain ulterior ends may, and often does, lower their value; but there seem plainly to be other kinds of poetry in which its value as poetry definitely and directly depends upon the ulterior ends involved. Consider the Psalms, Isaiah, the New Testament, Dante, the *Pilgrim's Progress*, Rabelais, any really universal satire, Swift, Voltaire, Byron.

In all these cases the consideration of ulterior ends has been certainly essential to the act of composing. That needs no arguing; but, equally, this consideration of the ulterior ends involved is inevitable to the reader.

Dr. Bradley puts this third position forward in a tentative form; he says that the ulterior *tends* to lower poetic value, an important reservation, but it would be better to distinguish two kinds of poetry, one to which his doctrine applies and one to which it does not. As illustrations of the cases in which his doctrine does apply, *The Ancient Mariner* and *Hartleap Well* may be mentioned. Here in both cases the experiences are of a kind into which no ulterior ends enter in any important degree. Thus when Coleridge and Wordsworth introduce moral considerations, the effect is undeniably one of intrusion. As Mrs. Meynell comically remarks, '*The Ancient Mariner* offends upon a deliberate plan. It denies the natural function of observation when it invents sanctions for the protection of a wild bird's life, and for the punishment of its slaughter. Coleridge intends to enforce a lesson by telling us that 200 mariners died of thirst because they had – with the superstition pardonable in their state of education – supposed an albatross to be the bringer of foggy weather, and had approved its slaughter, as almost all men implicitly approve the daily slaughter of innocent beast and bird.' But this charge against Coleridge is only reasonable if we make of this ulterior end, this 'lesson' against cruelty to animals, a vital part of the poem. Mrs. Meynell, we may think, takes Coleridge's moral too seriously. It may be this possibility which Coleridge had in mind when he said, long afterwards, that *The Ancient Mariner* did not contain enough of the moral. As the poem stands, it is of a kind into which ulterior ends do not enter. If we are to take this alien element, this lesson, into account in our judgement, we shall have deliberately to misread the poem, with Mrs. Meynell. The same considerations apply to *Hartleap Well*; and so far as Dr. Bradley is merely enforcing this point, we may agree; but he fails to notice – it is only fair to say that few critics seem ever to notice it – that poetry is of more than one kind, and that the different kinds are to be judged by different principles. There is a kind of poetry into the judgement of which ulterior ends directly and essentially enter; a kind part of whose value is directly derivable from the value of the ends with which it is associated. There are other kinds, into which ulterior ends do not enter in any degree, and there are yet other kinds whose value may be lowered by the intrusion of ends relatively trivial in value. Dr. Bradley is misled by the usual delusion that there is in this respect only one kind of poetry, into saying far more than the facts of poetic experience will justify.

The fourth point is of more general importance perhaps than these three. It is in fact the real point of disagreement between the view we are upholding and the doctrine which Dr. Bradley, together with the vast majority of modern critics, wishes to maintain. It is stated in the concluding sentence of the paragraph which I have quoted. He says of poetry that 'its nature is to be, not a part nor yet a copy of the real world, as we commonly understand that phrase, but to be a world by itself, independent, complete, autonomous. To possess it fully, you must enter that world, conform to its laws, and ignore, for the time being, the beliefs, aims, and particular conditions which belong to you in the other world of reality.' This doctrine insists upon a severance between poetry and what, in opposition, may be called life; a complete severance, allowing, however, as Dr. Bradley goes on to insist – an 'underground' connection. But this 'underground' connection is all important. Whatever there is in the poetic experience has come through it. The world of poetry has in no sense any different reality from the rest of the world and it has no special laws and no other-worldly peculiarities. It is made up of experiences of exactly the same kinds as those that come to us in other ways. Every poem, however, is a strictly limited piece of experience, a piece which breaks up more or less easily if alien elements intrude. It is more highly and more delicately organized than ordinary experiences of the street or of the hillside; it is fragile. Further it is communicable. It may be experienced by many different minds with only slight variations. That this should be possible is one of the conditions of its organization. It differs from many other experiences, whose value is very similar, in this very communicability. For these reasons when we experience it, or attempt to, we must preserve it from contamination, from the irruptions of personal particularities. We must keep the poem undisturbed by these or we fail to read it and have some other experience instead. For these reasons we establish a severance, we draw a boundary between the poem and what is not the poem in our experience. But this is no severance between unlike things but between different systems of the same activities. The gulf between them is no greater than that between the impulses which direct the pen and those which conduct the pipe of a man who is smoking and writing at once, and the 'disassociation' or severance of the poetic experience is merely a freeing of it from extraneous ingredients and influences. The myth of a 'transmutation' or 'poetization' of experience and that other myth of the 'contemplative' or 'aesthetic' attitude, are in part due to talking about Poetry and the 'poetic' instead of thinking about the concrete experiences which are poems.

The separation of poetic experience from its place in life and its ulterior worths, involves a definite lop-sidedness, narrowness, and incompleteness in those who preach it sincerely. No one, of course, would bring such charges against the author of *Shakespearean Tragedy*; his is that welcome and not unfamiliar case of the critic whose practice is a refutation of his principles. When genuinely held the view leads to an attempted splitting up of the experiencing reader into a number of distinct faculties or departments which have no real existence. It is impossible to divide a reader into so many men – an aesthetic man, a moral man, a practical man, a political man, an intellectual man, and so on. It cannot be done. In any genuine experience all these elements inevitably enter. But if it could be done, as many critics pretend, the result would be fatal to the wholeness and sanction of the critical judgement. We cannot e.g. read Shelley adequately while believing that all his views are moonshine – read *Prometheus Unbound* while holding that 'the perfectibility of man is an undesirable ideal' and that 'hangmen are excellent things'. To say that there is a purely aesthetic or poetic approach to, let us say, the *Sermon on the Mount*, by which no consideration of the intention or ulterior end of the poem enters, would appear to be merely mental timidity, the shrinking remark of a person who finds essential literature too much for him. Into an adequate reading of the greater kinds of poetry everything not private and peculiar to the individual reader must come in. The reader must be required to wear no blinkers, to overlook nothing which is relevant, to shut off no part of himself from participation. If he attempts to assume the peculiar attitude of disregarding all but some hypothetically-named aesthetic elements, he joins Henry James's Osmond in his tower, he joins Blake's Kings and Priests in their High Castles and Spires.

11

A SKETCH FOR A PSYCHOLOGY

> 'Wot's wot?' repeated one of the buccaneers in a deep growl.
> 'Ah, he'd be a lucky one as knowed that!'
>
> *Treasure Island*

M. Jules Romains recently observed[1] that psychology hitherto has merely contrived to say laboriously and obscurely, and with less precision, what we all know without its aid already. This is regrettably difficult to deny; any particular remark of a psychologist, if true, is unlikely to be startling. But at certain points new light has none the less crept in. Incoherences and flaws have been found in the common sense picture, adumbration rather, of the mind; connections between bits of our behaviour, which common-sense had missed, have been noted and, still more important, a general outline of the kind of thing a mind is has begun to take shape. The next age but two, if an oncoming Age of Relativity is to be followed as Mr. Haldane supposes[2] by an

---

[1] *Eyeless Sight*, p. 22.
[2] *Dædalus, or Science and the Future*, by J. B. S. Haldane.

Age of Biology, will be introduced by a recognition on the part of many minds of their own nature, a recognition which is certain to change their behaviour and their outlook considerably. We are still far removed from such an age. None the less enough is known for an analysis of the mental events which make up the reading of a poem to be attempted. And such an analysis is a primary necessity for criticism. The psychological distinctions which have hitherto served the critic are too few and his use of them in most cases too unsystematic, too vague, and too uncertain, for his insight to yield its full advantages.

The view put forward here is in many respects heterodox, a disadvantage in a sketch. But so many difficulties attend any exposition of psychology, however orthodox and however full, that the dangers of misunderstanding are outweighed by the advantages of a fresh point of view. It is the general outline and in particular the insistence upon an account of knowledge in terms merely of the causation of our thoughts which is contrary to received opinion. The detail of the analysis of poetic experience, the account of imagery, of emotion, of pleasure, of incipient action and so forth, although, so far as I am aware, no similar analysis has before been explicitly set out, may be taken as comparatively orthodox.

For our immediate purpose, for a clearer understanding of values and for the avoidance of unnecessary confusions in criticism, it is necessary to break away from the set of ideas by which popular and academic psychology alike attempt to describe the mind. We naturally tend to conceive it as a thing of a peculiar spiritual kind, fairly persistent though variable, endowed with attributes, three in number, its capacities namely for knowing, willing and feeling, three irreducible modes of being aware of or concerned with objects. A violent shock to this entity comes when we are forced by a closer examination of the facts to conceive it as doing all these three unconsciously as well as consciously. An unconscious mind is a fairly evident fiction, useful though it may be, and goings on in the nervous system are readily accepted as a satisfactory substitute. From this to the recognition of the conscious mind as a similar fiction is no great step, although one which many people find difficult. Some of this difficulty is due to habit. It wears off as we notice how many of the things which we believed true of the fiction can be stated in terms of the less fictitious substitute. But much of the difficulty is emotive, non-intellectual, more specifically religious, in origin.[1] It is due to desire, to fear, or to exaltation as the case may be, to emotion masquerading as thought and is a difficulty not so easily removed.

That the mind is the nervous system, or rather a part of its activity, has long been evident, although the prevalence among psychologists of persons with philosophic antecedents has delayed the recognition of the fact in an extraordinary fashion. With every advance of neurology – and a decided advance here was perhaps the only good legacy left by the War[2] – the evidence becomes more overwhelming. It is true that as our knowledge of the nervous system stands at present much of the detail of the identification is impenetrably obscure, and the account which we give must frankly be admitted to be only a degree less fictitious than one in terms of spiritual happenings. But the kind of account which is likely to be substantiated by future research has become clear, largely through the work of Behaviourists and Psycho-analysts, the assumptions and results of both needing to be corrected however in ways which the recent experimental and theoretical investigations of the 'Gesalt' School are indicating.

The view that we are our bodies, more especially our nervous systems, more especially still the higher or more central co-ordinating parts of it, and that the mind is a system of impulses

---

[1] Compare Chapter Thirty-four where the ways in which emotive factors interfere with thought are considered.
[2] Cf. Piéron, *Thought and the Brain*, Chapter I.

should not be described as Materialism. It might equally well be
called Idealism. Neither term in this connection has any scientific, any strictly symbolic meaning or reference. Neither stands
for any separable, observable group of things, or character in
things. Each is primarily an emotive term used to incite or support certain emotional attitudes. Like all terms used in the vain
attempt (vain because the question is nonsensical) to say what
things are, instead of to say how they behave, they state nothing.
Like all such terms they change in different hands from banners
to bludgeons, being each for some people an emotive agent
round which attitudes, aspirations, values are rallied, and for
other people a weapon of offence by which persons supposed
adverse to these attitudes, aspirations and values may, it is hoped,
be discomfited. That the Materialist and the Idealist believe
themselves to be holding views which are incompatible with
one another is but an instance of a very widespread confusion
between scientific statement and emotive appeal, with which we
shall in later chapters be much concerned. The Mind-Body problem is strictly speaking no problem; it is an *imbroglio* due to
failure to settle a real problem, namely, as to when we are making a statement and when merely inciting an attitude. A problem
simpler here than in many cases, since the alleged statement is of
an impossible form,[1] but complicated on both sides of the controversy by misunderstanding of the attitudes which the other
side is concerned to maintain. For if mental events are recognized as identical with certain neural events, neither the attitudes
which ensue towards them nor the attitudes they themselves will
warrantably take up, are changed so much as either Idealists or
Materialists have commonly supposed. To call anything mental
or spiritual, as opposed to material, or to call anything material
as opposed to mental, is only to point out a difference between

---

[1] Many apparent questions which begin with the words 'What' and 'Why' are
not questions at all, but requests for emotive satisfaction.

the two kinds. The differences which can actually be detected between a mental event, such as a toothache, and a non-mental event, such as a sunspot, remain when we have identified the mental event with a neural change. So recognized, it loses none of its observable peculiarities, only certain alleged unstatable and ineffable attributes are removed. It remains unlike any event which is not mental; it is as unparalleled as before. It retains its privileges as the most interesting of all events, and our relations to one another and to the world remain essentially as they were before the recognition. The extreme ecstasies of the mystic, like the attitudes of the engineer towards a successful contrivance, remain just as much and just as little appropriate with regard to the humblest or the proudest of our acts. Thus the identification of the mind with a part of the working of the nervous system, need involve, theology apart, no disturbance of anyone's attitude to the world, his fellow-men, or to himself. Theology, however, is still more implicit in current attitudes than traditional sceptics suspect.

The nervous system is the means by which stimuli from the environment, or from within the body, result in appropriate behaviour. All mental events occur in the course of processes of adaptation, somewhere between a stimulus and a response. Thus every mental event has an origin in stimulation, a character, and consequences, in action or adjustment for action. Its character is sometimes accessible to introspection. What it feels like, in those cases in which it feels or is felt at all, is consciousness, but in many cases nothing is felt, the mental event is unconscious. Why some events are conscious but not others is at present a mystery; no one has yet succeeded in bringing the various hints which neurology may offer into connection with one another. In some important respects conscious and unconscious mental events must differ, but what these are no one can as yet safely con-jecture. On the other hand there are many respects in which they are similar, and these are the respects which are at present most open to investigation.

The process in the course of which a mental event may occur, a process apparently beginning in a stimulus and ending in an act, is what we have called an impulse. In actual experience single impulses of course never occur. Even the simplest human reflexes are very intricate bundles of mutually dependent impulses, and in any actual human behaviour the number of simultaneous and connected impulses occurring is beyond estimation. The simple impulse in fact is a limit, and the only impulses psychology is concerned with are complex. It is often convenient to speak as though simple impulses were in question, as when we speak of an impulse of hunger, or an impulse to laugh, but we must not forget how intricate all our activities are.

To take the stimulus as a starting-point is in some ways misleading. Of the possible stimuli which we might at any moment receive, only a few actually take effect. Which are received and which impulses ensue depends upon which of our interests is active, upon the general set, that is, of our activities. This is conditioned in a large degree by the state, of satisfaction or unrest, of the recurrent and persistent needs of the body. When hungry and when replete we respond differently to the stimulus of a smell of cooking. A change in the wind unnoticed by the passengers causes the captain to reduce sail. Social needs in this respect are often as important as individual. Thus some people walking in a Gallery with friends before whom they wish to shine will actually receive far more stimulus from the pictures than they would if by themselves.

A stimulus then must not be conceived as an alien intruder which thrusts itself upon us and, after worming a devious way through our organism as through a piece of cheese, emerges at the other end as an act. Stimuli are only received if they serve some need of the organism and the form which the response to them takes depends only in part upon the nature of the stimulus, and much more upon what the organism 'wants', i.e. the state of equilibrium of its multifarious activities.

Thus experience has two sources which in different cases have very different importance. So far as we are thinking about or referring to certain definite things our behaviour in all probability will only be appropriate (i.e. our thoughts true) in so far as it is determined by the nature of the present and past stimuli we have received from those things and things like them. So far as we are satisfying our needs and desires a much less strict connection between stimulus and response is sufficient. A baby howls at first in much the same way, whatever the cause of his unrest, and older persons behave not unlike him. Any occasion may be sufficient for taking exercise, or for a quarrel, for falling in love or having a drink. To this partial independence of behaviour (from stimulus) is due the sometimes distressing fact that views, opinions and beliefs vary so much with our differing moods. Such variation shows that the view, belief or opinion is not a purely intellectual product, is not due to thinking in the narrower sense, of response that is governed by stimuli, present or past, but is an attitude adopted to satisfy some desire, temporary or lasting. Thought in the strictest sense varies only with evidence: but attitudes and feelings change for all manner of reasons.

The threefold division between the causes, character and consequences of a mental event, conscious or unconscious, corresponds, with certain qualifications, to the usual division in traditional psychology of thought (or cognition) feeling, and will (or cognition). To be cognisant of anything, to know it, is to be influenced by it; to desire, to seek, to will anything is to act towards it. In between these two are the conscious accompaniments, if any, of the whole process. These last, the conscious characters of the mental event, include evidently both sensations and feelings. (Cf. Chapter Sixteen, pp. 113–16.)

The correspondence is not by any means simple. Many things

are included under knowing, for example, which on this reconstruction of psychology would have to be counted as will-ing.[1] Expectation, usually described as a cognitive attitude, becomes a peculiar form of action, getting ready, namely, to receive certain kinds of stimuli rather than others. The opposite case is equally common. Hunger, a typical desire on the usual account, would become knowledge, giving us, when genuine hunger, obscure awareness of a lack of nourishment, when habit-hunger, awareness of a certain phase in a cyclic visceral process. These illustrations bring out clearly what is everywhere recognized, that the customary cognition-feeling-conation classification of mental goings on is not a pigeon-holing of exclusive processes. Every mental event has, in varying degrees, all three characteristics. Thus expectation as a preparation for certain stimuli may lower the threshold for them, and sometimes makes their reception more and sometimes less discriminating; hunger also is characteristically accompanied by a search for food.

The advantage of substituting the causation, the character and the consequences of a mental event as its fundamental aspects in place of its knowing, feeling, and willing aspects is that instead of a trio of incomprehensible ultimates we have a set of aspects which not only mental events but all events share. We have, of course, to introduce qualifications. Stimuli, as we have men-tioned above, are not the only causes of mental events. The ner-vous system is specialized to receive impressions through the organs of sense, but its state at any moment is also determined by a host of other factors. The condition of the blood and the position of the head are typical instances. Only that part of the

[1] 'Willing' is a bad word; I would use conation throughout were it not so likely to increase unnecessarily the difficulty which this chapter will unavoidably present to readers who are not familiar with psychological jargon. The essential thing is to think of willing (desiring, striving towards, trying) as an unconscious as much as a conscious process.

cause of a mental event which takes effect through incoming (sensory) impulses or through effects of past sensory impulses can be said to be thereby known. The reservation no doubt involves complications. But any plausible account of what knowledge is and how it happens is bound to be complicated.

Similarly, not all the effects of a mental event are to be counted as what that event wills or seeks after; apoplectic strokes, for example, can be ruled out. Only those movements which the nervous system is specialized to incite, which take place through motor impulses, should be included.

On all other accounts the relation between an awareness and what it is aware of is a mystery. We can name the relation as we please, apprehension, presentation, cognition or knowledge, but there we have to leave the matter. On this account we make use of the fact that an awareness, say of a variety of black marks on this page, is caused in a certain peculiar way, namely through impressions on a part of the brain (the retina) and various complicated connected goings on in other parts of the brain. To say that the mental (neural) event so caused is aware of the black marks is to say that it is caused by them, and here 'aware of' = 'caused by'. The two statements are merely alternative formulations.

In extending this account to more complicated situations where we know or, less ambiguously, refer to things which are past or future we have to make use of the fact that impressions are commonly *signs*, have effects which depend not on themselves alone but upon the other impressions which have co-operated with them in the past.

A sign[1] is something which has once been a member of a context or configuration that worked in the mind as a whole. When it reappears its effects are as though the rest of the context were present. In analysing complex events of referring we have

---

[1] This topic is discussed at length in *The Meaning of Meaning*.

to break them up artificially into the simpler sign-situations out of which they arise; not forgetting meanwhile how inter-dependent the parts of any interpretation of a complex sign are.

The detail of this procedure is most easily studied in connection with the use of words. We shall deal with it therefore in Chapter Sixteen, where the reading of a poem is discussed. Here only the general principle matters that to know anything is to be influenced by it, directly when we sense it, indirectly when the effects of past conjunctions of impressions come into play. More will be added later, in connection with the process of reading, about the receptive, the knowledge aspect of mental events. The other two aspects need less explanation. They are also more generally important for the understanding of poetic, musical and other experiences. For a theory of knowledge is needed only at one point, the point at which we wish to decide whether a poem, for example, is true, or reveals reality, and if so in what sense; admittedly a very important question. Whereas a theory of feeling, of emotion, of attitudes and desires, of the affective-volitional aspect of mental activity, is required at all points of our analysis.

12

PLEASURE

The poor benefit of a bewitching minute.
The Revenger's Tragedy

Sensation, imagery, feeling, emotion, together with pleasure, unpleasure and pain are names for the conscious characteristics of impulses. How they may best be sorted out is a problem whose difficulty is much aggravated by the shortcomings of language at this point. We speak, for instance, of pleasures and pains in the same fashion, as though they were of the same order, but, strictly, although pains as single self-sufficing modifications of consciousness are easily enough obtainable, pleasures by themselves do not seem to occur. Pleasure seems to be a way in which something happens, rather than an independent happening which can occur by itself in a mind. We have, not pleasures, but experiences of one kind or another, visual, auditory, organic, motor, and so forth, which are pleasant. Similarly we have experiences which are unpleasant. If, however, we call them painful we give rise to an ambiguity. We may be saying that they are unpleasant or we may be saying that they are accompanied by pains, which is a different matter. The use of the term pleasure, as though like pain it was itself a complete experience, instead of being something which attaches to or follows along with or after other experiences, has led to a number of confusions; especially in those critical theses, to which objection has already been taken in Chapter Nine, which identify value with pleasure.

The twenty or more distinct kinds of sensations, into which modern psychology has elaborated the old five senses, can be observed to differ very widely in the degree to which they are susceptible of and accompanied by pleasantness and unpleasantness. The higher senses, sight and hearing, in most persons seem to yield sensations which vary much less from neutrality or indifference than the others. We must be careful to understand this difference correctly however. An arrangement of colours and shapes, a sequence of notes or a musical phrase may, of course, in suitable people, be as intensely toned, pleasantly or unpleasantly, as any organic or taste sensations, for example. But even this is not usual. The right experiment is to compare a single colour, say, or a single note, with such a sensation as a uniform touch or temperature gives rise to, a bath for example, or with a simple uniform taste or smell, or with hunger, or nausea. Fair comparison is difficult, equivalent levels of simplicity and uniformity being impossible to discover, but few will doubt that the degree of pleasure-unpleasure aroused by tastes, for example, far exceeds that which auditory or visual sensations excite by themselves. We must of course be careful here to avoid confusing the intrinsic pleasure-unpleasure of the sensations with that which arises through memory, through the effects of other sensations, pleasant or unpleasant, which may have accompanied them in the past, and through expectations agreeable or disagreeable.

To speak of the intrinsic pleasure-unpleasure of a sensation is perhaps misleading. The pleasantness of a sensation as we know is a highly variable thing. It may alter completely while the strictly sensory characteristics of the sensation remain as before. The difference in the same smell of liquor, before and after an alcoholic excess is a striking example. A sound which is pleasant for a while may become very unpleasant if it continues and does not lapse from consciousness. And yet indisputably it may remain qua sensation the same. A sound-sensation may remain unchanged in tone, volume and intensity yet vary widely in pleasure-unpleasure. This difference is important. It is one of the chief reasons which have caused feeling (pleasure-unpleasure) to be distinguished from sensation as altogether of a different nature. Tone, volume and intensity are features in the sound closely dependent upon the stimulus, pleasantness is dependent not on external stimulus but upon factors, very obscure at present, in us. All here is conjecture. The close connection of stimulus with sensation we know because it happens to be comparatively accessible to experiment. And introspection of sensations of external origin is for that reason much more easy than introspection of most visceral or organic sensations. We can practise it freely and repeat it and so control our results. To a lesser extent those sensations of internal origin which we can in part consciously control, those due to voluntary movements, share this double accessibility. But all the rest of the multifarious conscious goings on in the nervous system remain obscure.

One broad fact, however, is important. The effects in the body of almost all stimuli of whatever nature are extraordinarily numerous and varied. 'You cannot show the observer a wall-paper pattern without by that very fact disturbing his respiration and circulation.'[1] And no man knows what other disturbances do not join in. The whole body resounds in what would seem to be a fairly systematic way. Whether the outpouring of this tide

---

[1] Titchener, *Text-book of Psychology*, p. 248.

of disturbance makes up a part of, gives a tone to consciousness, or whether only the incoming reports of the results can be conscious is a question upon which no conclusive evidence would seem to be yet available. The incoming reports of some at least of these disturbances certainly can become conscious. A lump in the throat, a yearning of the bowels, horripilation, breathlessness, these are their coarser and more obvious forms. Usually, they are less salient and fuse with the whole mass of internal sensations to form the *coenesthesia*, the whole bodily consciousness, tinging it, altering its general character in some one of perhaps a thousand different ways.

It has been much disputed whether pleasure-unpleasure is a quality of general bodily or organic consciousness, of some part of it perhaps, or whether it is something quite different from any quality of any sensation or set of sensations. As we have seen, it is not a quality of an auditory sensation in the sense in which its loudness, for instance, is a quality. There seem to be similar objections to making it a quality of any sensation of any kind. A sensation is what an impulse at a certain stage in its development feels like, and its sensory qualities are characters[1] of the impulse at that stage. The pleasure-unpleasure attaching to the impulse may be no character of the impulse itself, but of its fate, its success or failure in restoring equilibrium to the system to which it belongs.

This is perhaps as good a guess at what pleasure and unpleasure are as can yet be made, pleasure being successful activity of some kind, not necessarily of a biologically useful kind, and unpleasure being frustrated, chaotic, mal-successful activity. We shall consider this theory again at a later stage (cf. Chapter Twenty-four). The point to be made here is that pleasure and unpleasure are complicated matters arising in the course of activities which are directed to other ends. The old controversies as to

---

[1] Into conjectures as to what these are, it seems as yet not profitable to enter.

whether pleasure is the goal of all striving or whether avoidance of unpleasure the starting-point, are thus escaped. As Ribot pointed out[1] the exclusive quest of pleasure for itself, *plaisir-passion*, is a morbid form of activity and self-destructive. Pleasure on this view is originally an *effect* signifying that certain positive or negative tendencies have instinctively attained their aim and are satisfied. Later through experience it becomes a cause. Instructed by experience man and animal alike place themselves in circumstances which will arouse desire and so through satisfaction lead to pleasure. The gourmet, the libertine, the aesthete, the mystic do so alike. But when the pleasure which is the result of satisfying the tendency becomes the end pursued rather than the satisfying of the tendency itself, then an 'inversion of the psychological mechanism' comes about. In the one case the activity is propagated from below upwards, in the other from above downwards, from the brain to the organic functions. The result is often an exhaustion of the tendency, 'disillusionment' and the *blasé*, world-wearied attitude.

The evil results, as Ribot remarks, are largely confined to those individuals in whom the quest for pleasure has the force of an obsession. But on the view of pleasure, which we have indicated above, it is clear that all those doctrines, very common in critical literature, which set up pleasure as the goal of activity, are mistaken. Every activity has its own specific goal. Pleasure very probably ensues in most cases when this goal is reached, but that is a different matter. To read a poem for the sake of the pleasure which will ensue if it is successfully read is to approach it in an inadequate attitude. Obviously it is the poem in which we should be interested, not in a by-product of having managed successfully to read it. The orientation of attention is wrong if we put the pleasure in the forefront. Such a mistake is perhaps not common among instructed persons, but to judge by many

[1] *Problemes de Psychologie affective*, pp. 141–144.

remarks which appear in reviews and dramatic notices the per-centage of instructed persons among reviewers and theatre-goers does not seem high. This error, a legacy in part from the criticism of an age which had a still poorer psychological vocabulary[1] than our own, is one reason why Tragedy, for example, is so often misapproached. It is no less absurd to sup-pose that a competent reader sits down to read for the sake of pleasure, than to suppose that a mathematician sets out to solve an equation with a view to the pleasure its solution will afford him. The pleasure in both cases may, of course, be very great. But the pleasure, however great it may be, is no more the aim of the activity in the course of which it arises, than, for example, the noise made by a motorcycle – useful though it is as an indication of the way the machine is running – is the reason in the normal case for its having been started.

This very common mistake noted, the significance of pleasure and unpleasure may be insisted upon without misgiving. They are our most delicate signs of how our activities are thriving. But since even the most intense delight may indicate only a local success and the activity be generally detrimental, they are signs which need a very wary interpretation.

[1] It is probable that Wordsworth and certain that Coleridge if writing today would use quite other terms in place of pleasure for describing poetic values.

13

EMOTION AND THE COENESTHESIA

They are the silent griefs that cut the heart-strings.
The Broken Heart

In alluding to the coenesthesia we came very near to giving an account of emotion as an ingredient of consciousness. Stimulating situations give rise to widespread ordered repercussions throughout the body, felt as clearly marked colourings of consciousness. These patterns in organic response are fear, grief, joy, anger and the other emotional states. They arise for the most part when permanent or periodical tendencies of the individual are suddenly either facilitated or frustrated. Thus they depend far less upon the nature of the external stimulus than upon the general internal circumstances of the individual's life at the time the stimulus occurs.

These emotional states, with pleasure and unpleasure, are

customarily distinguished under the head of feeling[1] from sensations, which are, as we have seen, very closely dependent for their character upon their stimulus. Thus sensations are ranked together as cognitive elements, concerned, that is, with our knowledge of things rather than with our attitude or behaviour towards them, or our emotion about them. Pleasure, however, and emotion have, on our view, also a cognitive aspect. They give us knowledge; in the case of pleasure, of how our activities are going on, successfully or otherwise; in the case of emotion, knowledge primarily of our attitudes. But emotion may give us further knowledge. It is a remarkable fact that persons with exceptional colour sense apparently judge most accurately whether two colours are the same, for example, or whether they have or have not some definite harmonic relation to one another, not by attentive optical comparison or examination, but by the general emotional or organic reaction which the colours evoke when simply glanced at. This is an indirect way of becoming aware of the specific nature of the external world, but none the less a very valuable way. A similar method is probably involved in those apparently immediate judgements of the moral character of persons met with for the first time which many people make so readily and successfully. They may be quite unable to mention any definite feature of the person upon which their judgement could be based. It is none the less often extraordinarily just and discriminating. The remarkable sensitiveness to its mother's expression which the infant shows is a striking example. The part played by this kind of judgement in all aesthetic appreciation need not be insisted upon. It is notable that artists are often pre-eminently adepts at such judgements. The

---

[1] The fashion in which the term 'feeling' shifts about in psychology is notorious as a source of confusion. It would be convenient if it could be kept for pleasure-unpleasure, and used no longer as a synonym for 'emotion', since emotions can much more easily be regarded as built up from organic sensations.

topic is usually discussed under the wide and vague heading of intuition; a rubric which completely obscures and befogs the issues.

For such judgements are not a simpler and more direct way of taking cognisance of things, but a more indirect and more complex way. It is not thereby shown to be a less primitive process. On the contrary, simplified ways of thinking are commonly advanced products. The 'intuitive' person uses his coenesthesia as a chemist uses his reagents or a physiologist his galvanometer. As far as the sensations which the colour stimuli excite can be optically discriminated, no difference is perceptible. But an actual yet sensorily imperceptible difference becomes apparent through the difference in organic reaction. The process is merely one of adding further and more delicate signs to the situation, it is analogous to attaching a recording lever to a barograph.

The differences between sensitive or 'intuitive' and more 'rational' and obtuse individuals may be of two kinds. It may be that the sensitive person's organic response is more delicate. This is a difficult matter to decide. It is certain, however, that the chief difference (a derivative difference very likely) lies in the fact that the obtuse person has not learned to interpret the changes in his general bodily consciousness in any systematic fashion. The changes may occur and occur systematically, but they mean nothing definite to him.

This kind of intervention of organic sensation in perception plays a part in all the arts. Much neglected, it is probably of very great importance. What here needs to be noticed is that it is not a mode of gaining knowledge which differs in any essential way from other modes. No unique and peculiar relation of 'feeling' towards things needs to be introduced to explain it, any more than a unique and peculiar mode of 'cognitively apprehending' them needs to be introduced to explain ordinary knowing. In both instances their causes, which have to be assumed in any case, will suffice. When we sense something our sensation is caused by what we sense. When we refer to something absent, a present sensation similar to sensations which in the past have been coincident with it, is thereby a sign for it, and so on, through more and more intricate mnemic sign-situations. Here a present colour sensation gives rise to an organic response which has in the past accompanied a definite colour; the response becomes then a sign of that colour which the sensitive and discriminating person trusts, although he is optically unable to make sure whether that colour is present or merely one very like it. Other cases differ from this in complexity but not in principle. If it is objected that this account of referring or thinking in terms of causes gives us at best but a very indirect way of knowing, the reply is that the prevalence of error is itself a strong argument against a too direct theory of knowledge.

In popular parlance the term 'emotion' stands for those happenings in minds which accompany such exhibitions of unusual excitement as weeping, shouting, blushing, trembling, and so on. But in the usage of most critics it has taken an extended sense, thereby suffering quite needlessly in its usefulness. For them it stands for any noteworthy 'goings on' in the mind almost regardless of their nature. The true and profound emotions, as spoken of by critics, are often lacking in all the characteristics which govern the more refined linguistic usage of common people, and, as it happens, of psychologists also, for what may perhaps be regarded now as the standard usage in psychology, sets out from the very same bodily changes accompanying experience as were noted above.

Two main features characterize every emotional experience. One of these is a diffused reaction in the organs of the body brought about through the sympathetic system. The other is a tendency to action of some definite kind or group of kinds. These extensive changes in the visceral and vascular systems, characteristically in respiration and in glandular secretion, commonly take place in response to situations which call some instinctive tendency into play. As a result of all these changes a tide of sensations of internal bodily origin comes into consciousness. It is generally agreed that these sensations make up at least the main part of the peculiar consciousness of an emotion. Whether they are necessary to it or not is disputed. It may perhaps be suggested that insufficient attention has been paid in the theory of emotion to images of such sensations. The fact that fear, for example, may be felt in the absence of any detectable bodily changes of the kind described (a disputed fact) may be explained by supposing images of these sensations to be taking their place.

These sensations, or images of them, are then a main ingredient of an emotional experience and account for its peculiar 'colour' or tone, for the voluminousness and massiveness as well as for the extreme acuteness of emotions. But of equal or greater importance are the changes in consciousness due to reactions in the nervous systems which control movement, governing muscular response to the stimulating situation. These range, in the case of fear, from the awakening of a simple tendency, an impulse to run away or hide under the table, to such elaborate readjustments as we make when we prepare to counter a threat against some favourite opinion. As a rule a process of extraordinary complexity takes place between perceiving the situation and finding a mode of meeting it. This complicated process contributes the rest of its peculiar flavour to an emotional experience.

A more detailed discussion from the same angle of the points raised in this and the surrounding chapters will be found in The Meaning of Psychology (1926) by C. K. Ogden, where the author's view of mental activity is elaborated.

14

MEMORY

Within the surface of Time's fleeting river
Its wrinkled image lies, as then it lay
Immovably unquiet, and for ever
It trembles, but it cannot pass away!
Shelley, *Ode to Liberty*

So far we have alluded only casually to memory, to that apparent
revival of past experience to which the richness and complexity
of experience is due. Every stimulus which is ever received leaves
behind it, so it is said, an imprint, a trace capable of being
revived later and of contributing its quota to consciousness and
to behaviour. To these effects of past experience the systematic,
the organized character of our behaviour is due; the fact that
they intervene is the explanation of our ability to learn by
experience. It is a way peculiar to living tissue by which the past
influences our present behaviour across, as it might appear, a
gulf of time.

How we should conceive this influence is perhaps the most
puzzling point in psychology. The old theory of a kind of

Somerset House of past impressions has given place to an account in terms of facilitations of neural paths, lowered resistances in synapses, and so forth. It was natural that as the broad outlines of neural activity came to be known, psychologists should attempt to make use of them. But on close examination it is clear that their interpretations were far too crude. Fixed 'paths', one for every item of experience which has ever taken place, and others for every kind of connection into which the items come, however multitudinous we make them, no longer explain what can be observed in behaviour and experience. As Van Kries and, more recently, Koffka have insisted, the fact, for example, that we *recognize* things in cases where it is certain that quite different paths must be involved, is fatal to the scheme. And mere multiplication of the entities invoked leads to no solution. Semon even goes so far as to say that when we listen to a song for the hundredth time we hear not only the singer but a chorus of nine and ninety mnemic voices. This corollary by itself is almost a refutation of his theory.

We have to escape from the crude assumption that the only way in which what is past can be repeated is by records being kept. The old associationists supposed the records to be writ small inside separate cells. The more modern view was that they were scored large through a deepening of the channels of conduction. Neither view is adequate.

Imagine an energy system of prodigious complexity and extreme delicacy of organization which has an indefinitely large number of stable poises. Imagine it thrown from one poise to another with great facility, each poise being the resultant of all the energies of the system. Suppose now that the *partial* return of a situation which has formerly caused it to assume a stable poise, throws it into an unstable condition from which it most easily returns to equilibrium by reassuming the former poise. Such a system would exhibit the phenomena of memory; but it would keep no records though appearing to do so. The appearance would be due merely to the extreme accuracy and sensitiveness of the system and the delicacy of its balances. Its state on the later occasion would appear to be a *revival* of its state on the former, but this would not be the case any more than a cumulus cloud this evening is a revival of those which decorated the heavens last year.

This imaginary construction can be made more concrete by imagining a solid with a large number of facets upon any one of which it can rest. If we try to balance it upon one of its coigns or ridges it settles down upon the nearest facet. In the case of the neural system we are trying to suggest each stable poise has been determined by a definite set, or better, context of conditions. Membership of this context is what corresponds to nearness to a facet. The partial return of the context causes the system to behave as though conditions were present which are not, and this is what is essential in memory.

That this suggestion in the form here presented is unsatisfactory and incomplete is evident. It is wildly conjectural no doubt, but so are the Archival and Pathway Theories. Yet it does avoid the chief deficiencies of those theories, it does suggest why only some conjunctions of experiences become 'associated', those namely which yield a stable poise. And it suggests why a thing should be recognized as the same though appearing in countless different aspects; every time it appears different conditions occur which, none the less, lead to one and the same stable poise, as the polyhedron we imagined may settle down on one and the same facet from all the surrounding ridges.

One of the collateral advantages of such a view is that it removes some of the temptations to revert to animism from which psychologists, and especially literary psychologists, suffer. Dissatisfaction with current hypotheses as to the mechanism of reflex arcs is a main cause for the scientifically desperate belief in the soul. And apart from this, the special emotive factors which disturb judgement on this point are less obtrusive when this account is substituted for the usual story of the conditioned reflex, that sacrilegious contrivance of the mechanists.

There is no kind of mental activity in which memory does not intervene. We are most familiar with it in the case of images, those fugitive elusive copies of sensations with which psychology has been hitherto so much, perhaps too much, concerned. Visual images are the best known of them, but it is important to recognize that every kind of sensation may have its corresponding image. Visceral, kinaesthetic, thermal images can with a little practice be produced, even by people who have never noticed their occurrence. But individual differences as regards imagery are enormous, more in the degree to which images become conscious, however, than in their actual presence or absence on the needful occasion. Those people who, by their own report, are devoid of images, none the less behave in a way which makes it certain that the same processes are at work in them as in producers of the most flamboyant images.

15

ATTITUDES

My Sences want their outward motion
Which now within
Reason doth win,
Redoubled by her secret notion.
John Hoskins

The interventions of memory are not confined to sensation and emotion. They are of equal importance in our active behaviour. The acquisition of any muscular accomplishment, dancing or billiards, for example, shows this clearly. What we have already done in the past controls what we shall do in the future. If the perception of an object and the recognition that it is a tree, for example, involve a poise in the sensory system concerned, a certain completeness or 'closure', to use the term employed by Köhler, so an act, as opposed to a random movement, involves a similar poise in a motor system. But sensory and motor systems are not independent; they work together; every perception probably includes a response in the form of incipient action. We constantly overlook the extent to which all the while we are making preliminary adjustments, getting ready to act in one way or another. Reading Captain Slocum's account of the centipede which bit him on the head when alone in the middle of the Atlantic, the writer has been caused to leap right out of his chair by a leaf which fell upon his face from a tree. Only occasionally does some such accident show how extensive are the motor adjustments made in what appear to be the most unmuscular occupations.

This incipient activity stands to overt action much as an image stands to a sensation. But such 'imaginal' activity is, by its very nature, extraordinarily hard to detect or to experiment upon. Psychology has only dealt with fringes of the mind hitherto and the most accessible fringe is on the side of sensation. We have therefore to build up our conjectures as to the rest of mental happenings by analogy with the perhaps not entirely representative specimens which sensation supplies. This limitation has led the majority of psychologists to see in imaginal movement no more than images of the *sensations* from muscle, joint, and tendon, which would arise if the movement were actually made.

It is certain that before any action takes place a preliminary organization must occur which ensures that the parts do not get in one another's way. It appears to the writer that these preliminaries in his case make up part of consciousness, but there is a heavy weight of authority against him. The point is no doubt exceptionally hard to determine.

In any case, whether the consciousness of activity is due to sensations and images of movements alone, or whether the outgoing part of the impulse and its preparatory organization help to make up consciousness, there is no doubt about the importance of incipient and imaginal movement in experience. The work done by Lipps, Groos and others on *einfühlung*, or empathy, however we may prefer to restate their results, shows that when we perceive spatial or musical form we commonly accompany our perception with closely connected motor activity. We cannot leave this activity out of our account of what happens in the experiences of the arts, although we may think that those who have built upon this fact what they had put forward as a complete aesthetic – Vernon Lee, for example – have been far from clear as to what questions they were answering.

The extent to which any activity is conscious seems to depend very largely upon how complex and how novel it is. The primitive and in a sense natural outcome of stimulus is action; the more simple the situation with which the mind is engaged, the closer is the connection between the stimulus and some overt response in action, and in general the less rich and full is the consciousness attendant. A man walking over uneven ground, for example, makes without reflection or emotion a continuous adjustment of his steps to his footing; but let the ground become precipitous and, unless he is used to such places, both reflection and emotion will appear. The increased complexity of the situation and the greater delicacy and appropriateness of the movements required for convenience and safety, call forth far more complicated goings on in the mind. Besides his perception of the nature of the ground, the thought may occur that a false move would be perilous and difficult to retrieve. This, when accompanied by emotion, is called a 'realization' of his situation. The adjustment to one another of varied impulses – to go forward carefully, to lie down and grasp something with the hands, to go back, and so forth – and their co-ordination into useful behaviour alters the whole character of his experience.

Most behaviour is a reconciliation between the various acts which would satisfy the different impulses which combine to produce it; and the richness and interest of the feel of it in consciousness depends upon the variety of the impulses engaged. Any familiar activity, when set in different conditions so that the impulses which make it up have to adjust themselves to fresh streams of impulses due to the new conditions, is likely to take on increased richness and fullness in consciousness.

This general fact is of great importance for the arts, particularly for poetry, painting and sculpture, the representative or mimetic arts. For in these a totally new setting for what may be familiar elements is essentially involved. Instead of seeing a tree we see something in a picture which may have similar effects upon us but is *not* a tree. The tree impulses which are aroused have to adjust themselves to their new setting of other impulses due to our awareness that it is a *picture* which we are looking at. Thus an opportunity arises for those impulses to define themselves in a way in which they ordinarily do not.

This, of course, is only the most obvious and simple instance of the way in which, thanks to the unusual circumstances in which things depicted, or in literature described, come before us, the experiences that result are modified. To take another obvious example, the description or the theatrical presentation of a murder has a different effect upon us from that which would be produced by most actual murders if they took place before us. These considerations, of vast importance in the discussion of artistic form, will occupy us later (pp. 222–3). Here it is sufficient to point out that these differences between ordinary experiences and those due to works of art are only special cases of the general difference between experiences made up of a less and of a greater number of impulses which have to be brought into co-ordination with one another. The bearing of this point upon the problem of the aesthetic mode with its detachment, impersonality, etc., discussed in the second chapter, will be apparent. (Compare Chapter Thirty-two, p. 233.)

The result of the co-ordination of a great number of impulses of different kinds is very often that no *overt* action takes place. There is a danger here of supposing that no action whatever results or that there is something incomplete or imperfect about such a state of affairs. But imaginal action and incipient action which does not go so far as actual muscular movement are more important than overt action in the well-developed human being. Indeed the difference between the intelligent or refined, and the stupid or crass person is a difference in the extent to which overt action can be replaced by incipient and imaginal action. An intelligent man can 'see how a thing works' when a less intelligent man has to 'find out by trying'. Similarly with such responses as are aroused by a work of art. The difference between 'understanding' it and failing to do so is, in most cases, a difference between being able to make the required responses in an imaginal or incipient degree, adjusting them to one another at that stage, and being unable to produce them or adjust them except overtly and at their fullest development. Though the kinds of activity involved are different, the analogy with the case of the mathematician is not misleading. The fact that he will not make half so many marks on paper as a schoolboy does not show that he is any less active. His activity takes place at an earlier stage in which his responses are merely incipient or imaginal. In a similar manner the absence of any overt movements or external signs of emotion in an experienced reader of poetry, or concert-goer, compared to the evident disturbances which are sometimes to be seen in the novice, is no indication of any lack of internal activity. The response required in many cases by works of art is of a kind which can only be obtained in an incipient or imaginal stage. Practical considerations often prevent their being worked out in overt form, and this is, as a rule, not in the least to be regretted. For these responses are commonly of the nature of solutions to problems, not of intellectual research, but of emotional accommodation and adjustment, and can usually be best achieved while the different impulses which have to be reconciled are still in an incipient or imaginal stage, and before the matter has become further complicated by the irrelevant accidents which attend overt responses.

These imaginal and incipient activities or tendencies to action,

I shall call attitudes. When we realize how many and how different may be the tendencies awakened by a situation, and what scope there is for conflict, suppression and inter-play — all contributing something to our experience — it will not appear surprising that the classification and analysis of attitudes is not yet far advanced. A thousand tendencies to actions, which do not overtly take place, may well occur in complicated adjustments. For these what evidence there is must be indirect. In fact, the only attitudes which are capable of clear and explicit analysis are those in which some simple mode of observable behaviour gives the clue to what has been taking place, and even here only a part of the reaction is open to this kind of examination.

Among the experiences which are by the nature of the case hidden from observation are found almost all those with which criticism is concerned. The outward aspect and behaviour of a man reading The Prioresses' Tale and The Miller's Tale may well be indistinguishable. But this should not lead us to overlook how great a part in the whole experience is taken by attitudes. Many experiences which, if examined by introspection for their actual content of sensation and imagery, differ very little, are totally diverse in the kind and degree of implicit activity present. This aspect of experiences as filled with incipient promptings, lightly stimulated tendencies to acts of one kind or another, faint preliminary preparations for doing this or that, has been constantly overlooked in criticism. Yet it is in terms of attitudes, the resolution, inter-inanimation, and balancing of impulses — Aristotle's definiton of Tragedy[1] is an instance — that all the most valuable effects of poetry must be described.

---

[1] 'Tragedy is an imitation of an action . . . effecting through Pity and Terror the correction and refinement ($\kappa\acute{\alpha}\theta\alpha\rho\sigma\iota\varsigma$) of such passions.' Poetics, VI. Cf., p. 247, infra.

16

THE ANALYSIS OF A POEM

Toutes choses sont dites déjà mais comme personne
n'écoute il faut toujours recommencer.

André Gide

The qualifications of a good critic are three. He must be an adept
at experiencing, without eccentricities, the state of mind relevant
to the work of art he is judging. Secondly, he must be able to
distinguish experiences from one another as regards their less
superficial features. Thirdly, he must be a sound judge of values.

Upon all these matters psychology, even in its present
conjectural state, has a direct bearing. The critic is, throughout,
judging of experiences, of states of mind; but too often he is
needlessly ignorant of the general psychological form of the
experiences with which he is concerned. He has no clear ideas as
to the elements present or as to their relative importance. Thus,
an outline or schema of the mental events which make up the
experience of 'looking at' a picture or 'reading' a poem,
can be of great assistance. At the very least an understanding of
the probable structures of these experiences can remove certain

misconceptions which tend to make the opinions of individuals of less service to other individuals than need be.

Two instances will show this. There are certain broad features in which all agree a poem of Swinburne is unlike a poem of Hardy. The use of words by the two poets is different. Their methods are dissimilar, and the proper approach for a reader differs correspondingly. An attempt to read them in the same way is unfair to one of the poets, or to both, and leads inevitably to defects in criticism which a little reflection would remove. It is absurd to read Pope as though he were Shelley, but the essential differences cannot be clearly marked out unless such an outline of the general form of a poetic experience, as is here attempted, has been provided. The psychological means employed by these poets are demonstrably different. Whether the effects are also dissimilar is a further question for which the same kind of analysis is equally required.

This separation inside the poetic experience of certain parts which are means from certain other parts which are the ends upon which the poetic value of the experience depends, leads up to our other instance. It is unquestionable that the actual experiences, which even good critics undergo when reading, as we say, *the same poem*, differ very widely. In spite of certain conventions, which endeavour to conceal these inevitable discrepancies for social purposes, there can be no doubt that the experiences of readers in connection with particular poems are rarely similar. This is unavoidable. Some differences are, however, much more important than others. Provided the ends, in which the value of the poem lies, are attained, differences in the means need not prevent critics from agreement or from mutual service. Those discrepancies alone are fatal which affect the fundamental features of experiences, the features upon which their *value* depends. But enough is now known of the ways in which minds work for superficial and fundamental parts of experiences to be distinguished. One of the greatest living critics praises the line:

> The fringed curtain of thine eyes advance,

for the 'ravishing beauty' of the visual images excited. This common mistake of exaggerating personal accidents in the means by which a poem attains its end into the chief value of the poem is due to excessive trust in the commonplaces[1] of psychology.

In the analysis of the experience of reading a poem, a diagram, or hieroglyph, is convenient, provided that its limitations are clearly recognized. The spatial relations of the parts of the diagram, for instance, are not intended to stand for spatial relations between parts of what is represented; it is not a picture of the nervous system. Nor are temporal relations intended. Spatial metaphors, whether drawn as diagrams or merely imagined, are dangers only to the unwary. The essential service which pictures can give in abstract matters, namely, the simultaneous and compact representation of states of affairs which otherwise tend to remain indistinct and confused, is worth the slight risk of misunderstanding which they entail.

We may begin then with a diagrammatic representation of the events which take place when we read a poem. Other literary experiences will only differ from this in their greater simplicity.

The eye is depicted as reading a succession of printed words. As a result there follows a stream of reaction in which six distinct kinds of events may be distinguished.

I   The visual sensations of the printed words.
II   Images very closely associated with these sensations.

---

[1] The description of images belongs to the first steps in psychology, and it is often possible to judge the rank and standing of a psychologist by the degree of importance which he attaches to their peculiarities. On theoretical grounds it seems probable that they are luxury products (cf. *The Meaning of Meaning*, pp. 148–151) peculiarly connected with the reproduction of emotion. For a discussion of some experimental investigations into their utility, Spearman, *The Nature of Intelligence*, Ch. XII, may be consulted.

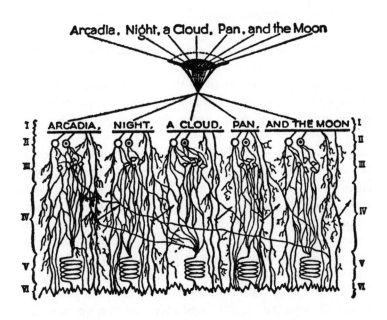

I — VISUAL SENSATIONS   ○ AUDITORY VERBAL IMAGE
II — TIED IMAGERY   ⊙ ARTICULATORY VERBAL IMAGE
III — FREE IMAGERY   Δ℘ FREE IMAGERY
IV — REFERENCES   ↗   REFERENCES
V — EMOTIONS   ⋐   EMOTIONS
VI — ATTITUDES   ⋀⋁⋀ ATTITUDES

III   Images relatively free.
IV   References to, or 'thinkings of', various things.
V   Emotions.
VI   Affective-volitional attitudes.

Each of these kinds of occurrences requires some brief description and explanation.

Upon the visual sensations of the printed words all the rest depends (in the case of a reader not previously acquainted with the poem); but with most readers they have in themselves no great importance. The individual shapes of the letters, their size and spacing, have only a minor effect upon the whole reaction. No doubt readers differ greatly in this respect; with some, familiarity plays a great part. They find it unpleasant and disturbing to read a poem in any but the edition in which they first became acquainted with it. But the majority of readers are less exigent. Provided that the print is clear and legible, and allows the habitual eye-movements of reading to be easily performed, the full response arises equally well from widely differing sensations. Those for whom this is true have, in the present state of economic organization, a decided advantage over the more fastidious. This does not show that good printing is a negligible consideration; and the primary place of calligraphy in the Chinese arts is an indication to the contrary. It shows merely that printing belongs to another branch of the arts. In the poetic experience words take effect through their associated images, and through what we are, as a rule, content to call their meaning. What meaning is and how it enters into the experience we shall consider.

Tied Images. – Visual sensations of words do not commonly occur by themselves. They have certain regular companions so closely tied to them as to be only with difficulty disconnected. The chief of these are the auditory image – the sound of the words in the mind's ear – and the image of articulation – the feel in the lips, mouth, and throat, of what the words would be like to speak.

Auditory images of words are among the most obvious of mental happenings. Any line of verse or prose slowly read, will, for most people, sound mutely in the imagination somewhat as it would if read aloud. But the degree of correspondence between the image-sounds, and the actual sounds that the reader would produce, varies enormously. Many people are able to imagine word-sounds with greater delicacy and discrimination than they can utter them. But the reverse case is also found. What importance then is to be attached to clear, rich and delicate sound imagery in silent reading? How far must people who differ in their capacity to produce such images differ in their total reactions to poems? And what are the advantages of reading aloud? Here we reach one of the practical problems of criticism for which this analysis is required. A discussion is best postponed until the whole analysis has been given. The principal confusion which prevents a clear understanding of the point at issue does, however, concern images and may be dealt with here. It is of great importance in connection with the topic of the following section.

The sensory qualities of images, their vivacity, clearness, fullness of detail and so on, do not bear any constant relation to their effects. Images differing in these respects may have closely similar consequences. Too much importance has always been attached to the sensory qualities of images. What gives an image efficacy is less its vividness as an image than its character as a mental event peculiarly connected with sensation. It is, in a way which no one yet knows how to explain, a relict of sensation and our intellectual and emotional response to it depends far more upon its being, through this fact, a representative of a sensation, than upon its sensory resemblance to one. An image may lose almost all its sensory nature to the point of becoming scarcely an image at all, a mere skeleton, and yet represent a sensation quite as adequately as if it were flaring with hallucinatory vividity. In other words, what matters is not the sensory *resemblance* of an image to the sensation which is its prototype, but some other relation, at present hidden from us in the jungles of neurology. (Cf. Chapter Fourteen.)

Care then should be taken to avoid the natural tendency to suppose that the more clear and vivid an image the greater will be its efficacy. There are trustworthy people who, according to their accounts, never experience any imagery at all. If certain views commonly expressed about the arts are true, by which vivid imagery is an all-important part of the experience, then these people are incapable of art experiences, a conclusion which is contrary to the facts. The views in question are overlooking the fact that *something* takes the place of vivid images in these people, and that, provided the image-substitute is efficacious, their lack of mimetic imagery is of no consequence. The efficacy required must, of course, include control over emotional as well as intellectual reactions. Needless perhaps to add that with persons of the image-producing types an increase in delicacy and vivacity in their imagery will probably be accompanied by increased subtlety in effects. Thus it is not surprising that certain great poets and critics have been remarkable for the vigour of their imagery, and dependent upon it. No one would deny the usefulness of imagery to some people; the mistake is to suppose that it is indispensable to all.

Articulatory imagery is less noticeable; yet the quality of silent speech is perhaps even more dependent upon these images than upon sound-images. Collocations of syllables which are awkward or unpleasant to utter are rarely delightful to the ear. As a rule the two sets of images are so intimately connected that it is difficult to decide which is the offender. In 'Heaven, which man's generation draws', the sound doubtless is as harsh as the movements required are cramping to the lips.

The extent to which interference with one set of images will change the other may be well seen by a simple experiment. Most people, if they attempt a silent recitation while opening the mouth to its fullest stretch or holding the tongue firmly between the teeth, will notice curious transformations in the auditory images. How the experiment should be interpreted is uncertain, but it is of use in making the presence of both kinds of verbal imagery evident to those who may have overlooked them hitherto. Images of articulation should not, however, be confused with those minimal actual movements which for some people (for all, behaviourists maintain) accompany the silent rehearsing of words.

These two forms of tied imagery might also be called verbal images, and supply the elements of what is called the 'formal structure' of poetry. They differ from those to which we now proceed in being images of words, not of things words stand for, and in their very close connection with the visual sensations of printed words.

Free Imagery. – Free images, or rather one form of these, visual images, pictures in the mind's eye, occupy a prominent place in the literature of criticism, to the neglect somewhat of other forms of imagery, since, as was remarked in a preceding chapter, for every possible kind of sensation there is a corresponding possible image.

The assumption, natural before investigation, that all attentive and sensitive readers will experience the same images, vitiates most of the historical discussions from that of Longinus to that of Lessing. Even in the present day, when there is no excuse for such ignorance, the mistake still thrives, and an altogether too crude, too hasty, and too superficial form of criticism is allowed to pass unchallenged. It cannot be too clearly recognized that individuals differ not only in the type of imagery which they employ, but still more in the particular images which they produce. In their whole reactions to a poem, or to a single line of it, their free images are the point at which two readings are most likely to differ, and the fact that they differ may very well be quite immaterial. Fifty different readers will experience not one common picture but fifty different pictures. If the value of the poem derived from the value qua picture of the visual image excited then criticism might well despair. Those who would stress this part of the poetic reaction can have but crude views on pictures.

But if the value of the visual image in the experience is not pictorial, if the image is not to be judged as a picture, how is it to be judged? It is improbable that the many critics, some of them peculiarly well qualified in the visual arts, who have insisted upon the importance of imagery, have been entirely wasting their time. It ought to be possible to give an account of the place of free imagery in the whole poetic experience which will explain this insistence. What is required will be found if we turn our attention from the sensory qualities of the imagery to the more fundamental qualities upon which its efficacy in modifying the rest of the experience depends. It has been urged above that images which are different in their sensory qualities may have the same effects. If this were not the case the absence of glaring differences between people of different image-types would be astonishing. But since images may represent sensations without resembling them, and represent them in the sense of replacing them, as far as effects in directing thought and arousing emotion go, differences in their mimetic capacity become of minor importance. As we have seen, it is natural for those whose imagery is vivid, to suppose that vivacity and clearness go together with power over thought and feeling. It is the power of an image over these that is as a rule being praised when an intelligent and sensitive critic appears merely to be praising the picture floating before his mind's eye. To judge the image as a picture is judged, would, as we have seen, be absurd; and what is sought in poetry by those painters and others whose interest in the world is primarily visual is not pictures but records of observation, or stimuli of emotion.

Thus, provided the images (or image-substitutes for the image-less) have the due effects, deficiencies in their sensory aspect do not matter. But the proviso is important. In all forms of imagery sensory deficiencies are for many people signs and accompaniments of defective efficacy, and the habit of reading so as to allow the fullest development to imagery in its sensory aspect is likely to encourage the full development of this more essential feature, its efficacy, if the freaks and accidents of the sensory side are not taken too seriously.

Some exceptions to this general recommendation will occur to the reader. Instances in plenty may be found in which a full development of the sensory aspect of images is damaging to their effects. Meredith is a master of this peculiar kind of imagery:

> Thus piteously Love closed what he begat
> The union of this ever diverse pair!
> These two were rapid falcons in a snare,
> Condemned to do the flitting of the bat.

The emotional as well as the intellectual effects of the various images here suggested are much impaired if we produce them vividly and distinctly.

Impulses and References. – We have now to consider those more fundamental effects upon which stress has been laid above as the true places of the values of the experience. It will be well at this point to reconsult the diagram. The vertical lines which run capriciously downwards from the visual sensations of the words, through their tied imagery and onward to the bottom of the diagram, are intended to represent, schematically, streams of impulses flowing through in the mind.

They start in the visual sensations, but the depiction of the tied imagery is intended to show how much of their further course is due to it. The placing of the free imagery in the third division is intended to suggest that while some free images may arise from visual words alone, they take their character in a large part as a consequence of the tied imagery. Thus the great importance of the tied imagery, of the formal elements, is emphasized in the diagram.

These impulses are the weft of the experience, the warp being the pre-existing systematic structure of the mind, that organized system of possible impulses. The metaphor is of course inexact, since weft and warp here are not independent. Where these impulses run, and how they develop, depends entirely upon the condition of the mind, and this depends upon the impulses which have previously been active in it. It will be seen then that impulses – their direction, their strength, how they modify one another – are the essential and fundamental things in any experience. All else, whether intellectual or emotional, arises as a consequence of their activity. The thin trickle of stimulation which comes in through the eye finds an immense hierarchy of systems of tendencies poised in the most delicate stability. It is strong enough and rightly enough directed to disturb some of these without assistance. The literal sense of a word can be grasped on the prompting of the mere sight of it, without hearing it or mentally pronouncing it. But the effects of this stimulation are immensely increased and widened when it is reinforced by fresh stimulation from tied images, and it is through these that most of the emotional effects are produced. As the agitation proceeds new reinforcement comes with every fresh system which is excited. Thus, the paradoxical fact that so trifling an irritation as the sight of marks on paper is able to arouse the whole energies of the mind becomes explicable.

To turn now to references, the only mental happenings which are as closely connected with visual words as their tied images are those mysterious events which are usually called thoughts.

Thus the arrow symbol in the hieroglyph should perhaps properly be placed near the visual impression of the word. The mere sight of any familiar word is normally followed by a thought of whatever the word may stand for. This thought is sometimes said to be the 'meaning', the literal or prose 'meaning' of the word. It is wise, however, to avoid the use of 'meaning' as a symbol altogether. The terms 'thought' and 'idea' are less subtle in their ambiguities, and when defined may perhaps be used without confusion.

What is essential in thought is its direction or reference to things. What is this direction or reference? How does a thought come to be 'of' one thing rather than another? What is the link between a thought and what it is 'of'? The outline of one answer to these questions has been suggested in Chapter Eleven. A further account must here be attempted. Without a fairly clear, although, of course, incomplete view, it is impossible to avoid confusion and obscurity in discussing such topics as truth in art, the intellect-*versus*-emotion *imbroglio*, the scope of science, the nature of religion and many others with which criticism must deal.

The facts upon which speculations as to the relations between thoughts and the things which they are 'of' have been based, have as a rule been taken from introspection. But the facts which introspection yields are notoriously uncertain, and the special position of the observer may well preclude success. Introspection is competent, in some cases, to discover the relations between events which take place within the mind, but cannot by itself give information as to the relations of these events with the external world, and it is precisely this which we are inquiring into when we ask, What connection is there between a thought and that which it is a thought of? For an answer to this question we must look further.

There is no doubt that causal relations hold between events in the mind and events outside it. Sometimes these relations are fairly simple. The striking of a clock is the cause of our thinking of its striking. In such a case the external thing is linked with the thought 'of' it in a fairly direct fashion, and the view here taken is that to be a thought 'of' the striking is to be merely a thought caused in this fashion by the striking. A thought of the striking is nothing else and nothing more than a thought caused by it.

But most thoughts are 'of' things which are not present and not producing direct effects in the mind. This is so when we read. What is directly affecting the mind is words on paper, but the thoughts aroused are not thoughts 'of' the words, but of other things which the words stand for. How, then, can a causal theory of thinking explain the relation between these remote things and the thoughts which are 'of' them? To answer this we must look at the way in which we learn what words stand for. Without a process of learning we should only think of the words.

The process of learning to use words is not difficult to analyse. On a number of occasions the word is heard in connection with objects of a certain kind. Later the word is heard in the absence of any such object. In accordance with one of the few fundamental laws known about mental process, something then happens in the mind which is like what would happen if such an object were actually present and engaging the attention. The word has become a sign of an object of that kind. The word which formerly was a part of the cause of a certain effect in the mind is now followed by a similar effect in the absence of the rest of the previous cause, namely, an object of the kind in question. This kind of causation appears to be peculiar to living tissue. The relation now between the thought and what it is 'of' is more indirect, the thought is 'of' something which formerly was part cause, together with the sign, of similar thoughts. It is 'of' the missing part of the sign, or more strictly 'of' anything which would complete the sign as a cause.

Thoughts by this account are general, they are of anything like such and such things, except when the object thought of and the thought are connected by direct causal relations, as, for instance, when we think of a word we are hearing. Only when these direct relations hold can we succeed in thinking simply of 'That'. We have to think instead of 'something of a kind'. By various means, however, we can contrive that there shall only be one thing of the kind, and so the need for particularity in our thoughts is satisfied. The commonest way in which we do this is by thoughts which make the kind spatial and temporal. A thought of 'mosquito' becomes a thought of 'mosquito there now' by combining a thought of 'thing of mosquito kind' with a thought of 'thing of there kind' and a thought of 'thing of now kind'. The awkwardness of these phrases, it may be mentioned, is irrelevant. Combined thoughts of this sort, we may notice, are capable of truth and falsity, whereas a simple thought – of 'whatever is now' for instance – can only be true. Whether a thought is true or false depends simply upon whether there is anything of the kind referred to, and there must be something now. It is by no means certain that there must be anything there always. And most probably no mosquito is where we thought it was then.

The natural generality and vagueness of all reference which is not made specific by the aid of space and time is of great importance for the understanding of the senses in which poetry may be said to be true. (Cf. Chapter Thirty-five.)

In the reading of poetry the thought due simply to the words, their *sense* it may be called, comes first; but other thoughts are not of less importance. These may be due to the auditory verbal imagery, and we have onomatopoeia,[1] but this is rarely

---

[1] Two kinds of onomatopoeia should be distinguished. In one the sound of the words (actual or imaginal) is like some natural sound (the buzzing of bees, galloping horses, and so forth). In the other it is not like any such sound but such as merely to call up free auditory images of the sounds in question. The second case is by far the more common.

independent of the sense. More important are the further thoughts caused by the sense, the network of interpretation and conjecture which arises therefrom, with its opportunities for aberrations and misunderstanding. Poems, however, differ fundamentally in the extent to which such further interpretation is necessary. The mere sense without any further reflection is very often sufficient thought, in Swinburne, for instance, for the full response —

> There glowing ghosts of flowers
>   Draw down, draw nigh;
> And wings of swift spent hours
>   Take flight and fly;
> She sees by formless gleams
> She hears across cold streams
>   Dead mouths of many dreams that sing and sigh.

Little beyond vague thoughts of the things the words stand for is here required. They do not have to be brought into intelligible connection with one another. On the other hand, Hardy would rarely reach his full effect through sound and sense alone —

> 'Who's in the next room?—who?
>   I seemed to see
> Somebody in the dawning passing through .
>   Unknown to me.'
> 'Nay: you saw nought. He passed invisibly'.

Between these and even more extreme cases, every degree of variation in the relative importance of sound, sense, and further interpretation, between form and content in short, can be found. A temptation to which few do not succumb is to suppose that there is some 'proper relation' for these different parts of the experience, so that a poem whose parts are in this relation must thereby be a greater or better poem than another whose parts are differently disposed. This is another instance of the commonest of critical mistakes, the confusion of means with ends, of technique with value. There is no more a 'proper place' for sound or for sense in poetry than there is one and only one 'proper shape' for an animal. A dog is not a defective kind of cat, nor is Swinburne a defective kind of Hardy. But this sort of criticism is extraordinarily prevalent. The objection to Swinburne On the ground of a lack of thought is a popular specimen.

Within certain types, needless to say, some structures are more likely to be successful than others. Given some definite kind of effect as the goal, or some definite structure already being used, a good deal can of course be said as to the most probable means, or as to what may or may not be added. Lyric cannot dispense with tied imagery, it is clear, nor can we neglect the character of this imagery in reading it. A prose composition has to be longer than a lyric to produce an equal definiteness of developed effect. Poems in which there is much turmoil of emotion are likely to be strongly rhythmical and to be in metre, as we shall see when we come to discuss rhythm and metre. Drama can hardly dispense with a great deal of conjecture and further interpretation which in most forms of the novel is replaced by analysis and explanation, and in narrative poetry is commonly omitted altogether; and so on.

But no general prescription that in great poetry there must always be this or that, – deep thought, superb sound or vivid imagery – is more than a piece of ignorant dogmatism. Poetry may be almost devoid even of mere sense, let alone thought, or *almost* without sensory (or formal) structure, and yet reach the point than which no poem goes further. The second case, however, is very rare. Almost always, what seems structureless proves to have still a loose and tenuous (it may be an intermittent) structure. But we can for example shift the words about very often in Walt Whitman without loss, even when he is almost at his best.

It is difficult to represent diagrammatically what takes place in thought in any satisfactory fashion. The impulse coming in from the visual stimulus of the printed word must be imagined as reaching some system in the brain in which effects take place not due merely to this present stimulus, but also to past occasions on which it has been combined with other stimulations. These effects are thoughts; and they in their groupings act as signs for yet other thoughts. The little arrows are intended to symbolize these references to things outside the mind.

Emotions, and Attitudes.

Feeling or emotion is not, we have insisted above, another and a rival mode of apprehending nature. So far as a feeling or an emotion does refer to anything, it refers in the way described, through its origin. Feelings, in fact, are commonly signs, and the differences between those who 'see' things by intuition, or 'feel' them, and those who reason them out, is commonly only a difference between users of signs and users of symbols. Both signs and symbols are means by which our past experience assists our present responses. The advantages of symbols, due to the ease with which they are controlled and communicated, their public nature, as it were, are obvious. Their disadvantages as compared with such relatively private signs as emotions or organic sensations are perhaps less evident. Words, when used symbolically or scientifically, not figuratively and emotively, are only capable of directing thought to a comparatively few features of the more common situations. But feeling is sometimes a more subtle way of referring, more dangerous also, because more difficult to corroborate and to control, and more liable to confusion. There is no inherent superiority, however, in feeling as opposed to thought, there is merely a difference in applicability; nor is there any opposition or clash between them except for those who are mistaken either in their thinking or in their feeling, or in both. How such mistakes arise will be discussed in Chapter Thirty-four.

As regards emotions and attitudes little need be added to what has already been said. Emotions are primarily signs of attitudes and owe their great prominence in the theory of art to this. For it is the attitudes evoked which are the all-important part of any experience. Upon the texture and form of the attitudes involved its value depends. It is not the intensity of the conscious experience, its thrill, its pleasure or its poignancy which gives it value, but the organization of its impulses for freedom and fullness of life. There are plenty of ecstatic instants which are valueless; the character of consciousness at any moment is no certain sign of the excellence of the impulses from which it arises. It is the most convenient sign that is available, but it is very ambiguous and may be very misleading. A more reliable but less accessible set of signs can be found in the readiness for this or that kind of behaviour in which we find ourselves after the experience. Too great insistence upon the quality of the momentary *consciousness* which the arts occasion has in recent times been a prevalent critical blunder. The Epilogue to Pater's *Renaissance* is the *locus classicus*. The after-effects, the permanent modifications in the structure of the mind, which works of art can produce, have been overlooked. No one is ever quite the same again after any experience; his possibilities have altered in some degree. And among all the agents by which 'the widening of the sphere of human sensibility' may be brought about, the arts are the most powerful, since it is through them that men may most co-operate and in these experiences that the mind most easily and with least interference organizes itself.

17

RHYTHM AND METRE

. . . when it approaches with a divine hopping.
The Joyful Wisdom

Rhythm and its specialized form, metre, depend upon repetition, and expectancy. Equally where what is expected recurs and where it fails, all rhythmical and metrical effects spring from anticipation. As a rule this anticipation is unconscious. Sequences of syllables both as sounds and as images of speech-movements leave the mind ready for certain further sequences rather than for others. Our momentary organization is adapted to one range of possible stimuli rather than to another. Just as the eye reading print unconsciously expects the spelling to be as usual, and the fount of type to remain the same, so the mind after reading a line or two of verse, or half a sentence of prose, prepares itself ahead for any one of a number of possible sequences, at the same time negatively incapacitating itself for others. The effect produced by what actually follows depends very closely upon this unconscious preparation and consists largely of the further twist which it gives to expectancy. It is in terms of the variation in these twists that rhythm is to be described. Both prose and verse vary immensely in the extent to which they excite this 'getting ready' process, and in the narrowness of the anticipation which is formed. Prose on the whole, with the rare exceptions of a Landor, a De Quincey, or a Ruskin, is accompanied by a very much vaguer and more indeterminate expectancy than verse. In such prose as this page, for example, little more than a preparedness for further words not all exactly alike in sound and with abstract polysyllables preponderating is all that arises. In short, the sensory or formal effect of words has very little play in the literature of analysis and exposition. But as soon as prose becomes more emotive than scientific, the formal side becomes prominent.

Let us take Landor's description[1] of a lioness suckling her young—

> On perceiving the countryman, she drew up her feet gently, and squared her mouth, and rounded her eyes, slumberous with content; and they looked, he said, like sea-grottoes, obscurely green, interminably deep, at once awakening fear and stilling and suppressing it.

After 'obscurely green' would it be possible (quite apart from sense) to have 'deeply dark' or 'impenetrably gloomy'? Why, apart from sense, can so few of the syllables be changed in vowel sound, in emphasis, in duration or otherwise, without disaster to the total effect? As with all such questions about sensory form and its effects, only an incomplete answer can be given. The expectancy caused by what has gone before, a thing which must be thought of as a very complex tide of neural settings, lowering the threshold for some kinds of stimuli and raising it for others,

---

[1] *Works*, II, 171.

and the character of the stimulus which does actually come, both play their part.

Even the most highly organized lyrical or 'polyphonic' prose raises as it advances only a very ambiguous expectation. Until the final words of the passage, there are always a great number of different sequences which would equally well fit in, which would satisfy the expectancy so far as that is merely due to *habit*, to the *routine of sensory stimulation*. What is expected in fact is not this sound or that sound, not even this kind of sound or that kind of sound, but some one of a certain thousand kinds of sounds. It is much more a negative thing than a positive. As in the case of many social conventions it is easier to say what disqualifies than to say what is required.

Into this very indeterminate expectancy the new element comes with its own range of possible effects. There is, of course, no such thing as *the* effect of a word or a sound. There is no one effect which belongs to it. Words have no intrinsic literary characters. None are either ugly or beautiful, intrinsically displeasing or delightful. Every word has instead a range of possible effects, varying with the conditions into which it is received. All that we can say as to the sorting out of words, whether into the 'combed' and 'slippery', the 'shaggy' and 'rumpled' as with Dante, or in any other manner, is that some, through long use, have narrower ranges than others and require more extraordinary conditions if they are to change their 'character'. What effect the word has is a compromise between some one of its possible effects and the special conditions into which it comes. Thus in Shakespeare hardly any word ever looks odd until we consider it; whereas even in Keats the 'cold mushrooms' in the *Satyrs' Song* give the mind a shock of astonishment, an astonishment which is full of delight, but none the less is a shock.

But with this example we have broken down the limitation to the mere sound, to the strictly formal or sensory aspect of word sequences, and in fact the limitation is useless. For the effect of a word as sound cannot be separated from its contemporaneous other effects. They become inextricably mingled at once.

The sound gets its character by compromise with what is going on already. The preceding agitation of the mind selects from a range of possible characters which the word might present, that one which best suits with what is happening. There are no gloomy and no gay vowels or syllables, and the army of critics who have attempted to analyse the effects of passages into vowel and consonantal collocations have, in fact, been merely amusing themselves. The way in which the sound of a word is taken varies with the emotion already in being. But, further, it varies with the sense. For the anticipation of the sound due to habit, to the routine of sensation, is merely a part of the general expectancy. Grammatical regularities, the necessity for completing the thought, the reader's state of conjecture as to what is being said, his apprehension in dramatic literature of the action, of the intention, situation, state of mind generally, of the speaker, all these and many other things intervene. The way the sound is taken is much less determined by the sound itself than by the conditions into which it enters. All these anticipations form a very closely woven network and the word which can satisfy them all simultaneously may well seem triumphant. But we should not attribute to the sound alone virtues which involve so many other factors. To say this is not in the least to belittle the importance of the sound; in most cases it is the key to the effects of poetry.

This texture of expectations, satisfactions, disappointments, surprisals, which the sequence of syllables brings about, is rhythm. And the sound of word comes to its full power only through rhythm. Evidently there can be no surprise and no disappointments unless there is expectation and most rhythms perhaps are made up as much of disappointments and postponements and surprises and betrayals as of simple, straightforward satisfactions. Hence the rapidity with which too simple rhythms, those which are too easily 'seen through', grow cloying or insipid unless hypnoidal states intervene, as with much primitive music and dancing and often with metre.

The same definition of rhythm may be extended to the plastic arts and to architecture. Temporal sequence is not strictly necessary for rhythm, though in the vast majority of cases it is involved. The attention usually passes successfully from one complex to another, the expectations, the readiness to perceive this rather than that, aroused by the one being either satisfied or surprised by the other. Surprise plays an equally important part here; and the difference in detail between a surprising and delightful variation and one which merely irritates and breaks down the rhythm, as we say, is here, as elsewhere, a matter of the combination and resolution of impulses too subtle for our present means of investigation. All depends upon whether what comes can be an ingredient in the further response, or whether the mind must, as it were, start anew; in more ordinary language, upon whether there is any 'connection' between the parts of the whole.

But the rhythmic elements in a picture or a building may be not successive but simultaneous. A quick reader who sees a word as a whole commonly overlooks misprints because the general form of the word is such that he is only able at that instant to perceive one particular letter in a particular place and so overlooks what is discrepant. The parts of a visual field exert what amounts to a simultaneous influence over one another. More strictly what is discrepant does not get through to more central regions. Similarly, with those far more intricate wholes, made up of all kinds of imagery and incipient action of which works of art consist. The parts of a growing response mutually modify one another and this is all that is required for rhythm to be possible.

We may turn now to that more complex and more specialized form of temporal rhythmic sequence which is known as metre.

This is the means by which words may be made to influence one another to the greatest possible extent. In metrical reading the narrowness and definiteness of expectancy, as much unconscious as ever in most cases, is very greatly increased, reaching in some cases, if rime also is used, almost exact precision. Furthermore, what is anticipated becomes through the regularity of the time intervals in metre virtually dated. This is no mere matter of more or less perfect correspondence with the beating of some internal metronome. The whole conception of metre as 'uniformity in variety', a kind of mental drill in which words, those erratic and varied things, do their best to behave as though they were all the same, with certain concessions, licences and equivalences allowed, should nowadays be obsolete. It is a survivor which is still able to do a great deal of harm to the uninitiated, however, and although it has been knocked on the head vigorously enough by Professor Saintsbury and others, it is as difficult to kill as Punch. Most treatises on the subject, with their talk of feet and of stresses, unfortunately tend to encourage it, however little this may be the aim of the authors.

As with rhythm with metre, we must not think of it as in the words themselves or in the thumping of the drum. It is not in the stimulation, it is in our response. Metre adds to all the variously fated expectancies which make up rhythm a definite temporal pattern and its effect is not due to our perceiving a pattern in something outside us, but to our becoming patterned ourselves. With every beat of the metre a tide of anticipation in us turns and swings, setting up as it does so extraordinarily extensive sympathetic reverberations. We shall never understand metre so long as we ask, 'Why does temporal pattern so excite us'? and fail to realize that the pattern itself is a vast cyclic agitation spreading all over the body, a tide of excitement pouring through the channels of the mind.

The notion that there is any virtue in regularity or in variety, or in any other formal feature, apart from its effects upon us, must be discarded before any metrical problem can be understood. The regularity to which metre tends acts through the definiteness of the anticipations which are thereby aroused. It is through these that it gets such a hold upon the mind. Once again, here too, the failure of our expectations is often more important than success. Verse in which we constantly get exactly what we are ready for and no more, instead of something which we can and must take up and incorporate as another stage in a total developing response is merely toilsome and tedious. In prose, the influence of past words extends only a little way ahead. In verse, especially when stanza-form and rime co-operate to give a larger unit than the line, it may extend far ahead. It is this knitting together of the parts of the poem which explains the mnemonic power of verse, the first of the suggestions as to the origin of metre to be found in the Fourteenth Chapter of *Biographia Literaria*, that lumber-room of neglected wisdom which contains more hints towards a theory of poetry than all the rest ever written upon the subject.

We do great violence to the facts if we suppose the expectations excited as we read verse to be concerned only with the stress, emphasis, length, foot structure and so forth of the syllables which follow. Even in this respect the custom of marking syllables in two degrees only, long and short, light and full, etc., is inadequate, although doubtless forced upon metrists by practical considerations. The mind in the poetic experience responds to subtler niceties than these. When not in that experience but coldly considering their several qualities as sounds by the ear alone, it may well find two degrees all that are necessary. In Chapter Thirteen we saw an analogous situation arising in the case of the discrimination of colours. The obvious comparison with the difference between what even musical notation can record in music and the player's interpretation can usefully be made here.

A more serious omission is the neglect by the majority of metrists of the pitch relations of syllables. The reading of poetry is of course not a monotonous and subdued form of singing. There is no question of definite pitches at which the syllables must be taken, nor perhaps of definite harmonic relations between different sounds. But that a rise and fall of pitch is involved in metre and is as much part of the poet's technique as any other feature of verse, as much under his control also, is indisputable. Anyone who is not clear upon this point may compare as a striking instance Milton's *Hymn on the Morning of Christ's Nativity* with Collins' *Ode to Simplicity* and both with the second Chorus of Hellas discussed in Chapter Eighteen. Due allowances made for the natural peculiarities of different readers, the scheme of pitch relations, in their contexts, of

> That on the bitter cross
> Must redeem our loss;

and of

> But com'st a decent maid,
> In Attic robe array'd,

are clearly different. There is nothing arbitrary or out of the poet's control in this, as there is nothing arbitrary or out of his control in the way in which an adequate reader will stress particular syllables. He brings both about by the same means, the modification of the reader's impulses by what has gone before. It is true that some words resist emphasis far more than perhaps any resist change of pitch, yet this difference is merely one of degree. It is as natural to lower the pitch in reading the word 'loss' as it is to emphasize it as compared with 'our' in the same context.

Here again we see how impossible it is to consider rhythm or metre as though it were purely an affair of the sensory aspect of syllables and could be dissociated from their sense and from the emotional effects which come about through their sense. One principle may, however, be hazarded. As in the case of painting the more direct means are preferable to the less direct (see Chapter Eighteen), so in poetry. What can be done by sound should not be done otherwise or in violation of the natural effects of sound. Violations of the natural emphases and tones of speech brought about for the sake of the further effects due to thought and feeling are perilous, though, on occasion, they may be valuable devices. The use of italics in *Cain* to straighten out the blank verse is as glaring an instance as any. But more liberties are justified in dramatic writing than elsewhere, and poetry is full of exceptions to such principles.[1] We must not forget that Milton did not disdain to use special spelling, 'mee', for example, in place of 'me', in order to suggest additional emphasis when he feared that the reader might be careless.

So far we have been concerned with metre only as a specialized form of rhythm, giving an increased interconnection between words through an increased control of anticipation. But it has other, in some cases even more important powers. Its use as an hypnotic agent is probably very ancient. Coleridge once again drops his incidental remark, just beside yet extremely close to the point. 'It tends to increase the vivacity and susceptibility both of the general feelings and of the attention. This effect it produces by the continued excitement of surprise, and by the quick reciprocations of curiosity still gratified and still re-excited, which are too slight indeed to be at any moment objects of distinct consciousness, yet become considerable in their

---

[1] It is worth remarking that any application of critical principles must be indirect. They are not any the less useful because this is so. Misunderstanding on this point has often led artists to accuse critics of wishing to make art a matter of rules, and their objection to any such attempt is entirely justified.

aggregate influence. As a medicated atmosphere, or as wine during animated conversation, they act powerfully, though themselves unnoticed.' (*Biographia Literaria*, Chapter Eighteen.) Mr Yeats, when he speaks of the function of metre being to 'lull the mind into a waking trance' is describing the same effect, however strange his conception of this trance may be.

That certain metres, or rather that a certain handling of metre should produce in a slight degree a hypnoidal state is not surprising. But it does so not as Coleridge suggests, through the surprise element in metrical effects, but through the absence of surprise, through the lulling effects more than through the awakening. Many of the most characteristic symptoms of incipient hypnosis are present in a slight degree. Among these susceptibility and vivacity of emotion, suggestibility, limitations of the field of attention, marked differences in the incidence of belief-feelings closely analogous to those which alcohol and nltrous oxide can induce, and some degree of hyperaesthesia (increased power of discriminating sensations) may be noted. We need not boggle at the word 'hypnosis'. It is sufficient to say, borrowing a phrase from M. Jules Romains, that there is a change in the régime of consciousness, which is directly due to the metre, and that to this régime the above-mentioned characteristics attach. As regards the hyperaesthesia, there may be several ways of interpreting what can be observed. All that matters here is that syllables, which in prose or in *vers libres* sound thin, tinny and flat, often gain an astonishing sonority and fullness even in verse which seems to possess no very subtle metrical structure.

Metre has another mode of action not hitherto mentioned. There can be little doubt that historically it has been closely associated with dancing, and that the connections of the two still hold. This is true at least of some 'measures'. Either motor images, images of the sensations of dancing, or, more probably, imaginal and incipient movements follow the syllables and make up their 'movement'. A place for these accompaniments should be found in the diagram in Chapter Sixteen. Once the metre has begun to 'catch on' they are almost as closely bound up with the sequence of the words as the tied 'verbal' images themselves.

The extension of this 'movement' of the verse from dance forms to more general movements is natural and inevitable. That there is a very close connection between the sense and the metrical movement of

> And now the numerous tramplings quiver lightly
> Along a huge cloud's ridge; and now with sprightly
> Wheel downward come they into fresher skies,

cannot be doubted whatever we may think of the rime.
   It is not less clear in

> Where beyond the extreme sea wall, and between the
>   remote sea gates,
> Waste water washes, and tall ships founder, and deep
>   death waits,

or in

> Ran on embattell'd Armies clad in Iron,

than it is in

> We sweetly curtsied each to each
> And deftly danced a saraband.

Nor is it always the case that the movement takes its cue from the sense. It is often a commentary on the sense and sometimes may qualify it, as when the resistless strength of Coriolanus in battle is given an appearance of dreadful ease by the leisureliness of the description,

> Death, that dark spirit, in's nervy arm doth lie
> Which being advanc'd declines, and then men die,

Movement in poetry deserves at least as much study as onomatopoeia.

This account, of course, by no means covers all the ways by which metre takes effect in poetry. The fact that we appropriately use such words as 'lulling', 'stirring', 'solemn', 'pensive', 'gay' in describing metres is an indication of their power more directly to control emotion. But the more general effects are more-important. Through its very appearance of artificiality metre produces in the highest degree the 'frame' effect, isolating the poetic experience from the accidents and irrelevancies of everyday existence. We have seen in Chapter Ten how necessary this isolation is and how easily it may be mistaken for a difference in kind. Much which in prose would be too personal or too insistent, which might awaken irrelevant conjectures or might 'overstep itself' is managed without disaster in verse. There are, it is true, equivalent resources in prose — irony, for example, very frequently has this effect — but their scope is far more limited. Metre for the most difficult and most delicate utterances is the all but inevitable means.

18

ON LOOKING AT A PICTURE

Hived in our bosoms like the bag o' the bee,
Think'st thou the honey with those objects grew?
Don Juan

The diagram and account given of the process which make up the reading of a poem may be easily modified to represent what happens when we look at a picture, a statue or building, or listen to a piece of music. The necessary changes are fairly obvious, and it will only be necessary here to indicate them briefly. Needless to say the importance to the whole response of different kinds of elements varies enormously from art to art; so much so as to explain without difficulty the opinion so often held by persons interested primarily in one of the arts – that the others (or some of them) are entirely different in nature. Thus painters often aver that poetry is so different, so indirect, so second-hand in the way in which it produces its results, as hardly to deserve the name of an art at all. But, as we shall see, the differences between separate arts are sometimes no greater than differences to be found in each of them; and close analogies can be discovered by careful analysis between all of them. These analogies indeed are among the most interesting features which such scrutiny as we are here attempting can make clear. For an understanding of the problems of one art is often of great service in avoiding misconceptions in another. The place of representation in painting, for example, is greatly elucidated by a sound comprehension of the place of reference or thought in poetry, just as a crude view on this latter point is likely to involve unfortunate mistakes upon the first. Similarly a too narrow view of music which would limit it to an affair merely of the appreciation of the pitch and time relations of notes may be corrected most easily by a comparison with the phenomena of colour in the plastic arts. Comparison of the arts is, in fact, far the best means by which an understanding of the methods and resources of any one of them can be attained. We must be careful of course not to compare the wrong features of two arts and not to find merely fanciful or insecurely grounded analogies. The dangers both of too close assimilation and too wide separation of the structures of different arts are well illustrated in criticism, both before and since the days of Lessing. Only a thorough psychological analysis will allow them to be avoided, and those whose experience leads them to doubt whether analogies are of service, may be asked whether their objection is not directed merely to attempts to compare different arts without a sufficient analysis. With such an analysis, comparison and the elaboration of analogies involve no attempt to make one art legislate for another, no attempt to blur their differences or to destroy their autonomy.

In analysing the experiences of the visual arts the first essential is to avoid the word 'see', a term which is treacherous in its ambiguity. If we say that we see a picture we may mean either that we see the pigment-covered surface, or that we see the image on the retina cast by this surface, or that we see certain planes or volumes in what is called the 'picture-space'. These senses are completely distinct. In the first case we are speaking of the source of the stimulus, in the second of the immediate effect of the stimulus on the retina, in the third we are referring to a complex response made up of perceivings and imaginings due to the intervention of mental structures left behind by past experience, and excited by the stimulus. The first case we may leave out of account as a matter of purely technical interest. The degree of similarity holding between the second and third, between the first effect of the stimulus and the whole visual response, will of course vary greatly in different cases. A perfectly flat, meticulously detailed depiction of conventionally conceived objects, such as is so often praised in the Academy for its 'finish', may be very nearly the same from its first impression on the retina to the last effort which vision can make upon it. At the other extreme a Cézanne, for example, which to the eye of a person quite unfamiliar with such a manner of painting may at first seem only a field or area of varied light, may, as the response develops, through repeated glances, become first an assemblage of blots and patches of colour, and then, as these recede and advance, tilt and spread relatively to one another and become articulated, a system of volumes. Finally, as the distances and stresses of their volumes become more definitely imagined, it becomes an organization of the entire 'picture-space' into a three-dimensional whole with the characters of the solid masses which appear in it, their weights, textures, tensions and what not, very definitely, as it seems, given. With familiarity the response is of course shortened. Its final visual stage is reached much sooner, and the stages outlined above become, through this telescoping, too fleeting to be noticed. None the less the great difference between the first retinal impression and the complete visual response remains. The retinal impression, the sign, that is, for the response, contains actually but a small part of the whole final product, an all-important part it is true, the seed in fact from which the whole response grows.

The additions made in the course of the response are of

several kinds. They may, perhaps, for our present purposes be spoken of without misunderstanding as images, or image-substitutes (see Chapter Sixteen). The eye, as is well known, is peculiar among our sense organs in that the receptor, the retina, is a part of the brain, instead of being a separate thing connected with the brain more or less remotely by a peripheral nerve. Moreover there are certain connections leading from other parts of the brain outwards to the retina as well as connections leading inwards. Thus there is some ground for supposing that through these outgoing connections actual retinal effects may accompany some visual images, which would thereby become much more like actual sensations than is the case with the other senses. However this may be, the process whereby an impression which, if interpreted in one way (e.g. by a person measuring the pigmented areas of a canvas), is correctly counted as a sign of a flat coloured surface, becomes, when differently interpreted, an intricately divided three-dimensional space – this process is one of the intervention of images of several kinds.

The order of these interventions probably varies from case to case. Perhaps the most important of the images which come in to give depth, volume, solidity to the partly imagined and partly perceived 'picture-space' are those which are relics of eye movements, kinaesthetic images of the convergence of the eyes and accommodation of the lenses according to the distance of the object contemplated. When, as it seems, we look past an object in a picture to some more distant object, seeming in so doing to change the focus of our eyes, we do not as a rule actually make any change. But certainly we feel as though we were focusing differently and as though the convergence were different. This felt difference which mainly gives the sense of greater distance is due to kinaesthetic imagery. Correspondingly the part of the 'picture-space' upon which we seem to be focusing, upon which we *are* imaginally focusing, become definite and distinct, and parts much nearer or much more distant become to some extent blurred and diffused. This effect is probably due to visual images, simulating the sensations which would normally ensue were we actually making a change of focus. The degree to which these last effects occur appears to differ very greatly from one person to another. Insufficient attention to the great variation in the means by which these images are involved by the painting is responsible for much bad criticism. Thus artists can commonly be found who are quite unable, when looking at paintings in which the means employed are unlike their own, to apprehend forms over which less specialized persons find no difficulty. In general most visitors to Galleries pay too little attention to the fact that few pictures can be instantaneously apprehended, that even ten minutes' study is quite inadequate in the case of unfamiliar kinds of work, and that the capacity for 'seeing' pictures (in sense three), an indispensable but merely an initial step to appreciating them, is something which has to be acquired. It is naturally of great assistance if many works by the same painter or of the same School can be seen together, for then the essential methods employed become clearer. In a general collection it is difficult not to look at too great a variety of pictures, and a confusion results, perhaps unnoticed, which is a serious obstacle to the coherent building up of any one picture. The fashion in which most Old Masters are hidden away under grime and glass and the efforts which are necessary in order to reconstruct them are additional obstacles. The neglect of these obvious facts is the chief explanation of the low level of appreciation and criticism from which the art of painting at present suffers.

Following upon the visual images are a swarm of others varying from picture to picture: tactile images giving the appearance of texture to surfaces, muscular images giving hardness, stiffness, softness, flexibility and so on to the volumes imagined – the lightness and insubstantiality of muslin, the solidity and fixity of rock being matters of the intervention of images due originally to the sensations we have received in the past from these materials. This muscular imagery is of course called up in differing ways in different cases. Primarily it is due to the imitation by the artist of subtleties in the light given off by the materials, or characteristic peculiarities in their form, but there are, as we shall see, more indirect but also less stable, less reliable and less efficacious ways by which they may be evoked. The same applies to the other images, thermal, olfactory, auditory and the rest, which may be involved in particular cases. There is a direct and an indirect way in which they can be evoked. They may spring up at the visual appeal or they may only respond at a later stage as a result of roundabout trains of thinking. Thus a silk scarf may look soft and light; or we may imagine it as light, it looking all the while iron-hard and heavy, because we know that it is a scarf and that scarves are soft and light. The two methods are very different. The second is a reversal of the natural order of perception and for this reason the condemnation so often heard from painters, of the literary or 'detective' approach to pictures, of which this would be a representative specimen, is well merited. We must, however, distinguish cases in which there is this reversal from those in which it does not occur, those namely in which by a process of inference we arrive at conclusions about the represented objects which could not possibly be directly given. But this question may be deferred until we come to discuss representation.

Hitherto in considering the growth of the three-dimensional imagined picture-space we have not explicitly mentioned the part played by colour nor the equally important effect of this growth in modifying the original colours of the first retinal impression. But not only may colour be the chief factor determining form, i.e. the three-dimensional organization of space but it is itself most vitally modified by form.

Colours as signs, that is to say even at the most optical and least elaborated stage, have certain very marked spatial characters of their own. Red, for example, seems to advance towards the eye and to swell out of its boundaries, while blue seems to retreat and to withdraw into itself.[1] Degree of saturation may also give recession in obvious and in more recondite ways. Pure colours in the foreground and greyed colours in the background are a simple example. Similarly opposition of colours is one of the main means by which the stresses and strains of volumes may be suggested.

These characters of colours, especially when they reinforce and co-operate with one another, may be made to play a very important part in determining the way in which the picture-space is constructed when we look at a picture.

Equally important are the less direct effects upon our picture-space imagining of the emotional or organic responses which we make to different colours. Individuals vary greatly in the extent to which they notice and can reflectively distinguish these responses, and probably also in the degree to which they actually make different responses. To persons sensitive in this respect, the colours excite each a distinct, well-marked emotion (and attitude) capable of being clearly differentiated from others. The sad poverty and vagueness of the colour vocabulary, however, misleads many people with regard to these. Each of the 'puces', 'mauves', 'magentas' etc. has to cover numbers of distinguishable colours, often with strikingly different effects upon us. Thus people who are content to say that pink is their favourite colour, or that green always suits them, are either quite undiscriminating in their attitude towards colour or little attentive to the actual effects produced upon them. A similar obtuseness or insincerity is evidenced when it is maintained, as is often done, that pink and green do not go together. Some pinks and some greens do

---

[1] This character of blue is the basis of the doctrine of Reynolds, that blue is unsuitable in foregrounds, which led Gainsborough, according to the well-known story, to paint The Blue Boy.

not, but some do, and the test of a colourist is just his ability to feel which are which. Few if any, in fact, of the colour relations with which the painter is concerned can be stated with the aid of such general terms – 'red', 'brown', 'yellow', 'grey', 'primrose', etc. – as are at present available. Each of these stands for a number of different colours whose relations to a given colour will commonly be different.

Taking 'colour' in this sense to stand for specific colours, not for classes or ranges of varying hues, sets of colours, where in certain spatial proportions and in certain relations of saturation, brightness and luminosity relatively to one another, excite responses of emotion and attitude with marked individual characteristics. Colours, in fact, have harmonic relations, although the physical laws governing these relations are at present unknown, and the relations themselves only imperfectly ascertained. For every colour another can be found such that the combined response to the two will be of a recognizable kind, whose peculiarities are due probably to the compatibility with one another of the impulses set up by each. This compatibility varies in a number of ways. The result is that for every colour a set of other colours is discoverable such that the response to each of them is compatible with the response to the tonic colour in a definite way.[1] A sensitive colourist feels these compatibilities as giving to these combinations of colours a definite character, which no other combinations possess. Similarly relations of incompatibility between colours can also be felt such that their combination yields no ordered response but merely a clash and confusion of responses. Colours which just fail to be complementary are a typical example. Similarly the primary colours in combination are offensive; should this precise kind

[1] This account of harmony also applies to music. Few modern authorities are content to regard harmony as an affair merely of the physical relationships 0f notes.

of offensiveness be part of the artist's purpose, he will, of course, make use of them.

The fact that roses, sunsets, and so forth are so often found to present harmonious combinations of colour may appear a little puzzling by this account. But the vast range of close gradations, which a rose petal, for example, presents, supplies the explanation. Out of all these the eye picks that gradation which best accords with the other colours chosen. There is usually some set of colours in some harmonious relation to one another to be selected out of the multitudinous gradations which natural objects in most lightings present; and there are evident reasons why the eye of a sensitive person should, when it can, pick out those gradations which best accord. The great range of different possible selections is, however, of importance. It explains the fact that we see such different colours for instance when gloomy and when gay, and thus how the actual selection made by an artist may reveal the kind and direction of the impulses which are active in him at the moment of selection.

Needless to say in the absence of a clear nomenclature and standardization of colours the task of describing and recording colour relations is of great difficulty, but the unanimity of competent, that is, sensitive persons as to which colours are related in specific ways to which, is too great to be disregarded. It is as great as the unanimity among musicians as to the harmonic relations of notes to one another. The great differences between the two cases are not likely to be overlooked. The presence of physical laws in many cases connecting notes harmonically related and the absence of similar known physical laws connecting colours is a glaring difference. But it should not be forgotten that these physical laws are, as it were, an extra-musical piece of knowledge. What matters to the musician is not the physical connections between notes but the compatibilities and incompatibilities in the responses of emotion and attitude which they excite. The musical relations between the notes would be the same even though the physical relations between the stimuli which arouse them were quite different.

Naturally enough the analogy with the harmonic relations of music has been the chief guide to those who have systematically investigated colour relations. Whatever may be the precise limits to which it may profitably be carried, for anyone who wishes to form a general conception of the emotional effects of colours in combination it is of very great value.

Colour is of course primarily the cause and controlling factor of emotional response to painting, but, as we have said, it may, and commonly does, help to determine form. Parts of a picture which are through their colour out of all emotional connection with the rest of the picture, tend, other things being equal, to fall out of the picture altogether, appearing as patches accidentally adhering to the surface or as gaps through which something else irrelevant is seen. This is the extreme instance, but the influence of colour upon form through the emotional relations of colours to one another is all-pervading. Sometimes colour strengthens and solidifies the structure, sometimes it fights against it, sometimes it turns into a commentary, as it were, the colour response modifying the form response and *vice versa*. The great complexity of the colour and form interactions needs no insistence. They are so various that no rule can possibly be laid down as to a right relation for all cases. All depends upon what the whole response which the painter is seeking to record may be. As with attempts to define a universal proper relation of rhythm to thought in poetry (e.g. the assertion that rhythm should echo or correspond to thought, etc.), so with general remarks as to how form and colour should be related. All depends upon the purpose, the total response to which both form and colour are merely means. Mistakes between means and ends, glorifying particular techniques into inexplicable virtues are at least as common in the criticism of painting as with any other of the arts.

One other aspect of the picture-space needs consideration. It is not necessarily a fixed and static construction, but may in several ways contain elements of movement. Some of these may be eye movements, or kinaesthetic images of eye movements. As the eye wanders imaginally from point to point the relations between the parts of the picture-space change; thus an effect of movement is induced. Equally important are the fusions of successive visual images which may be suggested by drawing. As we watch, for example, an arm being flexed, the eye receives a series of successive and changing retinal impressions. Certain combinations of these, which represent not the position and form of the arm at any instant, but a compromise or fusion of different positions and forms, have an easily explicable capacity to represent the whole series, and thus to represent movement. The use of such fused images in drawing may easily be mistaken for distortion, but when properly interpreted it may yield normal forms in movement. Many other means by which movement is given in painting might be mentioned. One means by which colour may suggest it, for example, is well indicated in the following description by Signac of *Muley-abd-er Rahman entouré de sa garde:* 'la tumulte est traduit par l'accord presque dissonant de grand parasol vert sur le bleu du ciel, surexcité déjà par l'orangé des murailles'.[1] It need hardly be pointed out that the response made to the picture-space varies enormously according to whether the forms in it are seen as in rest or in movement.

So far we have merely discussed what may be described as the sensory elements in the picture, and the responses in emotion and attitude due to these elements. But in most painting there are further elements essentially involved. It has been asserted that all further elements are irrelevant, at least to appreciation; and as a reaction to common views that seem to overlook the sensory elements altogether the doctrine is comprehensible and perhaps

[1] *D'Eugène Delacroix au Néo-Impressionisme,* p. 39.

not without value. For too many people do look at pictures primarily with intent to discover what they are 'of', what they represent, without allowing the most important thing in the picture, its sensory stimulation through colour and form, to take effect. But the reaction goes too far when it denies the relevance of the representative elements in all cases. It may be freely granted that there are great pictures in which nothing is represented, and great pictures in which what is represented is trivial and may be disregarded. It is equally certain that there are great pictures in which the contribution to the whole response made through representation is not less than that made more directly through form and colour. To those who can accept the general psychological standpoint already outlined, or indeed any modern account of the working of the mind, the assertion that there is no reason why representative and formal factors in an experience should conflict, but much reason why they should co-operate, will need no discussion. The psychology of 'unique aesthetic emotions' and 'pure art values' upon which the contrary view relies is merely a caprice of the fancy.

The place of representation in the work of different masters varies enormously and it is not true that the value of their works varies correspondingly. From Raphael and Picasso at one extreme to Rembrandt, Goya and Hogarth at the other, Rubens, Delacroix and Giotto occupying an intermediate position, all degrees of participation between non-representative form and represented subject in the building up of the whole response can be found. We may perhaps hazard, for reasons indicated already, as a principle admitting of exception, that what can be done by sensory means should not be done indirectly through representation. But to say more than this is to give yet another instance of the commonest of critical mistakes: the exaltation of a method into an end.

Representation in painting corresponds to thought in poetry. The same battles over the Intellect-Emotion *imbroglio* rage in both fields. The views recently so fashionable that representation has no place in art and that treatment not subject is what matters in poetry spring ultimately from the same mistakes as to the relation of thinking to feeling, from an inadequate psychology which would set up one as inimical to the other. Reinforced as they are by the illusion, supported by language, that Beauty is a quality of things, not a character of our response to them, and thus that all beautiful things as sharing this Beauty must be alike, the confusion which such views promote is a main cause of the difficulty which is felt so widely in appreciating both the arts and poetry. They give an air of an esoteric mystery to what is, if it can be done at ail, the simplest and most natural of proceedings.

The fundamental features of the experiences of reading poetry and of appreciating pictures, the features upon which their value depends, are alike. The means by which they are brought about are unlike, but closely analogous critical and technical problems arise, as we have seen, for each. The misapprehensions to which thought is liable recur in all the fields in which it is exercised, and the fact that it is sometimes more easy to detect a mistake in one field than in another is a strong argument for comparing such closely allied subjects.

19

SCULPTURE AND THE CONSTRUCTION OF FORM

Thus men forgot
That All Deities reside in the Human breast.
The Marriage of Heaven and Hell

The initial signs from which the work of art is built up psychologically in the case of sculpture differ in several respects from the initial signs of painting. There are of course forms of sculpture for which the difference is slight. Some bas-reliefs, for example, can be considered as essentially drawings, and sculpture placed as a decorative detail in architecture so that it can only be viewed from one angle has necessarily to be interpreted in much the same manner. Similarly some primitive sculpture in which only one aspect is represented may be considered as covered by what has been said about painting, although the fact that the relief and the relation of volumes is more completely given and less supplied by imaginative effort is of some consequence. Further, the changes, slight though they may be, which accompany slight movements of the contemplator have their effect. His total attitude is altered in a way which may or may not be important according to circumstances.

With sculpture in which a number (four for example) of aspects are fully treated without any attempt to fill in the intermediate connecting aspects, the whole state of affairs is changed, since there arises the interpretative task of uniting these aspects into a whole.

This connection of a number of aspects into a whole may be made in varying ways. The signs may receive a *visual* interpretation and the form be mainly built up of visual images combined in sequences or fused. This, however, is an unsatisfactory method. It tends to leave out or blur too many of the possible responses to the statue and there is usually something unstable about such syntheses. The form so constructed is insubstantial and incomplete. Thus those sculptors whose work primarily asks for such a visual interpretation are commonly felt to be lacking in what is called a 'sense of form'. The reasons for this are to be found in the nature of visual imagery and in the necessarily limited character of our purely visual awareness of space.

But the connection may be made, not through visual combination, but through combination of the various muscular images whereby we feel, or imaginatively construct the tensions, weights, stresses, etc. of physical objects. Each sequence of visual impressions as we look at the statue from varying standpoints calls up a group of these muscular images, and these images are capable of much more subtle and stable combinations than the corresponding visual images. Thus two visual images which are incompatible with one another may be each accompanied by muscular images (feelings of stress, tension, etc.) which are perfectly compatible and unite to form a coherent whole free from conflict. By this means we may realize the solidity of forms far more perfectly than if we rely upon visual resources alone, and since it is mainly through the character of the statue as a solid that the sculptor works, this muscular interpretation has, as a rule, obvious and overwhelming advantages.

None the less a place remains for sculpture whose primary interpretation is in visual terms. Looking at any of the more recent work of Epstein, for example, a feeling of quick and active intelligence on the part of the contemplator arises, and this sense of own activity is the source of much that follows in his response. By contrast a work of Rodin seems to be not so much exciting activity in him as active itself. The correlation of visual aspects, in other words, is a conscious process compared with the automatic correlation of muscular image responses. The first we seem to be doing ourselves; the second seems to be something which belongs to the statue. This difference as we have described it is of course a technical difference and by itself involves nothing as to the value of the different works concerned. A similar difference may be found in the apprehension of form in painting.

These two modes are not as separate as our account would suggest; neither occurs in purity. Their interaction is further complicated through the highly representational character of most sculpture, and through the interlinking of different interpretations due to the congruences and incompatibilities of the emotional responses to which they give rise.

With sculpture perhaps more than with any other of the plastic arts we are in danger of overlooking the work of the contemplator's imagination in filling out and interpreting the sign. What we transport from Egypt to London is merely a set of signs, from which a suitable interpreter setting about it rightly can produce a certain state of mind. It is this state of mind which matters and which gives its value to the statue. But so obscure to ordinary introspection are the processes of the interpretation that we tend to think that none occur. That we interpret a picture or a poem is obvious upon very little reflection. That we interpret a mass of marble is less obvious. The historical accident that speculation upon Beauty largely developed in connection with sculpture is responsible in great degree for the fixity of the opinion that Beauty is something inherent in physical objects, not a character of some of our responses to objects.

From certain visual signs, then, the contemplator constructs, muscularly as well as visually, the spatial form of the statue. We have seen that the picture-space is a construction, similarly the statue-space is a construction, and the proportions and relations of the volumes which in this statue-space make up the statue are by no means necessarily the same as those of the mass of marble from which we receive our signs. In other words, the scientific examination of the statue and the imaginative contemplation of it do not yield the same spatial results. Thus the process of measuring[1] statues with a view to discovering a numerical formula for Beauty is little likely to be fruitful. And the work of those, such as Havard Thomas, who have attempted to use this method, show the features which we should expect. Their merits derive from factors outside the range of the theory. The psychological processes involved in the construction of space are too subtle, and the differences between the actual configuration of the marble and the configuration of the statue in the statue-space are brought about in too many ways for any correlation to be established.

Among the factors which intervene in the building up of the imaginative form the most obvious are the lighting, and the material.

With change of lighting, change of form follows at once

---

[1] This remark applies equally strongly to the attempts which are from time to time made to find formulae for the proportions of buildings. No one with an adequate idea of the complexity of the factors which determine our responses is likely to attach great importance to these investigations, interesting though they are. The interpretation of the results is not within sight of even the most optimistic of psychologists.

through change in the visual signs, and since stone is often a translucent not an opaque material, lighting is by no means such a simple matter as is sometimes supposed. More is involved than the avoidance of distracting cast shadows and the disposal of the brightest illumination upon the right portions of the statue. The general aim should obviously be to reproduce the lighting for which the sculptor designed his work, an aim which requires very sensitive and full appreciation for its success. An aim, moreover, which in the case of works transported from North to South and *vice versa* is sometimes impossible of realization.

The interpretation of form is an extraordinarily complex affair. 'The consequences of the asymmetricality of space as we construct it must be noted. Up and down have distinct characters which differ from those of right and left, which differ again from those of away and towards us. A measured vertical distance does not seem to us the same as an equal horizontal distance. Nor does an equal distance away from us seem equal to either. These effects are modified again, sometimes reinforced, sometimes reduced, by effects due to quite a different source, to the relative ease or difficulty with which the eye follows certain lines. The greater and less compatibility of certain eye movements with others is the cause of much of what is confusedly called Rhythm in the plastic arts. After certain lines we expect others, and the success or failure of our expectation modifies our response. Unexpectedness, of course, is an obvious technical resource for the artist. The intervention here of the representational factor cannot be overlooked. An eye movement which encounters difficulty for any of a number of possible reasons, among which so-called rhythmical factors deserve special notice, is interpreted as standing for a greater distance than an equal but more easy movement. This is only a rough rule, for yet other psychological factors may come in to nullify or even reverse the effect; for example, an explicit recognition of the difficulty. Yet another determining condition in our estimation of intervals of space is the uniformity of their filling. Thus a hue one inch long hatched across will generally seem longer than an equal line unhatched, and a modulated surface seem larger than a smooth one.

These instances of the psychological factors which help to make the imaginatively constructed statue-space different from the actual space occupied by the marble will be enough to show how intricate is the interpretation by which we take even the first step towards the appreciation of a statue. Our full response of attitude and emotion is entirely dependent upon how we perform the initial operations. It is of course impossible to make these interpretations separately, consciously and deliberately. Neural arrangements over which we have little or no direct control perform them for us. Thanks to their complexity the resultant effect, the imagined form of the statue, will vary greatly from individual to individual and in the same individual from time to time. It might be thought therefore that the hope that a statue will be a vehicle of the same experience for many different individuals is vain. Certain simplifications, however, save the situation.

Form, as we have seen, is, through our selection among the possible signs present, within certain limits what we like to make it. As it varies, so do our further or deeper responses of feeling and attitude vary. But just as there are congruences and compatibilities among the responses we make, in the case of colour, which tend, given certain colours, to make us pick out of a range of possible colours one which will give us a congruent (or harmonious) response, so it is with form. Out of the multitude of different forms which we might construct by stressing certain of the signs rather than others, the fixing even temporarily of a part of the form tends to bias us towards so interpreting the rest as to yield responses accordant with those already active. Hence a great reduction of the disparity of the interpretations which arise, hence also the danger of an initial misapprehension which perverts the rest of the interpretation.

This Chapter, like the last, is intended as an indication, merely, of the ways in which a psychological analysis may assist the critic and help to remove misconceptions. The usual practice of alluding to Form as though it were a simple unanalysable virtue of objects – a procedure most discouraging to those who like to know what they are doing, and thus very detrimental to general appreciation – will lapse when a better understanding of the situation becomes general. None the less there are certain very puzzling facts as to the effects of forms when apprehended which in part explain this way of talking. These are perhaps best considered in connection with Music, the most purely formal of the arts.

20

THE *IMPASSE* OF MUSICAL THEORY

> Will twenty chapters render plain
> Those lonely lights that still remain
> Just breaking over land and main?

For fairly obvious reasons the psychology of Music is often regarded as more backward than that of the other arts; and the *impasse* which has here been reached more baffling and more exasperating. But such advance as has been possible in the theory of the other arts has been mainly concerned with them as representational or as serviceable. For poetry, for painting, for architecture there still remain problems as perplexing as any which can be raised about music. For example, what is the difference between good and bad blank verse in its formal aspect, between delightful and distressing alliteration, between euphony and cacophony, between metrical triumph and metrical failure? Or in the case of Painting, why do certain forms excite such marked responses of emotion and attitude and others, so very like them geometrically, excite none or produce merely confusion? Why have colours their specific responses and how is it that their combinations have such subtle and yet definite effects? Or what is the reason that spaces and volumes in Architecture affect us as they do? These questions are at present as much without answers as any that we can raise about Music; but the fact that in these arts other questions arise which can in part be answered, whereas in Music questions about the effects of form over-whelmingly preponderate, has in part obscured the situation.

Other effects are of course also involved; in programme music something analogous to representation in painting; in opera and much other music, dramatic action; and so forth. But these effects, although often contributing to the total value, are plainly subordinate in music to its more direct influence as sound alone. The difficulties which they raise have such close analogies in painting and poetry that a separate discussion may be omitted. The problem of 'pure form' arises, however, with peculiar insistence in music.

More than forty years ago Gurney summed up the state of musical theory as follows: 'When we come to actual forms, and to the startling differences of merit which the very simplest known to us present, the musical faculty defies all explanation of its action and its judgements. The only conceivable explanation indeed would be an analogy, and we know not where to look for it'.[1] And the work done since has added remarkably little. As he so admirably insisted, even though we confine ourselves to the responses of onc individual, all general explanations of the musical effect apply equally to the ineffective, to the distressing and the delightful, to the admirable and the atrocious alike. But the same is true of all attempts to explain the effects upon us of any forms which neither represent something nor are in obvious ways serviceable. Whether they are forms seen or heard, whether

[1] *The Power of Sound*, p. 176.

they are made up of notes or of movements, of intervals of time or of images of speech, the same is true of them all.

Whatever effects cannot be traced to some practical use we might make of them (as we use a plate to eat from or a house to live in), or to some interference with or threat against the ways in which we might act, or to some object practically interesting to us, which they represent – all such effects arc necessarily very difficult to explain.

There is nothing in the least mysterious, however, about the difficulty of explaining them. The facts required happen to be beyond our present powers of observation. They belong to a branch of psychology for which we have as yet no methods of investigation. It seems likely that we shall have to wait a long while, and that very good advances must first be made in neurology before these problems can profitably be attacked. But however regrettable this may be, there is no justification what-ever for the invention of unique faculties and ultimate, analys-able, indefinable entities. To say that a thing is unanalysable may be to assert either that it is simple or that we do not know yet how to analyse it. Musical effects, like the effects of forms in general, are inexplicable in the second sense only. To pretend that they are inexplicable in the first sense is mere mystery-mongering. To take two parallel cases, trade booms and fine weather were until recently inexplicable, and are doubtless still in many respects difficult to account for. But no one would pretend that these blessings require us to assume unique *sui generis* tendencies in economic or meteorological affairs.

But the practice of describing the 'musical faculty' and the formal effects of the arts in general as *sui generis* has another cause in addition to intellectual bewilderment. Many people think that to say that a mental activity is unique, or *sui generis*, in some way gives it a more exalted standing than if it were recognized as merely too complicated or too inaccessible to experiment to be at present explained. In part this is a relic of the old opinion that explanation is itself derogatory, an opinion which only those who are, in this respect, uneducated, still entertain. Partly also this preference for 'unique' things is due to confusion with the sense in which St. Paul's may be said to be unique. But the experience of 'seeing stars' after a bang on the nose is just as 'unique' as any act of musical appreciation and shares any exalted quality which such uniqueness may be supposed to confer.

Every element in a form, whether it be a musical form or any other, is capable of exciting a very intricate and widespread response. Usually the response is of a minimal order and escapes introspection. Thus a single note or a uniform colour has for most people hardly any observable effect beyond its sensory characteristics. When it occurs along with other elements the form which they together make up may have striking con-sequences in emotion and attitude. If we regard this as an affair of mere summation of effects it may seem impossible that the effect of the form can be the result of the effects of the elements, and thus it is natural and easy to invent ultimate properties of 'forms' by way of pseudo-explanation. But a little more psycho-logical insight makes these inventions appear quite unnecessary. The effects of happenings in the mind rarely add themselves up. Our more intense experiences are not built up of less intense experiences as a wall is built up of bricks. 'The metaphor of addition is utterly misleading. That of the resolution of forces would be better, but even this does not adequately represent the behaviour of the mind. The separate responses which each element in isolation would tend to excite are so connected with one another that their combination is, for our present know-ledge, incalculable in its effects. Two stimuli which, when separ-ated by one interval of time or space, would merely cancel one another, with another interval produce an effect which is far beyond anything which either alone could produce. And the combined response when they are suitably arranged may be of quite another kind than that of either. We may, if we like, think of the effects of impulses at various intervals of time upon a pendulum, but this metaphor is, as we have suggested, insufficient. It is over simple. The intricacies of chemical reactions come nearer to being what we need. The great quantities of latent energy which may be released by quite slight changes in conditions suggest better what happens when stimuli are combined. But even this metaphor incompletely represents the complexity of the interactions in the nervous system. It is only by conjecture that its working can as yet be divined. What is certain is that it is the most complex and the most sensitive thing of which we know.

The unpredictable and miraculous differences, then, in the total responses which slight changes in the arrangement of stimuli produce, can be fully accounted for in terms of the sensitiveness of the nervous system; and the mysteries of 'forms' are merely a consequence of our present ignorance of the detail of its action. We have spoken above of the 'elements' of a form, but in fact we do not yet know which these are. Any musical sound, for example, is plainly complex, though how complex it is from the point of view of its musical effects is still very uncertain. It has pitch, it has *timbre*, the characters which change as it is played upon one kind of instrument or another, the characters which are sometimes called its colour. Its effects also vary with its loudness and with its volume. It may be far more complex still. Its relations again to other musical sounds may be of at least three kinds: pitch relations, harmonic relations and temporal relations, complicated, all of them, in the utmost degree by Rhythm. Possibly other relations still are involved. There would be no advantage here in entering into the detail of the analysis of these qualities and relations. The one point of importance for our present purpose is the immense scope for the resolution, interinanimation, conflict and equilibrium of impulses opened up by this extraordinary complexity of musical sounds and of their possible arrangement. It is not in the least surprising that so few invariable correspondences between stimuli and total responses have as yet been discovered.

The same state of affairs recurs wherever forms by themselves, dissociated from all practical uses and from all representation produce immediate effects upon the mind. In painting, in sculpture, in architecture and in poetry, we need equally to be on our guard against those who would attribute peculiar, unique and mystic virtues to forms in themselves. In every case their effect is due to the interplay (not the addition) of file effects which their elements excite. Especially we do well to beware of empty speculations upon 'necessary and inevitable relations' as the source of the effect. Of course in a given case a certain relation, a certain arrangement, may be necessary, in the sense that the elements if differently disposed would have a quite different combined effect. But this is not the sense in which necessity is usually claimed. It is necessity, in the metaphysical sense, some here utterly obscure kind of 'logical necessity' which is the favourite toy of a number of art critics. To those who have some familiarity both with Logic and with Psychology the regular appearance of the term 'logical' in describing these relations is the clearest indication that nothing definite or adequately considered is being said. The fact that, given certain elements arranged in a certain way, a certain further element can usually be introduced in one way and one way only if *a certain total effect is to be produced*, does, it is true, give a certain 'inevitability' to the artist's work. But what the effect is and whether the effect is worth while have still to be considered, and this inevitably has nothing to do with a priori rightness and is a matter simply of cause and effect. The salt required to make a soup palatable is 'logically necessitated' in this sense as much as any relation in a picture. The value lies not in the apprehension, conscious or subconscious, of the rightness of the relations, but in the total mental effect which, since they are right (i.e. since they work), they produce.

21

A THEORY OF COMMUNICATION

For surely once, they feel, we were
Parts of a single continent.
Matthew Arnold

Artificial mysteries are as prevalent in unreflecting and even in elaborately excogitated opinion upon communication as elsewhere. On the one hand are some who define communication as the actual transference of experiences in the strictest possible sense of transference – the sense in which a penny can be transferred from one pocket to another – and are led to most fantastic hypotheses. Blake seems sometimes to have believed that one single, the same, identical state of mind, imagined as a being or power, can occupy now one mind, now another, or many minds at once. Other thinkers, in less picturesque manners have fallen back upon no less transcendental considerations as necessities in the explanation of communication. We must suppose, it is alleged, that human minds are wider than we ordinarily believe, that parts of one mind may pass over to become parts of another, that minds interpenetrate and intermingle, or even that particular minds are merely an illusory appearance and the underlying reality one mind whose facets or aspects are many. In this way it is easy to enter the maze. Probably some wanderings in it are unavoidable for all speculative persons at some period of their mental development. The only escape from it is by the original entrance.

For communication defined as strict transference of or participation in identical experiences does not occur. This is not a heartbreaking conclusion. No general theory, in fact, as to the nature or conditions of experiences can affect their value. For value is prior to all explanations. If actual transference and participation did occur we should of course be compelled to adopt a transcendental theory. It does not occur[1] and no arguments which assume it have the least weight.

All that occurs is that, under certain conditions, separate minds have closely similar experiences. Those who are unable to accept this view reject it not on grounds of evidence, not through the ways in which the world influences them, but on grounds of desire, due to the influence of the contrary opinion on their attitudes to their fellows. At moments anyone may wish it otherwise; severance seems a deprivation; caught in a moment of maladjustment we feel that our essential insularity is a blight

---

[1] The very strange and important phenomena of apparent telepathy, and the feats of some 'psychometrists' and 'clairvoyants', although they may call for a great extension of our ideas as to how minds influence one another, do not require any such desperate devices as transference of or participation in, identical experiences. If they did, the possibility of investigating them by the only technique with which anything has ever been successfully investigated would be remote. On any 'identity' or 'participation' theory, communication becomes an ineffable and irremovable mystery. There may, of course, be any number of strange events occurring about which we cannot know, but to discuss such events is unprofitable.

and a defect, and to accept the facts and upon them to found a new and more perfect adjustment is for all sensitive people in some situations difficult. But the true belief does not, and perhaps no true belief can, really deprive anyone of any values. Sad cases of bad systematizations there doubtless are, for which no readjustment is possible. A false belief may become an indispensable condition for the most important activities of individuals who without it break down into confusion. So it is with many religious beliefs; and in saying that the removal of such beliefs need involve no loss, and may involve great gains in values, we do not say that there are not certain individuals whose values will be destroyed in the process. We say only that adaptable people will find that most of their values can be retained after rejecting their errors, that compensations and equivalents for their losses are available, and that whole sets of fresh values become open to them through their better adjustment to the actual world in which they live. This is the justification for the opinion which has so often been held, that knowledge is the greatest of all goods. The opinion appears to be warranted. Knowledge *is* we are slowly finding out, an indispensable condition for the attainment of the widest, most stable, and most important values.

We start then from the natural isolation and severance of minds. Their experiences at the best, under the most favourable circumstances, can be but similar. Communication, we shall say, takes place when one mind so acts upon its environment that another mind is influenced, and in that other mind an experience occurs which is like the experience in the first mind, and is caused in part by that experience. Communication is evidently a complicated affair, and capable of degrees at least in two respects. The two experiences may be more or less similar, and the second may be more or less dependent upon the first. If A and B are walking in the street together and A touches B and says, 'There is the Lord Chief Justice,' B's experience while he contemplates the dignitary is only adventitiously dependent upon A's experience. But if A, having met the Lord Chief Justice, describes him to a friend afterwards in a quarry at Portland, for example, his friend's experience will depend very largely upon the particular judges he may himself have encountered, and for the rest will derive its special features from A's description. Unless A has remarkable gifts of description and B extraordinarily sensitive and discriminating receptive ability, their two experiences will tally at best but roughly. They may completely fail to tally without either being clearly aware of the fact.

In general, long and varied acquaintanceship, close familiarity, lives whose circumstances have often corresponded, in short an exceptional fund of common experience is needed, if people, in the absence of special communicative gifts, active and receptive, are to communicate, and even with these gifts the success of the communication in difficult cases depends upon the extent to which past similarities in experience can be made use of. Without such similarities communication is impossible. Difficult cases are those in which the speaker must himself supply and control a large part of the causes of the listener's experience; in which correspondingly the listener has to struggle against the intrusions of elements from his own past experience which are irrelevant. When A can point and B gaze, the matter is sometimes easy; although, as is well known, a complex object, for example a landscape, where many different selections are possible corresponding to different emphases of interest, cannot be dealt with in so simple a manner. Less complex things in which the interesting feature is more salient, for example, a gentleman asleep in Church, may be merely indicated with more confidence of communication, although here again one person may feel indignation and another amusement at the sight.

In difficult cases the vehicle of communication must inevitably be complex. The effect of a word varies with the other words among which it is placed. What would be highly ambiguous by itself becomes definite in a suitable context. So it is throughout; the effect of any element depends upon the other elements present with it. Even in such shallow communication as is involved in merely making out the letters in a handwriting this principle is all-important, and in the deepest forms of communication the same principle holds good. To this is due the superiority of verse to prose for the most difficult and deepest communications, poetry being by far the more complex vehicle. A similar instance is the increased ambiguity of a monochromatic reproduction as compared with the original painting. What difficulty of communication depends upon we have already considered. It should not be confused with the difficulty of the matter communicated, although the two are often connected. Some very difficult calculations, for example, can be communicated with ease. Depth of communication likewise is not necessarily connected with difficulty. It is a name for the degree of completeness in the response required. A glance at the diagram on p. 107 will make this use of the term clear. Communications involving attitudes are deeper than those in which references alone are concerned. Abstract and analytic prose, in fact, depends for its success upon the shallowness of its draught. It must avoid any stirring of the emotions lest its required distinctions become obscured.

22

THE AVAILABILITY OF THE POET'S EXPERIENCE

That he is the wisest, the happiest and the best, inasmuch as he is a poet, is equally incontrovertible; the greatest poets have been men of the most spotless virtue, of the most consummate prudence, and, if we would look into the interior of their lives, the most fortunate of men.

The Defence of Poetry

The special communicative gifts, either active or passive, which have been alluded to, are no peculiar irreducible abilities. They can be described in terms of activities already mentioned. The use of past similarities in experience and the control of these elements through the dependence of their effects upon one another, make up the speaker's, the active communicator's gift. Discrimination, suggestibility, free and clear resuscitation of elements of past experience *disentangled from one another*, and control of irrelevant personal details and accidents, make up the recipient's gift. We may now consider these more closely.

Certain favourable and unfavourable special circumstances in the temperaments or characters of the persons concerned may be set aside. Thus courage or audacity, enterprise, goodwill, absence of undue pride or conceit, honesty, humaneness, humility in its finest sense, humour, tolerance, good health, and the Confucian characteristics of the 'superior man' are favourable general conditions for communication. But we will assume them present in sufficient degree and pass on to the less evident because more fundamental conditions. In the first place all those which we have enumerated as desirable in the recipient are also necessary in the artist. He is pre-eminently accessible to external influences and discriminating with regard to them. He is distinguished further by the freedom in which all these impressions are held in suspension and by the ease with which they form new relations between themselves. The greatest difference between the artist or poet and the ordinary person is found, as has often been pointed out, in the range, delicacy, and freedom of the connections he is able to make between different elements of his experience. 'All the images of nature were still present to him,' says Dryden, with felicity, of Shakespeare, 'and he drew them not laboriously but luckily.' It is this available possession of the past which is the first characteristic of the adept in communication, of the poet or the artist.

Availability, not mere possession, however, is what is essential. Many people are endowed with memories of marble upon which time can do little to efface even the slightest mark, but they benefit little from their endowment. A merely repetitive retention is rather a disability than an asset in communication, since it makes the separation of the private and irrelevant from the essential so difficult. Persons to whom the past comes back as a whole are likely to be found in an asylum.

What is in question here is not memory, in the stricter sense in which past experience is dated and placed, but free reproduction. To be able to revive an experience is not to remember when and where and how it occurred, but merely to have that peculiar state of mind available. Why some experiences are available and others not is unfortunately still a matter for conjecture merely. The difficulty upon most accounts, Semon's for example, is to explain why *all* our past experience is not being revived all the time. But some plausible conjectures are not difficult to make, and the absence of clear evidence or conclusive proof should not prevent our making them if they are recognized for conjectures.

How far an experience is revivable would seem to depend in the first place upon the interests, the impulses, active in the experience. Unless similar interests recur its revival would seem to be difficult. The original experience is built upon a number of impulses; it came about only through these impulses. We may even say that it is those impulses. The first condition for its revival is the occurrence of impulses similar to *some* of these.

The patient in the asylum occupied in reliving the same piece of experience indefinitely does so (if he does) because he is limited very strictly in the range of his possible impulses, other impulses not being allowed to intervene. Hence the completeness with which he is said to reconstruct the past. Most revival is distorted because only some of the original impulses are repeated, new impulses being involved and a compromise resulting.

The impulses implicated in experiences may be many and varied or few and alike. An experience which has a very simple impulse structure will, we may suppose, tend to come back only when these impulses are again relatively dominant. Other things being equal it will have less chance of revival than an experience with a more complex structure. Recalling the illustration used in Chapter Fourteen, the broader the facet the more numerous are the positions from which the polyhedron will settle down on that facet. It is a first principle of psychology that the partial return only of a situation may reinstate the whole, and since most impulses have belonged in the past to many varied wholes there must evidently be much rivalry as to which wholes do actually recur. What seems to decide the dispute more than anything else is the character of the original connections between the parts. As has recently been emphasized by the exponents of *Gestaltpsychologie*, mere original contiguity or simultaneity is comparatively powerless to control revival. Compare the learning of a geometric theorem by heart with understanding it, or even a brief study of some building with mere daily familiarity.

What then is the difference between understanding a situation and the more usual reactions to it? It is a difference in the degree of organization of the impulses which it arouses. It is the difference between a systematized complex response, or ordered sequence of responses, and a welter of responses. We must not take 'understanding' in too specialized a sense here, or we shall overlook the immense importance of this difference in determining revival. We are accustomed to make an artificial distinction between intellectual or theoretical and non-intellectual or emotional mental activities. To understand a situation in the sense here intended is not necessarily to reflect upon it, to inquire into its principles and consciously distinguish its characters, but to respond to it as a whole, in a coherent way which allows its parts their due share and their proper independence in the response. Experience which has this organized character, it is reasonable to suppose, has more chance of revival, is more available as a whole and in parts, than more confused experience.

Contrast the behaviour of the sleepy and the fully awake, of the normal man with the lightly and the more deeply anaesthetized patient, of the starved or fevered with the healthy. To describe these differences in neural potency, and to mark the degree of physiological efficiency, Dr. Head has recently[1]

---

[1] Henry Head, 'The Conception of Nervous and Mental Energy' in the *British Journal of Psychology*, Oct. 1923, Vol. XIV, p. 126.

suggested the term *vigilance*, a useful addition to our symbolic machinery. In a high state of vigilance the nervous system reacts to stimuli with highly adapted, discriminating, and ordered responses; in a lowered state of vigilance the responses are less discriminating, less delicately adapted. Whether we are considering the decerebrate preparation or the intact poet, the simplest automatisms or the most highly conscious acts, what happens in a given stimulus situation varies with the vigilance of the appropriate portion of the nervous system. The point as regards revival can be put conveniently by saying that experiences of high vigilance are the most likely to be available. The degree of vigilance of the individual at the moment at which revival is attempted is, of course, equally but more evidently an important factor.

The answer then, at least in part, to the problem of how the poet's experience is more than usually available to him is that it is, as he undergoes it, more than usually organized through his more than usual vigilance. Connections become established for him which in the ordinary mind, much more rigid and exclusive in its play of impulses, are never effected, and it is through these original connections that so much more of his past comes to be freely revivable for him at need.

The same explanation may be put in another way. In order to keep any steadiness and clarity in his attitudes the ordinary man is under the necessity on most occasions of suppressing the greater part of the impulses which the situation might arouse. He is incapable of organizing them; therefore they have to be left out. In the same situation the artist is able to admit far more without confusion. Hence the fact that his resultant behaviour is apt to cause dismay, irritation or envy, or to seem incomprehensible. The wheeling of the pigeons in Trafalgar Square may seem to have no relation to the colour of the water in the basins, or to the tones of a speaker's voice or to the drift of his remarks. A narrow field of stimulation is all that we can manage and we overlook the rest. But the artist does not, and when he needs it, he has it at his disposal.

The dangers to which he is exposed, the apparent inconsequence, the difficulty on many occasions of co-operating with him, of relying upon him, of predicting what he will do, are evident and often expatiated upon. His superficial resemblance to persons who are merely mental chaoses, unorganized, without selective ability and of weak and diffused attention, is likewise clear. Essentially he is the opposite of these.

23

TOLSTOY'S INFECTION THEORY

> Beauty is no quality in things themselves; it exists merely in the mind which contemplates them.
>
> *Hume*

It is strange that the speculations upon the arts should so rarely have begun from the most obvious fact about them. Mr. Roger Fry, in his interesting Retrospect, records the shock with which Tolstoy's insistence upon communication struck contemporary students in England. 'What remained of immense importance was the idea that a work of art was not the record of beauty already existent elsewhere, but the expression of an emotion felt by the artist and conveyed to the spectator.'[1] It will be useful to examine Tolstoy's account. He formulates his theory[2] as follows:

[1] *Vision and Design*, p. 194.
[2] *What is Art*, Sect. XV.

'Art becomes more or less infectious in consequence of three conditions:

i   In consequence of a greater or lesser peculiarity of the sensation conveyed.
ii In consequence of a greater or lesser clearness of the transmission of this sensation.
iii In consequence of the sincerity of the artist, that is, of the greater or lesser force with which the artist himself experiences the sensation which he is conveying.'

He adds, in curious contradiction to his other view which we have already discussed, 'Not only is the infectiousness a certain sign of art, but the degree of the infection is the only standard of the value of art.'

This contradiction we may perhaps remove or at least mitigate if we notice that 'degree of infection' is a highly ambiguous phrase. It may be equivalent to —

i   the number of persons who may be infected,
ii the completeness with which the experience is reproduced in them.

These are the two most relevant senses here, and both are involved in Tolstoy's exposition. The first would bring this view into connection with his doctrine that only so far as art is accessible to all men is it valuable. The second, however, cannot be reconciled with that view, but that he held it cannot be doubted. 'The more the sensation to be conveyed is special,' he goes on, 'the more strongly does it act upon the receiver; the more special the condition of the mind is, to which the reader is transferred, the more willingly and the more powerfully does he blend with it.'

This is plainly untrue. What Tolstoy would have said with more reflection is that some special experiences are interesting and owe their attraction partly to their strangeness, their unusual character. But many unusual and special experiences are unattractive and repellent. Dyspeptics, amateurs of psycho-analysis, fishermen, and golfers, have very often most remarkable things to recount. We shun having to listen precisely because they are so special. Further, many experiences by their very oddness are incommunicable.

Only so far as common interests are aroused does the ease and completeness of transmission depend upon the rarity and strangeness of the experience communicated. With this proviso Tolstoy's remark is obviously justified. That he should have stressed it is an indication of his sincerity and candour. So much of his doctrine is a simple denial that special experiences are a fit subject for art. A division between experiences which though special are yet in the main path of humanity and accessible to all men if they are sufficiently finely developed in normal direc-tions, and those other special experiences which are due to abnormality, disease, or eccentric and erratic specialization, is what he would have added if his attention had been drawn to the point. He would have enjoyed classifying the fashionables and intellectuals, the etiolate cultured classes, among the insane.

The second condition of infectiousness, the greater or less clearness of the transmission of the sensation, is more important. How to obtain clear transmission is precisely the problem of communication. We have seen that it is a matter of the avail-ability of common experiences, the elicitation of these by a suitable vehicle, and the control and extrusion of irrelevant elements, so far as they arise, through the complexity of the vehicle.

The third condition, the sincerity of the artist, is more obscure. Tolstoy's own elucidation carries us but a little way. What is this force with which an experience occurs? Certainly experiences may be of the utmost intensity without thereby being any more easy to convey. A lightning flash, for example, which just misses one upon a summit, is much more difficult to describe than the same flash seen from the valley. Tolstoy, however, is speaking of the experience as evoked by the artist in the course of communication, of the 'emotion, kindred to that which was before the subject of contemplation', which then 'is gradually produced and does itself exist in the mind', to quote Wordsworth's celebrated account of the source of poetry. He is speaking of the fullness, steadiness and clearness with which the experience to be communicated develops in the mind of the communicator at the moment of expression. Inrushes of emotion, accompanied by scraps and odd bits of imagery, thought and incipient activity, are not uncommon, and the process of jotting down what comes to mind at the moment is all that the would-be poet can achieve.

> Round him much embryo, much abortion lay,
> Much future ode and abdicated play:
> Nonsense precipitate like running lead,
> Which slipped through cracks and zigzags of the head.

Opposed to him is the poet who 'described in *ideal* perfection, brings the whole soul of man into activity. . . . ' His is 'a more than usual state of emotion, with more than usual order; judgement ever awake, and steady self-possession, with enthusiasm and feeling profound or vehement.'[1] As so often, Coleridge drops the invaluable hint almost inadvertently. The wholeness of the mind in the creative moment is the essential consideration, the free participation in the evocation of the experience of all the impulses, conscious or unconscious, relevant to it, without suppressions or restrictions. As we have seen, this completeness or wholeness is the rarest and the most difficult condition required for supreme communicative ability. How it works we have also

[1] *Biographia Literaria*, Vol. II, Ch. XIV, p. 12.

seen, and if this is, as doubtless it must be, what Tolstoy meant by sincerity, however queer some of his tests for it were, we have found yet another indication of how great his contribution to critical theory, under happier circumstances, might have been.

24

THE NORMALITY OF
THE ARTIST

Prose is an uninterrupted, polite warfare with poetry . . . every
abstraction wants to have a jibe at poetry and wishes to be
uttered with a mocking voice.

The Joyful Wisdom

If the availability of his past experience is the first characteristic
of the poet, the second is what we may provisionally call his
normality. So far as his experience does not tally with that of
those with whom he communicates, there will be failure. But
both the sense in which it must tally and the sense in which the
artist is normal need to be carefully considered.

Within racial[1] boundaries, and perhaps within the limits of

---

[1] The degree of racial difference is peculiarly difficult to estimate. In view of the
extent of mixture which has taken place it may be of great importance in
considering even the art of one culture or tradition alone. Cf. F. G. Crookshank,
The Mongol in our Midst.

certain very general types,[1] many impulses are common to all men. Their stimuli and the courses which they take seem to be uniform. At the same time there are many other impulses which are not uniform. It is difficult to give instances, since there are so few names for impulses, but sounds are fairly uniform while words used in isolation are fairly ambiguous stimuli. Impulses could, if we knew enough, be arranged in an order of general uniformity or stability. Some impulses remain the same, taking the same course on the same occasions, from age to age, from prehistoric times until to-day. Some change as fashions change. Between the two extremes are the vast majority; neither, when the nervous system is vigilant, very fixed nor very erratic; set off by a given stimulus and taking the course they do because other impulses are also active or have just been active.

For successful communication a number of impulses with their effective stimuli must be common to the communicators, and further the general ways in which impulses modify one another must be shared. We evidently cannot expect that many total situations and responses will have been common, and it is not necessary that they should be. Within limits the disparities can be overcome by what is called imagination.

There is nothing peculiarly mysterious about imagination. It is no more marvellous than any other of the ways of the mind. Yet it has so often been treated as an arcanum that we naturally approach it with caution. It is desirable at least to avoid part of

[1] These types if they must be admitted, have not yet been described satisfactorily. The defects of such attempts as those of Jung, for example, are shown by the fact that individuals change so readily and so freely from 'type' to 'type', being extrovert one hour and introvert the next, rationalist and intuitive from moment to moment. This is, of course, denied by the Zürich School but not by the majority of observers. To point it out is not to overlook much that is valuable in these distinctions. A satisfactory classification would doubtless be very complex, and perhaps of the form: An individual of Type A is extrovert under these conditions, introvert under those, etc.

the fate which befell Coleridge,[1] and our account will be devoid of theological implications.

Given some impulses active others are thereby aroused in the absence of what would otherwise be their necessary stimuli. Such impulses I call imaginative, whether images occur or not, for image-production is not at all essentially involved in what the critic is interested in as imagination. Which other impulses are brought in is in part determined by which were co-operative together originally when all the impulses had their own stimuli, that is to say, in the non-imaginary experiences from which the imaginary experience derives. In so far as this factor comes in the imagination may be said to be *repetitive*. The imagination we are concerned with may be called *formative*[2] by way of distinction. For present circumstances are at least as important. Remember in a changed mood a scene which took place under a strong emotion. How altered is its every aspect! The selection of the impulses which take effect is changed; the impulses are distorted, they run in different courses. The imaginative construction is always at least as much determined by what is going on in the present as by what went on in the past, *pasts* rather, whence it springs.

Many of the most curious features of the arts, the limitation of their number, their formal characteristics and the conditions of

[1] *Biographia Literaria*, Ch. XIII. 'The primary IMAGINATION I hold to be the living Power and prime Agent of all human perception, and as a repetition in the finite mind of the eternal act of creation in the infinite I AM.' The luminous hints dropped by Coleridge in the neighbourhood of this sentence would seem to have dazzled succeeding speculators. How otherwise explain why they have been overlooked.

[2] Coleridge's distinction between IMAGINATION and Fancy was in part the same as this. But he introduced value considerations also, Imagination being such combination or fusion of mental elements as resulted in certain valuable states of mind, and Fancy being a mere trivial playing with these elements. The discussion of this distinction will be postponed to Chapter Thirty-two, where the different uses of the term 'imagination' are separated.

impersonality, detachment and so forth, which have given rise to much confused discussion of the 'aesthetic' state for example, are explained by this fact. In difficult communication the artist must find some means of so controlling a part of the recipient's experience that the imaginative development will be governed by this part and not left to the accidents of repetition which will differ naturally from individual to individual. As a basis for every art, therefore, will be found a type of impulse which is extraordinarily uniform, which fixes the framework, as it were, within which the rest of the response develops. These are among the most uniform impulses, among those which come nearest to having a one-one correlation with their stimuli, of all those which we experience.

In poetry, rhythm metre and tune or cadence; in music, rhythm pitch timbre and tune; in painting, form and colour; in sculpture, volume and stress; in all the arts, what are usually called the formal elements are the stimuli, simple or complex, which can be most depended upon to produce uniform responses. It is true that these responses are not so uniform as the reflexes, as sneezing or blinking for example. But even these are to a considerable extent subject to interference and modification by impulses of higher levels. What communication requires is responses which are uniform, sufficiently varied, and capable of being set off by stimuli which are physically manageable. These three requisites explain why the number of the arts is limited and why formal elements have such importance.

They are the skeleton or scaffolding upon or within which the further impulses involved in the communication are supported. They supply the present dependable part of the experience by which the rest, the more erratic, ambiguous part of the imaginative development, is controlled. By themselves (although there has been a natural tendency in criticism to maintain the contrary opinion) they are often quite inadequate. As we have seen, differences of all degrees, both between and within the arts, exist.

The fashion in which the poet's impulses must tally with those of his readers, will now be moderately clear. The poet is in the least favourable position, perhaps, among the artists, but as a compensation the range and fullness of the communications open to him is, if he can overcome the difficulties, very great. But evidently the least eccentricity on his part, either in the responses which he makes to rhythms and verbal tunes, or in the ways in which these govern and modify his further responses or are modified by them, will be disastrous. It is the same for all the arts. A defective or eccentric colour sensibility, a common defect as is well known, may play havoc with an artist's work, *qua* communication, without necessarily involving any deficiency of value in his own experience. It is theoretically possible for an individual to develop in himself states of mind of very high value and yet to be so unusual in his own sensibility as to seem ridiculous or be incomprehensible to others. The question then arises as to which is in the right, the artist or his uncomprehending critics. This frequent dilemma raised alike by great innovating artists and by nincompoops brings us back to the problem of normality.

To be normal is to be a standard, but not, as things are and are likely to remain, an average; and to inquire into the characters of the norm or to ask who are normal is to raise a question as to value. The artist departs from the average, but so do other people. His departure, however, is one of the reasons why we attend to his work; other people's departures may be reasons why we should not. What are the main differences which decide whether a departure is a merit or a defect?

The theory of value outlined above indicates some of these differences. If the artist's organization is such as to allow him a fuller life than the average, with less unnecessary interference between its component impulses, then plainly we should do well to be more like him, if *we can* and as far as we can. But the qualification, if *we can*, has far-reaching consequences. Politically it might be better for the community to be organized on the model of ant and bee communities, but, since it cannot, the question whether we should try to make it so does not arise. Similarly, if the artist's organization[1] is so eccentric as to make general approximation to it impossible, or if a general approximation would involve (people being what they are) greater losses than gains, then however admirable it may be in itself, we shall be justified in neglecting it. The case, if it indeed occurs, is exceptional but instructive theoretically. What is excellent and what is to be imitated are not necessarily the same. But it is interesting to note that mentalities to which the usual ordinary man is not capable of approximating without loss can almost always be shown to be defective, and that the defects themselves are the barrier to approximation. Certain mystical poets are perhaps as good an example of this as any. However admirable the experience of a Boehme or a Blake, of a Nietzsche or of the Apocalypst, the features which prevent general participation in it, the barriers to communication, are not the features upon which its value chiefly depends. It is the inchoate part of Blake's personality which makes him incomprehensible, not the parts which were better organized than those of every one else.

The explanation of the rarity of admirable though utterly eccentric experience is not difficult. The metaphorical remark that we are all branches of the same tree is its most compendious form. So much must be alike in the nature of all men, their situation in the world so much the same, and organization building upon this basis must depend upon such similar processes, that variation both wide and successful is most unlikely. That we are apt to exaggerate the differences between men is well known. If we consider what is usually called mind, alone, we may well

---

[1] It is useful in this discussion to distinguish between the artist's personality as involved in his work and such other parts of it as are not involved. With these last we are not here concerned.

suppose that minds may differ *toto caelo*, but if we look more carefully, taking account of the whole man, including his spinal reflexes for example, seeing his mind as but the most delicate and most advanced part of his total organization, we shall not be tempted to think him so diverse. People of course do seem extraordinarily different in the ways in which they think and feel. But we are specialized to detect these differences. Further, we tend constantly to overlook differences in situation which would explain differences in behaviour. We assume to a ridiculous extent that what is stimulating us will stimulate others in the same way, forgetting that what will happen depends upon what has happened before and upon what is already happening within, about which we can usually know little.

The ways then in which the artist will differ from the average will as a rule presuppose an immense degree of similarity. They will be further developments of organizations already well advanced in the majority. His variations will be confined to the newest, the most plastic, the least fixed part of the mind, the parts for which reorganization is most easy. Thus his differences are far less serious obstacles to communication than, shall we say, such differences as divide the hypochondriac from the healthy. And, further, so far as they require reorganization there will commonly be good reasons why this should be carried out. We should not forget that finer organization is the most successful way of relieving strain, a fact of relevance in the theory of evolution. The new response will be more advantageous than the old, more successful in satisfying varied appetencies.

But the advantages may be localized or general, minor as well as major. The artist stands at the parting of a multitude of ways. His advance may be and often is in a direction which if followed up would be generally disadvantageous although for the moment it leads to an increase of value. The metaphor is of course insufficient. We can improve it by substituting a manifold of many dimensions for the cross-roads. Which way is the mind to grow and which ways are compatible with which is the question. There are specialist and universal poets, and the specialist may be developing in a manner either consistent or inconsistent[1] with general development, a consideration of extreme importance in judging the value of his work. Its bearing upon the permanence of his work will be discussed later.

At any moment, in any situation, a variety of attitudes is possible. Which is the best is decided not only by the impulses which gain organized satisfaction in the attitude but also by the effect of the attitude upon the rest of the organization of the individual. We should have to consider the whole system and all the possibilities of all probable situations which might arise if we were to be sure that any one attitude is the best. Since we cannot do this, but can only note the most obvious objections to some, we have to be content if we can avoid those attitudes which are most evidently wasteful.

For the normality of the poet is to be estimated in terms of waste. Most human attitudes are wasteful, some to a shocking degree. The mind which is, so far as can be seen, least wasteful, we take as a norm or standard, and, if possible, we develop in our degree similar experiences. The taking of the norm is for the most part done unconsciously by mere preference, by the shock of delight which follows the release of stifled impulse into organized freedom. Often the choice is mistaken, the advantage which leads to preference is too localized, involves losses in the end, losses round the next corner as it were.

Little by little experience corrects such illusory preference, not through reflection — almost all critical choices are irreflective, spontaneous, as some say — but through unconscious reorganization of impulses. We rarely change our tastes, we rather find

[1] A weakness of the modern Irish school (even at its best, in Mr. Yeats) or of the exquisite poetry of Mr. Dc la Mare, may be that its sensibility is a development out of the main track. It is this which seems to make it minor poetry in a sense in which Mr. Hardy's best work or Mr. Eliot's *The Waste Land* is major poetry.

them changed. We return to the poems which made us weep tears of delight when we were young and find them dusty rhetoric. With a tender hurt inside we wonder what has happened.

Sometimes, of course, experience corrects nothing. There may be nothing which needs correcting, or too much. The localized advantage, the sweet aching thrill of the Boosey Ballad —

> I have a rose, a white, white rose,
>   'Twas given me long ago,
> When the winds had fallen to silence,
>   And the stars were dim and low.
> It lies in an old book faded,
>   Between the pages white,
> But the ages cannot dim the dream
>   It brings to me tonight!

The localized advantage may be irresistible in its appeal; the personality will not surrender it, no matter what of greater worth is forgone for its sake, or what possibilities passing by are lost, unglimpsed in the enthralment.

25

BADNESS IN POETRY

Il faut dissiper un malentendu: nous sommes pourris d'art!
Le Corbusier-Saugnier

The theory of badness in poetry has never received the study which it deserves, partly on account of its difficulty. For with bad art even more than with good unless we are careful to distinguish the communicative from the value aspects, even when these are connected, we shall find the issues obscured. Sometimes art is bad because communication is defective, the vehicle inoperative; sometimes because the experience communicated is worthless; sometimes for both reasons. It would perhaps be best to restrict the term bad art to cases in which genuine communication does to a considerable degree take place, what is communicated being worthless, and to call the other cases defective art. But this is not the usual practice of critics, any work which produces an experience displeasing to the critic being commonly called bad, whether or not this experience is like that responsible for the work.

Let us begin by considering an instance of defective communication; choosing an example in which it is likely that the original experience had some value.

THE POOL
Are you alive?
I touch you.
You quiver like a sea-fish.
I cover you with my net.
What are you – banded one?

I take a complete work to avoid possible unfairness. Here we have the whole of the link which is to mediate between the experiences of the author and of the reader. Aristotle, in a different connection, it is true, and for different reasons, affirmed that a work of art must possess a certain magnitude, and we can adapt his remark here. Not the brevity only of the vehicle, but its simplicity, makes it ineffective. The sacrifice of metre in free verse needs, in almost all cases, to be compensated by length. The loss of so much of the formal structure leads otherwise to tenuousness and ambiguity. Even when, as here, the original experience is presumably slight, tenuous and fleeting, the mere correspondence of matter to form is insufficient. The experience evoked in the reader is not sufficiently specific. A poet may, it is true, make an unlimited demand upon his reader, and the greatest poets make the greatest claim, but the demand made must be proportional to the poet's own contribution. The reader here supplies too much of the poem. Had the poet said only, 'I went and poked about for rocklings and caught the pool itself' the reader, who converts what is printed above into a poem, would still have been able to construct an experience of equal value; for what results is almost independent of the author.

To pass to a case in which communication is successful, where the objection lies to what is communicated:

After the fierce midsummer all ablaze
    Has burned itself to ashes and expires
    In the intensity of its own fires,
Then come the mellow, mild, St. Martin days
Crowned with the calm of peace, but sad with haze.
    So after Love has led us, till he tires
    Of his own throes and torments, and desires,
Comes large-eyed Friendship : with a restful gaze

He beckons us to follow, and across
    Cool, verdant vales we wander free from care.
    Is it a touch of frost lies in the air?
Why are we haunted with a sense of loss?
    We do not wish the pain back, or the heat;
    And yet, and yet, these days are incomplete.

As to the success of the communication there can be no question. Both the popularity of the author, Ella Wheeler Wilcox, of whose work this is a favourable specimen, and records of the response made by well-educated persons, who read it without being aware of the authorship, leave this beyond doubt. It reproduces the state of mind of the writer very exactly. With a very numerous class of readers pleasure and admiration ensue. The explanation is, probably, in the soothing effect of aligning the very active Love-Friendship groups of impulses with so settled yet rich a group as the Summer-Autumn simile brings in. The mind finds for a moment an attitude in which to contemplate a pair of situations (Love and Friendship) together, situations which are for many minds particularly difficult to see together. The heavy regular rhythm, the dead stamp of the rimes, the obviousness of the descriptions ('mellow, mild, St. Martin'; 'cool verdant vales') their alliteration, the triteness of the close, all these accentuate the impression of conclusiveness. The restless spirit is appeased, one of its chief problems is made to seem as if, regarded from a lofty, all-embracing standpoint, it is no problem but a process of nature.

This reconciliation, this appeasement, is common to much good and to much bad poetry alike. But the value of it depends upon the level of organization at which it takes place, upon whether the reconciled impulses are adequate or inadequate. In this case those who have adequate impulses as regards *any* of the four main systems involved, Summer, Autumn, Love, Friendship, are not appeased. Only for those who make certain conventional, stereotyped maladjustments instead, does the magic work.

The nature and source of these stock conventional attitudes is of great interest. Suggestion is very largely responsible for them. The normal child under the age of ten is probably free from them, or at least with him they have no fixity or privileged standing. But as general reflection develops the place of the free direct play of experience is taken by the deliberate organization of attitudes, a clumsy and crude substitute. 'Ideas', as they are commonly called, arise. A boy's 'Idea' of Friendship or of Summer or of his Country is not, though the name would seem to imply it, primarily an intellectual affair. It is rather an attitude, or set of attitudes, of tendencies to act in certain fashions rather than others. Now reflection, unless very prolonged and very arduous, tends to fix the attitude by making us dwell in it, by *removing us from experience*. In the development of any attitude there are stages, points of rest, of relatively greater stability. These, as we dwell in them, become more and more difficult to pass, and it is not surprising that most people remain all their lives in various halfway houses.

These stages or levels of emotional adjustment seem, for the most part, to be fixed not by any special suitability to circumstances, certainly not to present circumstances, but much more by social suggestion and by accidents which withdraw us from actual experience, the one force which might push us further. At present bad literature, bad art, the cinema, etc., are an influence of the first importance in fixing immature and actually inapplicable attitudes to most things. Even the decision as to what constitutes a pretty girl or a handsome young man, an affair apparently natural and personal enough, is largely determined by magazine covers and movie stars. The quite common opinion that the arts have after all very little effect upon the community shows only that too little attention is being paid to the effects of bad art.

The losses incurred by these artificial fixations of attitudes are evident. Through them the average adult is worse, not better adjusted to the possibilities of his existence than the child. He is even in the most important things functionally unable to face facts: do what he will he is only able to face fictions, fictions projected by his own stock responses.

Against these stock responses the artist's internal and external conflicts are fought, and with them the popular writer's triumphs are made. Any combination of these general Ideas, hit at the right level or halting point of development, is, if suitably advertised, certain of success. Best-sellers in all the arts, exemplifying as they do the most general levels of attitude development, are worthy of very close study. No theory of criticism is satisfactory which is not able to explain their wide appeal and to give clear reasons why those who disdain them are not necessarily snobs.

The critic and the Sales Manager are not ordinarily regarded as of the same craft, nor are the poet and the advertising agent. It is true that some serious artists are occasionally tempted into poster designing. It is, however, doubtful whether their work pays. But the written appeals which have the soundest financial prospects as estimated by the most able American advertisers are such that no critic can safely ignore them. For they do undoubtedly represent the literary ideals present and future of the people to whom they are addressed.[1] They are tested in a way which few other forms of literature are tested, their effects are watched by adepts whose livelihood depends upon the accuracy of their judgement, and they are among the best indices available of what is happening to taste. Criticism will justify itself as an applied science when it is able to indicate how an advertisement may be profitable without necessarily being crass. We shall see later under what conditions popularity and possible high value are compatible.

The strongest objection to, let us say, the sonnet we have quoted, is that a person who enjoys it, through the very organization of his responses which enables him to enjoy it, is debarred from appreciating many things which, if he could appreciate them, he would prefer. We must not, of course, forget those variations in psychological efficiency discussed in Chapter Twenty-two as degrees of vigilance. Even a good critic at a sufficiently low ebb of neural potency might mistake such a sonnet for one of Shakespeare's or with more ease for one of Rossetti's. But when vigilance was restored he would see, or at least feel, the differences. The point is that a reader who, at a high degree of vigilance, thoroughly enters into and enjoys this class of verse, is necessarily so organized that he will fail to respond to poetry. Time and much varied experience might change him sufficiently, but by then he would no longer be able to enjoy such verse, he would no longer be the same person.

A general statement such as this about the incompatibility of inexpressibly complex adjustments must naturally be incapable of strict proof. Individuals with alternating personalities and subject to fugues would have to be considered. So would the phenomena of 'mutations of régime' unaccompanied by change of

[1] A specimen: 'The thoughtful man, the man on business bent, wends his way to Wembley with definite purpose. He seeketh knowledge, desireth increase of commerce or willeth to study new epoch-making inventions.' – *Official Advertisement*.

vigilance if such occur. None the less very much evidence substantiates the statement. The experience of all those who have passed through the stages in the development of attitudes presupposed by great poetry is probably conclusive.

Even though the intricacies of the nervous system should be capable of getting round this objection, there remain sufficient other reasons why indulgence in verse of this character should be condemned. There can be no doubt whatever that the value of the experience which results from it is small. On a pleasure theory of value there might well be doubt, since those who do enjoy it certainly appear to enjoy it in a high degree. But on the theory here maintained, the fact that those who have passed through the stage of enjoying the *Poems of Passion* to that of enjoying the bulk of the contents of the *Golden Treasury*, for example, do not return, settles the matter. We must bear in mind, of course, the conditions which have to be satisfied before this test is conclusive. That a man who has passed through the stage of drinking nothing but beer to the stage of drinking nothing but brandy rarely returns, does not prove that brandy is the better drink. It merely proves that it is the more efficient intoxicant. We have to ask in applying the test what the responses in question are, and in the case of poetry they are so varied, so representative of all the activities of life, that actual universal preference on the part of those who have tried both kinds fairly is the same (on our view) as superiority in value of the one over the other. Keats, by universal qualified opinion, is a more efficient poet than Wilcox, and that is the same thing as saying that his works are more valuable.

26

JUDGEMENT AND DIVERGENT READINGS

> *The Prime Minister* – The misunderstanding – in so far as it is
> a misunderstanding – is purely a misunderstanding. . . .
> *The Leader of the Opposition* – With the utmost goodwill on
> this side, I find myself with far less grasp of the whole sub-
> ject than I had. . . .
>
> *The Times*, 8th July 1924.

Ambiguity in a poem, as with any other communication, may be
the fault of the poet or of the reader. The ambiguities due to
erratic reading are as important for criticism as others, and practically more troublesome. There are strong social incentives for
overlooking them. Talking to one another we assume, in nine
cases out of ten like the merest simpletons, that our readings
agree, and that when we differ in our opinions it is something
else, not our experiences but our judgements about them which
are at variance. Most discussion about works of art is waste of
time as *communication* for this reason. It may, of course, have great

value as a means by which people may severally develop their own reactions.

These assumptions which so densely obscure the issue raise innumerable practical difficulties both for criticism and for the construction of a theory of criticism. It is well worth while to analyse typical situations a little further.

The closing lines of the Fifth Sonnet of Wordsworth's River Duddon series will afford a convenient instance:

> Sole listener, Duddon! to the breeze that played
> With thy clear voice, I caught the fitful sound
> Wafted o'er sullen moss and craggy mound,
> Unfruitful solitudes that seemed to upbraid
> The sun in heaven! – but now, to form a shade
> For thee, green alders have together wound
> Their foliage; ashes flung their arms around;
> And birch trees risen in silver colonnade.
> And thou hast also tempted here to rise,
> Mid sheltering pines, this cottage rude and grey;
> Whose ruddy children, by the mother's eyes
> Carelessly watched, sport through the summer day,
> Thy pleased associates – light as endless May
> On infant bosoms lonely nature lies.

Two readers who found themselves, as they thought, in entire agreement as to the excellence of this sonnet, and especially as to the beauty of its close, were surprised shortly afterwards to discover that they had been reading quite different poems. By the one the last sentence was interpreted as saying that the gloom of lonely nature, of sullen moss and craggy ground, however it might seem late on in life, had no oppressive effect upon the children. By the other it was read as saying that however barren and gloomy might be the scene, actually lonely nature there in itself had no such character, but was, as it were, floating 'light as endless May on infant bosoms'. The two readings, by throwing their effect back upon what had preceded and in addition completely altering the rhythm of the close, produced what it is no exaggeration to describe as two different poems. Neither would be uncharacteristic of Wordsworth, although doubtless the first reading is the one to be accepted.

This exemplifies what is perhaps the rarest case,[1] that in which agreement as to value covers an actual grave difference in the experiences valued. More usually there is some genuine source for the agreement, to be found in some common character of the experiences. What this common character is may be difficult to discover. It may be merely the rhythm, or the cadence of some phrase, or the form of a sequence of references. But sometimes, if it is a more obvious part, such as a description or metaphor, a discussion between critical readers, who are aware that their experiences differ, will bring it to light.

Another common case is exemplified by some famous discussions of *Hamlet*. It is curious that people with such different conceptions of the character of Hamlet himself and of the action of the play, have been able to agree none the less as to its value as a whole, apart, of course, from its incidental values. Much has to be discounted in estimating this agreement. On some interpretations praise of the play as a whole is certainly insincere. On the interpretation which makes Claudius the hero, whose tragic frailty lies in the fact that his long-suffering patience with the baseless suspicions of the crazy nuisance Hamlet breaks down in the end and brings the noble monarch to disaster, there would be little beyond the playwright's subtlety which could honestly be commended. But with all allowances it seems certain that widely different interpretations have seemed to good critics to result in the same peculiar high value of tragedy. The explanation is that tragic value is a general not a specific character of

[1] For another instance see Browning, *Parting at Morning*.

responses. Just as a collision between motor-cars and a collision between ships are equally collisions, so the impulses whose equilibrium produces the *catharsis* of tragedy may be very varied; provided that their relations to one another are correct.

Very many of the values of the arts are of this general kind. Besides the experiences which result from the building up of connected attitudes, there are those produced by the breaking down of some attitude which is a clog and a bar to other activities. From Blake's 'Truly, my Satan, thou art but a dunce',[1] to Voltaire's 'Bon père de famille est capable de tout', such works can be found in all degrees. It matters little what the detail of the impulses which make up the obstructing attitude for different people in each case may be. This often varies, but when the attitude collapses the effect can be agreed upon. The great masters of irony – Rabelais and the Flaubert of *Bouvard et Pécuchet* – are the chief exponents of this kind of exorcism.

[1] *The Keys of the Gates: To the Accuser who is the God of this World.*

27

LEVELS OF RESPONSE AND THE WIDTH OF APPEAL

L'art n'est pas chose populaire, encore moins 'poule de luxe'. . . .
        L'art est d'essence hautaine.

Le Corbusier-Saugnier

There still remains the most interesting of the cases in which apparent agreement disguises real differences, that in which a work occasions valuable responses of the same kind at a number of different levels. *Macbeth* is as good an example as any. Its very wide popularity is due to the fact that crude responses to its situations integrate with one another, not so well as more refined responses, but still in something of the same fashion. At one end of the scale it is a highly successful, easily apprehended, two-colour melodrama, at the other a peculiarly enigmatic and subtle tragedy, and in between there are various stages which give fairly satisfactory results. Thus people of very different capacities for discrimination and with their attitudes developed in very different degrees can join in admiring it. This possibility of being enjoyed at many levels[1] is a recognized characteristic of Elizabethan Drama. *The Pilgrim's Progress, Robinson Crusoe, Gulliver's Travels*, the Ballads, are other instances. The differences between such things and, for example, the work of Donne, Milton, Blake, Landor, Stendhal, Henry James, Baudelaire . . . raise some of the most interesting of critical problems.

There is a common opinion, sometimes very strongly held, that a work which appeals to all kinds and all degrees of men is thereby proved to be greater, more valuable, than one which appeals only to some. There may be a confusion in this opinion. The sum of value yielded, since men actually are of different degrees, the social value that is to say of such work, will naturally be greater. But it does not follow that the maximum value for the reader of the highest level need be greater. The common belief that it is necessarily greater, that the work of wide appeal must be in itself a more admirable thing than work which appeals only to those who discriminate finely, is due to the assumption that it appeals everywhere for the same reasons and thus is shown to touch something essential and fundamental in human nature. But no one in a position to judge, who has, for example, some experience of the teaching of English, will maintain that Shakespeare's appeal, to take the chief instance, is homogeneous. Different people read and go to see the same play for utterly different reasons. Where two people applaud we tend to assume, in spite of our better knowledge, that their experiences have been the same: the experience of the first would often be nauseous to the second, if by accident they were exchanged, and the first would be left helpless, lost and bewildered. On this false

---

[1] We must, of course, distinguish art of this kind from the Christmas party or magazine kind of production, in which the author provides something (different and in a different place) for everybody. The works of Dickens might be cited as examples.

assumption it is easy to build up a formidable theory about art's concern with the basic elements of human nature and to arraign modern art for superficiality. But there have always been these two kinds, work with the wide, and work with only the special appeal. What actually are the differences between them?

The one, the art which keeps the child from play and the old man from his chimney-corner, evidently builds up its attitudes with the simplest, most aboriginal impulses, and it handles them so that the undeveloped mind can weave them into some sort of satisfying fabric while the more mature mind, qualifying and complicating them until they perhaps lose all likeness to their earlier form, still finds them serve its needs. The other is built up from impulses which, except in a personality capable of very nice adjustments, do not unite in any valuable way, and often the impulses themselves are of a kind of which only a highly developed mind or one with special experience is capable. This last point, however, is separable, and raises a question which will be discussed later.

Plainly each of the two methods has its advantages. The poet of wide appeal, it is tempting to suppose, has an advantage in that the impulses involved are general, have been interested all through life and are very representative of experience. And he has the further advantage perhaps of avoiding a certain dangerous finality. Impulses which adjust themselves at so many levels may go on doing so perhaps indefinitely. There may be something in the suggestion that Shakespeare wrote better than he knew. Certainly it is a serious charge against much of Henry James, for example; that when the reader has once successfully read it there is nothing further which he can do. He can only repeat his reading. There is often a point at which the parts of the experience click together, the required attitude is achieved, and no further development is possible. Together with this goes the sense in the reader that all had to be just as it is and not otherwise, whereas with much of Shakespeare we feel that anything might have been different and the result the same. 'Not laboriously but luckily.'

But this is only sometimes true of the sophisticated poet who makes no appeal below a certain level. It is not true of Pope, for example, or of Walt Whitman, to choose two unlike authors who at their best are not generally appreciated. And as a counter-balancing advantage for such poets their greater freedom must be noticed. Perhaps the chief reason for the decline of drama in the seventeenth century (social factors apart) was the exhaustion of the best themes which could be used in order to appeal at all levels. Drama, to secure audiences large enough to be encouraging, must make a widespread appeal; but the limitations which this condition imposes upon action are very strict. There are no similar restrictions for lyric poetry, and it is significant that the greatest lyrics have so often a high-level appeal only. The Mad Song of Blake, The Phoenix and the Turtle, The Hymn of Pan, most great sonnets, are instances in point.

There is, too, no good reason why impulses which only begin to make up valuable attitudes in highly organized and discriminating minds should lead to attitudes less valuable or more fragile, more fixed and final than others. We must not allow the unique instance of Shakespeare to weigh too heavily; after all, King Lear, the most inexhaustible of his works, is not a thing which has great popular appeal.

28

THE ALLUSIVENESS OF MODERN POETRY

> Tehee! Tehee! O sweet delight!
> He tickles this age who can
> Call Tullia's ape a marmosyte,
> And Leda's goose a swan!
> *Anon.*

We have distinguished between impulses which are involved at all stages of development, their course and fate naturally varying with the stage, and those which do not go off at all except in developed minds. The responses of the non-mathematical and the mathematical mind to a formula illustrate the difference. It is the use of responses not available without special experience, which more than anything else narrows the range of the artist's communication and creates the gulf between expert and popular taste.

In the second chorus of *Hellas* in the middle of the second stanza the rhythm, tune, and handling, though not the metre, become suddenly uncharacteristic of Shelley. A fullness of tone, a queer, gentle cadence, and a leisurely ease of movement belong to the fifth and following lines:

> A mortal shape to him
> Was like the vapour dim
> Which the orient planet animates with light.
> Hell, sin, and slavery, came,
> Like bloodhounds mild and tame,
> Nor preyed until their Lord had taken flight.

And this tone and the movement are in clear contrast with the fever, the impetuosity, the shrillness and rapidity of the first stanza, or of the closing lines of the second:

> The moon of Mahomet
> Arose and it shall set:
> While, blazoned as on heaven's immortal noon,
> The Cross leads generations on.

The difference is difficult to describe except perhaps by the aid of a musical notation. It is like the difference between two voices, and in spite of the highly characteristic matter[1] of the lines, the reader feels that not Shelley but some other poet is speaking. What Shelley is doing becomes unmistakable in the third and last stanza. The corresponding lines, again in clear contrast with the lines surrounding them, have the same strange modulation:

---

[1] Cf. *Promethus Unbound*, Act I: 'the air around them
      looks radiant as the air around a star';
also *Triumph of Life*: 'as veil by veil the silent splendour drops
                    From Lucifer'.

> So fleet, so faint, so fair,
> The Powers of Earth and Air
> Fled from the folding-star of Bethlehem.
> Apollo, Pan and Love,
> And even Olympian Jove,
> Grew weak, for killing Truth had glared on them.

In a manner more familiar perhaps in music than in poetry Shelley is echoing another poem, borrowing, as it were, Milton's voice though not his words, making in fact a musical quotation, a poetical allusion of an exquisite felicity.

But by so doing he is necessarily restricting the number of the readers who will fully appreciate him.

Such allusions are a normal and regular part of the resources of all poets who belong to the literary tradition, that is to say, of the vast majority of poets in modern times. They are not often so unobtrusive and the place which they are given in the structure of the poem varies. Sometimes, as in this instance, a failure on the part of the reader has no important consequences. One familiar with the *Hymn on the Morning of Christ's Nativity* will respond more fully and with a deeper sense of the situation; but a reader unfamiliar with it is not deprived of any major part of the poem. In other cases the loss is more serious. Another instance from Shelley will illustrate this, and it is interesting for its own sake. The Shape which guides the Chariot in the *Triumph of Life* is described and identified for the reader in a large degree through another Miltonic quotation for allusion:

> A Shape
> So sate within, as one whom years deform,
> Beneath a dusky hood and double cape,
> Crouching within the shadow of a tomb,
> And o'er *what seemed the head* a cloud-like crape
> Was bent.

Shelley, it is known, crystallized much of his philosophy in the sentence: 'Death is the veil which those who live call life', and the reference[1] here to the guardian of Hell Gate,

> What seem'd his head
> The likeness of a Kingly Crown had on,

is not accidental or unimportant for the understanding of the poem.

Some care is needed in considering the problem of allusions. There may be worthy and unworthy motives behind their employment *and* their enjoyment. There are some to whom a familiarity with literature occasions a sense of superiority over others which is trivial and mean. The pleasure of recognition, proportional as it is to the difficulty of unobtrusiveness of the allusion is a thing of slight value, not to be confused with literary or poetic values. It is perfectly possible for a reader, familiar with the *Nativity Hymn*, for example, to receive all that Shelley intended without ever noticing the allusion, without, that is to say, any recognition. But the erudite often forget that this happens. To turn the capacity of recognizing recondite references into a shibboleth by which culture may be estimated is a perversion to which scholarly persons are too much addicted. The point is worth mentioning, since this snobbishness, percolating down (or, if the metaphor be preferred, by repercussion) is responsible for much insincerity and timidity, for wrong attitudes of many kinds towards literature, for irritation and oppression developing into distaste and neglect of poetry. Allusion is a trap for the writer almost as effective as for the academic critic. It invites insincerity. It may encourage and disguise laziness. When it becomes a habit it is a disease. But these dangers form no ground for denying to allusion, and the similar

---

[1] *Paradise Lost*, Bk. II, line 672.

resources of which it is typical, a fit and justifiable place in poetry.

Allusion is the most striking of the ways in which poetry takes into its service elements and forms of experience which are not inevitable to life but need to be specially acquired. And the difficulty which it raises is merely a special instance of a general communicative difficulty which will probably increase for the poetry of the future. All the thought and feeling of recent man goes on in terms of experience which is much more likely to be special and peculiar to the individual, than, let us say, the experience of medieval man. The survival of medieval man on such a vast scale among us should not mislead in this matter. The people who are most keenly and variously interested, that is to say, the people whose lives are most valuable on our theory of value, the people for whom the poet writes and by his appeal to whom he is judged, inevitably build up their minds with far more varied elements than has even been the case before. And the poet, in so far as he is equal to his opportunities, does the same. It is hard, and, in fact, impossible, to deny him his natural and necessary resources on the ground that a majority of his readers will not understand. This is not his fault but the fault of the social structure. Given present conditions and future developments in the directions indicated by the changes of the last two hundred years, it is extremely probable that poets will become not less but more allusive, that their work will depend more and more not only upon other poetry but upon all manner of special fields of familiarity.[1] Many of the finest and most

---

[1] A very interesting contemporary example in connection with which the problem arises perhaps more acutely than ever before is Mr. Eliot's *The Waste Land* already mentioned. The impatience of so many critics and the fact that they have complained of the presence and necessity of notes well illustrates the confusion which prevails upon this question. A more reasonable complaint would have been that Mr. Eliot did not provide a larger apparatus of elucidation. (See Appendix.)

widely significant experiences, and those therefore most suitable for poetry, come nowadays, for example, through reading pieces of advanced research. There is nothing new in this, of course, nothing that was not happening when Donne wrote. The difficulty springs from the fact that research is so much further ahead than it used to be.

29

PERMANENCE AS A CRITERION

Wherewith being crown'd,
Crooked eclipses 'gainst his glory fight.
Shakespeare, *Sonnet LX*

The permanence of poetry is a subject closely connected with the foregoing. Just as there is a prejudice in favour of work with a wide popular appeal, so there is another in favour of work which lasts, which has 'stood the verdict of the centuries', or is thought likely to stand it. Both are in part due to critical timidity; if we cannot decide ourselves, let us at least count hands and go with the majority.

But circumstances which have nothing to do with value sometimes determine survival, and work which is of great value must often perish for that very reason. It never gets printed, none will look at it or listen to it. And immortality often attaches itself to the bad as firmly as to the good. Few things are worse than *Hiawatha* or *The Black Cat*, *Lorna Doone* or *Le Crime de Silvestre*

Bonnard, and some of the greatest favourites[1] of the anthologies figure there through their 'bad eminence'.

There are, however, reasons for connecting persistence of appeal with a certain type of structure, and, which is more interesting, instant fame with a failure to appeal to subsequent generations. Work which relies upon ready-made attitudes, without being able to reconstitute similar attitudes when they are not already existent, will often make an appeal to one generation which is a mystery to the generations with different attitudes which follow. But this disadvantage from the point of view of permanence of communication does not necessarily involve any lack of value for those to whom the experiences are accessible. Very often, of course, it will accompany low value; but this need not be so.

The permanence of some art has often been an excuse for fantastic hypotheses. Such art has been thought to embody immortal essences, to reveal special kinds of 'eternal' truths. But such debilitating speculations here no less than elsewhere should be avoided. Those are not the terms in which the matter may best be discussed. The uniformity of the impulses from which the work of art starts is a sufficient explanation of its permanence. Where the impulses involved are only accidentally touched off through being temporarily in a heightened state of excitability, we may reasonably expect that there will be little permanence. As a catchword will work one year like magic, since certain attitudes are for social reasons ready poised on a hair-trigger adjustment, and the next year be inoperative and incomprehensible, so, on a larger scale and in less striking degree, men's special social circumstances often provide opportunities for works of art which at other times are quite inadequate stimuli. There are fashions in the most important

---

[1] E.g. *'When lovely woman stoops to folly,'* *Heraclitus*, *The Miller's Daughter*, *Alexander Selkirk*, and (its best known parts at least) *The Skylark*.

things as in the least, but for the artist to profit by them is usually to forgo permanence. The greater the ease of communication under such conditions the greater the danger of obsolescence.

Far more of the great art of the past is actually obsolete than certain critics pretend, who forget what a special apparatus of erudition they themselves bring to their criticism. The *Divina Commedia* is a representative example. It is true that for adequately equipped readers who can imaginatively reproduce the world outlook of Aquinas, and certain attitudes to woman and to chastity, which are even more inaccessible, there is no obsolescence. But this is true of the most forgotten poems. Actual obsolescence is not in general a sign of low value, but merely of the use of special circumstances for communication. That a work reflects, summaries and is penetrated by its age and period is not a ground for assigning it a low value, and yet this saturation more than anything else limits the duration of its appeal. Only so far as a work avoids the catchword type in its method, and relies upon elements likely to remain stable, formal elements for example, can it escape the touch of time. That Dante is neglected is due only indirectly to his present-day obscurity; he is still as accessible as ever through his formal side. It is the labour required from readers who are not content with a partial approach which explains why he is so little read even by the scholarly. What can be translated in him, the content, is precisely what is of least present and future interest, and at the same time most difficult to understand.

30

THE DEFINITION OF A POEM

Men take the words they find in use among their neighbours, and that they may not seem ignorant what they stand for use them confidently without much troubling their heads about a certain fixed meaning . . . it being all one to draw these men out of their mistakes, who have no settled notions, as to dispossess a Vagrant of his habitation, who has no settled abode. This I guess to be so; and everyone may observe in himself or others whether it be so or not.

Locke

It may be useful to collect here some of the results of the foregoing sections and consider them from the point of view of the practising critic. The most salient perhaps is the desirability of distinguishing clearly between the communicative and the value aspects of a work of art. We may praise or condemn a work on either ground or upon both, but if it fails entirely as a vehicle of communication we are, to say the least, not well placed for denying its value.

But, it may be said, it will then have no value for *us* and its value or disvalue for us is all that we as critics pretend or should pretend to judge. To make such a reply, however, is to abdicate as a critic. At the least a critic is concerned with the value of things for himself and for people like him. Otherwise his criticism is mere autobiography. And any critic worth attention makes a further claim, a claim to sanity. His judgement is only of general interest in so far as it is representative and reflects what happens in a mind of a certain kind, developed in a certain fashion. The services of bad critics are sometimes not less than those of good critics, but that is only because we can divine from their responses what other people's responses are likely to be.

We must distinguish between standard or normal criticism and erratic or eccentric criticism. As critics Lamb or Coleridge are very far from normal; none the less they are of extraordinary fertility in suggestion. Their responses are often erratic even when of most revelatory character. In such cases we do not take them as standards to which we endeavour to approximate, we do not attempt to see eye to eye with them. Instead we use them as means by which to make quite different approaches ourselves to the works which they have characteristically but eccentrically interpreted.

The distinction between a personal or idiosyncratic judge-ment and a normative is sometimes overlooked. A critic should often be in a position to say, 'I don't like this but I know it is good', or 'I like this and condemn it', or 'This is the effect which it produces upon me, and this quite different effect is the one it should produce.' For obvious reasons he rarely makes any such statements. But many people would regard praise of a work which is actually disliked by the praiser as immoral. This is a confusion of ideas. Any honest reader knows fairly well the points at which his sensibility is distorted, at which he fails as a normal critic and in what ways. It is his duty to take these into consideration in passing judgement upon the value of a work. His rank as a critic depends at least as much upon his ability to discount these personal peculiarities as upon any hypothetical impeccability of his actual responses.

So far we have been considering those cases in which the vehicle is sufficiently adequate and the critic sufficiently representative and careful for the response to be a good index of the value of the poem. But these cases are comparatively rare. The superstition which any language not intolerably prolix and uncouth encourages that there is something actual, *the poem*, which all readers have access to and upon which they pass judgement, misleads us. We naturally talk about poems (and pictures, etc.) in a way which makes it impossible for anybody to discover what it is we are talking about. Most critical discussion, in other words, is primarily emotive with only a very loose and fourfold equivocal reference. We may be talking about the artist's experience, such of it as is relevant, or about the experience of a qualified reader who made no mistakes, or about an ideal and perfect reader's possible experience, or about our own actual experience. All four inmost cases will be qualitatively different. Communication is perhaps never perfect, so the first and the last will differ. The second and third differ also, from the others and from one another, the third being what we ought unrestrictedly to experience, or the best experience we could possibly undergo, whereas the second is merely what we ought to experience as things are, or the best experience that we can expect.

Which of these possible definitions of a poem shall we adopt? The question is one of convenience merely; but it is by no means easy to decide. The most usual practice is to mean by *the poem* either the first or the last; or, by forgetting what communication is, to mean both confusedly together. The last involves the personal judgement to which exception was taken on the previous page, and has the further disadvantage that there would be for every sonnet as many poems as readers. A and B, discussing *Westminster Bridge* as they thought, would unwittingly be discussing two different things. For some purposes, for the disentanglement of some misunderstandings, it is convenient to define a poem temporarily in this manner.

To define the poem as the artist's experience is a better solution. But it will not do as it stands since nobody but the artist has that experience. We must be more ingenious. We cannot take any single experience as the poem; we must have a class of more or less similar experiences instead. Let us mean by *Westminster Bridge* not the actual experience which led Wordsworth on a certain morning about a century ago to write what he did, but the class composed of all actual experiences, occasioned by the words, which do not differ within certain limits from that experience. Then anyone who has had one of the experiences comprised in the class can be said to have read the poem. The permissible ranges of variation in the class need (of course) very careful scrutiny. To work them out fully and draw up a neat formal definition of a poem would be an amusing and useful occupation for any literary logician with a knowledge of psychology. The experiences must evidently include the reading of the words with fairly close correspondence in rhythm and tune. Pitch difference would not matter, provided that pitch relations were preserved. Imagery might be allowed to vary indefinitely in its sensory aspect but would be narrowly restricted otherwise. If the reader will run over the diagram of a poetic experience given in Chapter Sixteen and consider in what respects his and his friends' experiences must agree if they are to be able to refer to them indifferently as though they were one and the same without confusion or misunderstanding, he will see what kind of thing a detailed definition of a poem would be.

This, although it may seem odd and complicated, is by far the most convenient, in fact it is the only workable way of defining a poem; namely, as a class of experiences which do not differ in any character more than a certain amount, varying for each character, from a standard experience. We may take as this standard experience the relevant experience of the poet when contemplating the completed composition.[1]

Anyone whose experience approximates in this degree to the standard experience will be able to judge the poem and his remarks about it will be about some experience which is included in the class. Thus we have what we want, a sense, namely, in which a critic can be said to have not read the poem or to have misread it. In this sense unrecognized failures are extremely common.

The justification for this outbreak of pedantry, as it may appear, is that it brings into prominence one of the reasons for the backwardness of critical theory. If the definition of a poem is a matter of so much difficulty and complexity, the discussion of the principles by which poetry should be judged may be expected to be confused. Critics have as yet hardly begun to ask themselves what they are doing or under what conditions they work. It is true that a recognition of the critic's predicament need not be explicit in order to be effective, but few with much experience of literary debate will underestimate the extent to which it is disregarded or the consequences which ensue from this neglect. The discussions in the foregoing chapters are intended as no more than examples of the problems which an explicit recognition of the situation will admit and of the ways in which they will he solved.

[1] Difficulties even here arise, e.g., the poet may be dissatisfied without reason. Coleridge thought *Kubla Khan* merely 'a psychological curiosity' without poetic merits, and may have been justified in some degree. If he was not, it is his dream experience which we should presumably have to take as our standard.

31

ART, PLAY, AND CIVILIZATION

L'heure est à la construction, pas au badinage.
Le Corbusier-Saugnier

The value of the experiences which we seek from the arts does
not lie, so we have insisted, in the exquisiteness of the moment
of consciousness; a set of isolated ecstasies is not a sufficient
explanation. Its inadequacy is additional evidence that the theories of value and of the mind upon which it rests are defective. We
must now consider what wider explanations are made possible
by the theory of value and the outline account of mental activity
and of communication above indicated. The ground, in part at
least, is cleared. What now can be said as to why the arts are
important and why good taste and sound criticism are not mere
luxuries, trivial excrescences grafted upon an independent
civilization?

A number of accounts of varying adequacy each in some
degree interesting but needing careful interpretation have been
put forward. The arts communicate experiences, it has been said,

and make states of mind accessible to the many which otherwise would be only possible to few. To this it might be added that the arts are also a means by which experiences arise in the mind of the artist which would never otherwise come about. Both as an occasion for a collectedness and concentration difficult to attain in the ordinary course of life, and as the means by which human effort may acquire a continuity analogous to but more subtle than the continuity of science, the study and practice of the arts can give immensely increased power to the artist, preserving him from that diffusion of his energies which is perhaps his greatest danger. All this is true, but it does not go to the root of the matter.

Again the educational aspect of the arts is constantly being stressed, sometimes in a manner which does them disservice. 'Message' hunting – the type of interest which discovers in *Macbeth* the moral that 'Honesty is the best policy'; in *Othello* a recommendation to 'Look before you leap', in *Hamlet* perhaps a proof that 'Procrastination is the Thief of Time', or in *King Lear* an indication that 'Your sins will find you out',[1] in Shelley an exhortation to Idealism, in Browning comfort for the discouraged and assurances as to a future life; but in Donne or Keats no 'message' – this mode of interpreting the phrase 'a criticism of life', though to a minute degree on the right lines, is probably more damaging than those entirely erratic theories, of which 'Art for Art's sake' is an example, with which we have been more concerned.

None the less but in subtler ways the educational influence of the arts is all-pervasive. We must not overlook bad art in estimating it. 'I should be said to insist absurdly on the power of my own confraternity' wrote a novelist of the 19th century 'if I were to declare that the bulk of the young people in the upper and middle classes receive their moral teaching chiefly from the

---

[1] Even Coleridge was not exempt from this failing. Cf. his comments on Gloster.

novels that they read. Mothers would no doubt think of their own sweet teaching; fathers of the examples which they set; and schoolmasters of the excellence of their instructions. Happy is the country which has such mothers, fathers and schoolmasters! But the novelist creeps in closer than the father, closer than the schoolmaster, closer almost than the mother. He is the chosen guide, the tutor whom the young pupil chooses for herself. She retires with him, suspecting no lesson . . . and there she is taught how she shall learn to love; how she shall receive the lover when he comes; how far she should advance to meet the joy; why she should be reticent and not throw herself at once into this new delight.'

The influence is also exerted in more indirect ways. There need be, we must remember, no discernible connection or resemblance whatever between the experience due to the work of art and the later behaviour and experience which is modified through it. Without such resemblance the influence may easily be overlooked or denied, but not by anyone who has a sufficient conception of the ways in which attitudes develop. No one who has repeatedly lived through experiences at the level of dis-crimination and coordination presupposed by the greater writers, can ever, when fully 'vigilant', be contented with ordin-ary crudities, though a touch of liver may of course suspend these superior responses. And conversely, keen and vigilant enjoyment of Miss Dell, Mr. Burroughs, Mrs. Wilcox or Mr. Hutchinson, when untouched by doubts or the joys of ironic contemplation, is likely to have as a consequence not only an acceptance of the mediocre in ordinary life, but a blurring and confusion of impulses and a very widespread loss of value.

These remarks apply even more evidently to the Cinema People do not much imitate what they see upon the screen or what they read of in best-sellers. It would matter little if they did. Such effects would show themselves clearly and the evil would be of a manageable kind. They tend instead to develop stock

attitudes and stereotyped ideas, the attitudes and ideas of producers: attitudes and ideas which can be 'put across' quickly through
a medium that lends itself to crude rather than to sensitive handling. Even a good dramatist's work will tend to be coarser than
that of a novelist of equal ability. He has to make his effects more
quickly and in a more obvious way. The Cinema suffers still
more than the stage from this disability. It has its compensating
advantages in the greater demands which it makes of the audience, but hitherto very few producers have been able to turn
them to account. Thus the ideas and attitudes with which the
'movie fan' becomes familiar tend to be peculiarly clumsy and
inapplicable to life. Other causes, connected with the mentality
of producers, increase the effect.

The danger lies not in the fact that school-girls are sometimes
incited to poke revolvers at taximen, but in much subtler and
more insinuating influences. Most films indeed are much more
suited to children than to adults, and it is the adults who really
suffer from them. No one can intensely and wholeheartedly
enjoy and enter into experiences whose fabric is as crude as that
of the average super-film without a disorganization which has its
effects in everyday life. The extent to which second-hand experience of a crass and inchoate type is replacing ordinary life offers
a threat which has not yet been realized. If a false theory of the
severance and disconnection between 'aesthetic' and ordinary
experience has prevented the value of the arts from being understood, it has also preserved their dangers from recognition.

Those who have attempted to find a place in the whole structure of life for the arts have often made use of the conception of
Play; and Groos and Herbert Spencer are famous exponents of
the theory. As with so many other Aesthetic Doctrines the opinion that Art is a form of Play may indicate either a very shallow
or a very penetrating view. All depends upon the conception of
Play which is entertained. Originally the view arose in connection with survival values. Art, it was thought, had little practical

value of the obvious kinds, so some indirect means must be found by which it could be thought to be of service. Perhaps, like play, it was a means of harmlessly expending superfluous energy. A more useful contribution was made when the problem of the value of play itself was seriously attacked. The immense practical utility of most forms of play then became evident. Characteristically play is the preparatory organization and development of impulses. It may easily become too narrowly specialized, and the impulses active may be such as never to receive 'serious' exercise. None the less with our present understanding of the amazingly recondite interactions between what appear to be totally different activities of the nervous system, the importance of play is not likely to need much insistence.

There are many human activities which, fortunately or unfortunately as the case may be, are no longer required of or possible to civilized man. Yet their total discontinuance may lead to grave disturbances. For some of these play serves as an opportunity. The view that art provides in some cases an analogous outlet through vicarious experience has naturally been put forward, notably by Mr. Havelock Ellis. 'We have lost the orgy, but in its place we have art.'[1] If we do not extend the 'sublimation' theory too far or try to bring under this Safety-valve heading work with which it has no concern, it may be granted that in some cases the explanation is in place. But the temptation to extend it, and so to misconceive the whole matter, is great.

The objection to the Play Theory, unless very carefully stated, lies in its suggestion that the experiences of Art are in some way incomplete, that they are substitutes, meagre copies of the real thing, well enough for those who cannot obtain better. 'The moralizing force of Art lies, not in its capacity to present a timid imitation of our experiences, but in its power to go beyond our

---

[1] Essay on Casanova, in *Affirmations*, p. 115.

experience, satisfying and harmonizing the unfilled activities of our nature.'[1] The Copy View, with the antithesis between Life and Literature which so often accompanies it, is a devastating misconception. Coupled with the suggestion involved by the word 'Play', that such things are for the young rather than for the mature, and that Art is something one grows out of, it has a large share of the responsibility for the present state of the Arts and of Criticism. Its only rival in obscuring the issues is its close cousin the Amusement or Relaxation Theory.

The experiences which the arts offer are not obtainable, or but rarely, elsewhere. Would that they were! They are not incomplete; they might better be described as ordinary experiences completed. They are not such that the most adequately equipped person can dispense with them and suffer no loss, and this loss is not momentary, but recurrent and permanent; the best equipped are precisely the people who most value these experiences. Nor is Art, as by way of corollary is sometimes maintained, a thing which had its function in the youth of the world, but with the development of Science becomes obsolete. It may very possibly decline and even disappear, but if it does a biological calamity of the first order will have occurred. Nor again is it something which may be postponed while premillennial man grapples with more immediate problems. The raising of the standard of response is as immediate a problem as any, and the arts are the chief instrument by which it may be raised or lowered.

Hitherto we have been concerned chiefly with more or less specific effects of the experiences of the arts, with the effects, upon single definite groups or system of impulses, of their exercise in these experiences. The Play Theory tends to limit us to these consequences. Important though they are, we must not overlook the more general effects which any well-organized

[3] *Affirmations*, p. 115.

experience produces. They may in certain cases be extraordinarily widespread. Such an apparently irrelevant test as the ability to stand upon one foot without unsteadiness has recently been employed, by Mr. Burt, as an index to mental and especially to emotional organization. All our activities react upon one another to a prodigious extent in ways which we can only as yet conjecture.

Finer adjustment, clearer and more delicate accommodation or reconciliation of impulses in any one field tends to promote it in others. A step in mathematical accomplishment, other things being equal, facilitates the acquisition of a new turn in ski-ing. Other things are rarely equal it should perhaps be remarked. If this is true even of such special narrowly restricted impulses as are involved in a scientific technique, it is far more evident when the major, the most widespread systems, those active in our responses to human beings and to the exigences of existence, are engaged.

There is abundant evidence that removal of confusion in one sphere of activity tends to be favourable to its removal elsewhere. The ease with which a trained mind approaches a new subject is the plainest example, but equally a person whose ordinary emotional experience is clear, controlled and coherent, is the least likely to be thrown into confusion by an unheard-of predicament. Complications sometimes obscure this effect: a mathematician approaching psychology may attempt to apply methods which are inappropriate, and the sanest people may prove stupid in their dealings with individuals of other races. The specialist, either intellectual or moral, who is helpless outside his own narrow field is a familiar figure in inferior comedy. But what would have to be shown before the principle is invalidated is that, granted equal specialization, the successful specialist is not better fitted for life in general than his unsuccessful confrère. Few people, however, will dispute the assertion that transference of ability frequently occurs although the mode by which it comes about may be obscure.

When very widespread and very fundamental impulses are implicated, where attitudes constantly taken up in ordinary life are aroused, this transference effect may be very marked. Everybody knows the feeling of freedom, of relief, of increased competence and sanity, that follows any reading in which more than usual order and coherence has been given to our responses. We seem to feel that our command of life, our insight into it and our discrimination of its possibilities, is enhanced, even for situations having little or nothing to do with the subject of the reading. It may be a chapter of *Gösta Berling* or of *The ABC of Atoms*, the close of the *Vanity of Human Wishes*, or the opening of *Harry Richmond*; whatever the differences the refreshment is the same. And conversely everybody knows the diminution of energy, the bafflement, the sense of helplessness, which an ill-written, crude, or muddled book, or a badly acted play, will produce, unless the critical task of diagnosis is able to restore equanimity and composure.

Neither the subject nor the closeness of correspondence between the experience and the reader's own situation has any bearing upon these effects. But indeed, to anyone who realizes what kind of a thing an experience is, and through what means it comes about, the old antithesis between subject and treatment ceases to be of interest (cf. Chapter Sixteen). They are not separable or distinct things and the division is of no service. In this case the effects we are considering depend only upon the kind and degree of organization which is given to the experiences. If it is at the level of our own best attempts or above it (but not so far above as to be out of reach) we are refreshed. But if our own organization is broken down, forced to a cruder, a more wasteful level, we are depressed and temporarily incapacitated, not only locally but generally. It is when what we are offered, and inveigled into accepting, is only slightly inferior to our own developed capacity, so that it is no easy matter to see what is wrong, that the effect is greatest. Stuff of an evident and extreme badness is exhilarating rather than depressing when taken from a discriminating standpoint; and there need be nothing snobbish or self-congratulatory in such reading. What is really discomposing and damaging to the critical reader is the mediocre, the work which falls just below his own standards of response. Hence the rage which some feel at the productions of Sir James Barrie, Mr. Locke, or Sir Hall Caine, a rage which work comparatively devoid of merits fails to excite.

These effects are not merely momentary or evanescent; if we would understand the place of the arts in civilization we must consider them more closely. An improvement of response is the only benefit which anyone can receive, and the degradation, the lowering of a response, is the only calamity. When we take into account not merely the impulses actually concerned in the experience but all the allied groups which thrive or suffer with it, and all the far-reaching effects of success or failure upon activities which may seem to be independent, the fact that some people feel so keenly about the arts is no longer surprising.

Underestimation of the importance of the arts is nearly always due to ignorance of the workings of the mind. Experiences such as these, into which we willingly and whole-heartedly enter, or into which we may be enticed and inveigled, present peculiar opportunities for betrayal. They are the most formative of experiences, because in them the development and systematization of our impulses goes to the furthest lengths. In ordinary life a thousand considerations prohibit for most of us any complete working out of our response; the range and complexity of the impulse-systems involved is less; the need for action, the comparative uncertainty and vagueness of the situation, the intrusion of accidental irrelevancies, inconvenient temporal spacing – the action being too slow or too fast – all these obscure the issue and prevent the full development of the experience. We have to jump to some rough and ready solution. But in the 'imaginative experience' these obstacles are removed. Thus what happens here, what precise stresses, preponderances, conflicts, resolutions and interinanimations, what remote relationships between different systems of impulses arise, what before unapprehended and inexecutable connections are established, is a matter which, we see clearly, may modify all the rest of life. As a chemist's balance to a grocer's scales, so is the mind in the imaginative moment to the mind engaged in ordinary intercourse or practical affairs. The comparison will bear pressing. The results, for good or evil, of the untrammelled response are not lost to us in our usual trafficking.

32

THE IMAGINATION

> Reason, in itself confounded,
> Saw division grow together;
> To themselves yet either neither,
> Simple were so well compounded.
> *The Phœnix and the Turtle*

At least six distinct senses of the word 'imagination' are still current in critical discussion. It is convenient to separate them before passing on to consider the one which is most important.

(i) The production of vivid images, usually visual images, already sufficiently discussed, is the commonest and the least interesting thing which is referred to by imagination.

(ii) The use of figurative language is frequently all that is meant. People who naturally employ metaphor and simile, especially when it is of an unusual kind, are said to have imagination. This may or may not be accompanied by imagination in the other senses. It should not be overlooked that metaphor and simile – the two may be considered together –

have a great variety of functions in speech. A metaphor may be illustrative or diagrammatical, providing a concrete instance of a relation which would otherwise have to be stated in abstract terms. This is the most common scientific or prose use of metaphor. It is rare in emotive language and in poetry; Shelley's 'Dome of many-coloured glass' is almost the only example which springs to mind. More usually the elucidation is a mere pretence; some attitude of the speaker to his subject or to his audience is using the metaphor as a means of expression. 'The freedom of my writings has indeed provoked an implacable tribe,' said Gibbon, 'but as I was safe from the stings, I was soon accustomed to the buzzing of the hornets'. But metaphor has yet further uses. It is the supreme agent by which disparate and hitherto unconnected things are brought together in poetry for the sake of the effects upon attitude and impulse which spring from their collocation and from the combinations which the mind then establishes between them. There are few metaphors whose effect, if carefully examined, can be traced to the logical relations involved. Metaphor is a semi-surreptitious method by which a greater variety of elements can be wrought into the fabric of the experience. Not that there is any virtue in variety by itself, though the list of critics who seem to have thought so would be lengthy; a page of the dictionary can show more variety than any page of poetry. But what is needed for the wholeness of an experience is not always naturally present, and metaphor supplies an excuse by which what is needed may be smuggled in. This is an instance of a very strange phenomenon constantly appearing in the arts. What is most essential often seems to be done as it were inadvertently, to be a by-product, an accidental concomitant. Those who look only to the ostensible purposes for the explanation of the effects, who make prose analyses of poems, must inevitably find them a mystery. But why overt and evident intention should so often destroy the effect is certainly a difficult problem.

(iii) A narrower sense is that in which sympathetic reproducing of other people's states of mind, particularly their emotional states, is what is meant. 'You haven't enough imagination,' the dramatist says to the critic who thinks that his persons behave unnaturally. This kind of imagination is plainly a necessity for communication, and is covered by what has already been said in Chapter Twenty-four. It has no necessary connection with senses of imagination which imply value. Bad plays to be successful require it as much as good.

(iv) Inventiveness, the bringing together of elements which are not ordinarily connected, is another sense. According to this Edison is said to have possessed imagination, and any fantastic romance will show it *in excelsis*. Although this comes nearer to a sense in which value is implied, it is still too general. The lunatic will beat any of us at combining odd ideas: Dr. Cook outstrips Peary, and Bottomley outshines Sir John Bradbury.

(v) Next we have that kind of relevant connection of things ordinarily thought of as disparate which is exemplified in scientific imagination. This is an ordering of experience in definite ways and for a definite end or purpose, not necessarily deliberate and conscious, but limited to a given field of phenomena. The *technical* triumphs of the arts are instances of this kind of imagination. As with all ordering, value considerations are very likely to be implied, but the value may be limited or conditional.

(vi) Finally we come to the sense of imagination with which we are here most concerned. The original formulation[1] was

---

[1] Coleridge's debt here to Schelling has been over-estimated. Such borrowings as he made were more hampering to him than helpful.

Coleridge's greatest contribution to critical theory, and except in the way of interpretation, it is hard to add anything to what he has said, though, as we have already noted in Chapter Twenty-four, some things might be taken away from it with advantage.

> "That synthetic and magical power, to which we have exclusively appropriated the name of imagination ... reveals itself in the balance or reconciliation of opposite or discordant qualities ... the sense of novelty and freshness, with old and familiar objects; a more than usual state of emotion, with more than usual order; judgement ever awake and steady self-possession with enthusiasm and feeling profound or vehement.' 'The sense of musical delight ... with the power of reducing multitude into unity of effect, and modifying a series of thoughts by some one predominant thought or feeling" these are gifts of the imagination. It was natural, we shall shortly see why, for Coleridge to carry his further speculations upon Imagination into the realms of Transcendentalism, but setting this aside, there is enough in this description and in the many applications and elucidations scattered through the *Biographia* and the *Lectures* to justify Coleridge's claim to have put his finger more nearly than anyone else upon the essential characteristic of poetic as of all valuable experience.

In describing the poet we laid stress upon the availability of his experience, upon the width of the field of stimulation which he can accept, and the completeness of the response which he can make. Compared with him the ordinary man suppresses nine-tenths of his impulses, because he is incapable of managing

---

[1] *Biographia Literaria*, II, pp. 12, 14.

them without confusion. He goes about in blinkers because what he would otherwise see would upset him. But the poet through his superior power of ordering experience is freed from this necessity. Impulses which commonly interfere with one another and are conflicting, independent, and mutually distractive, in him combine into a stable poise. He selects, of course, but the range of suppression which is necessary for him is diminished, and for this very reason such suppressions as he makes are more rigorously carried out. Hence the curious local callousness of the artist which so often strikes the observer.

But these impulses active in the artist become mutually modified and thereby ordered to an extent which only occurs in the ordinary man at rare moments, under the shock of, for example, a great bereavement or an undreamt-of happiness; at instants when the 'film of familiarity and selfish solicitude', which commonly hides nine-tenths of life from him, seems to be lifted and he feels strangely alive and aware of the actuality of existence. In these moments his myriad inhibitions are weakened; his responses, canalized – to use an inappropriate metaphor – by routine and by practical but restricted convenience, break loose and make up a new order with one another; he feels as though everything were beginning anew. But for most men after their early years such experiences are infrequent; a time comes when they are incapable of them unaided, and they receive them only through the arts. For great art has this effect, and owes thereto its supreme place in human life.

The poet makes unconsciously a selection which outwits the force of habit; the impulses he awakens are freed, through the very means by which they are aroused, from the inhibitions that ordinary circumstances encourage; the irrelevant and the extraneous is excluded; and upon the resulting simplified but widened field of impulses he imposes an order which their greater plasticity allows them to accept. Almost always too the chief part of his work is done through those impulses which we have seen to be most uniform and regular, those which are aroused by what are called the 'formal elements'. They are also the most primitive, and for that reason commonly among those which are most inhibited, most curtailed and subordinated to super-imposed purposes. We rarely let a colour affect us purely as a colour, we use it as a sign by which we recognize some coloured object. Thus our responses to colours in themselves become so abbreviated that many people come to think that the pigments painters use are in some way more colourful than Nature. What happens is that inhibitions are released, and at the same time mutual interactions between impulses take place which only sunsets seem to evoke in everyday experience. We have seen in discussing communication one reason for the pre-eminence of 'formal elements' in art, the uniformity of the responses which they can be depended upon to produce. In their primitiveness we find another. The sense that the accidental and adventitious aspect of life has receded, that we are beginning again, that our contact with actuality is increased, is largely due to this restoration of their full natural powers to sensations.

But this restoration is not enough; merely looking at a land-scape in a mirror, or standing on one's head will do it. What is much more essential is the increased organization, the heightened power of combining all the several effects of formal elements into a single response, which the poet bestows. To point out that 'the sense of musical delight is a gift of the imagination' was one of Coleridge's most brilliant feats. It is in such resolution of a welter of disconnected impulses into a single ordered response that in all the arts imagination is most shown, but for the reason that here its operation is most intricate and most inaccessible to obser-vation, we shall study it more profitably in its other manifestations.

We have suggested, but only by accident, that imagination characteristically produces effects similar to those which accom-pany great and sudden crises in experience. This would be mis-leading. What is true is that those imaginative syntheses which most nearly approach to these climaxes, Tragedy for example, are the most easy to analyse. What clearer instance of the 'balance or reconciliation of opposite and discordant qualities' can be found than Tragedy. Pity, the impulse to approach, and Terror, the impulse to retreat, are brought in Tragedy to a reconciliation which they find nowhere else, and with them who knows what other allied groups of equally discordant impulses. Their union In an ordered single response is the *catharsis* by which Tragedy is recognized, whether Aritotle meant anything of this kind or not. This is the explanation of that sense of release, of repose in the midst of stress, of balance and composure, given by Tragedy, for there is no other way in which such impulses, once awakened, can be set at rest without suppression.

It is essential to recognize that in the full tragic experience there is no suppression. The mind does not shy away from anything, it does not protect itself with any illusion, it stands uncomforted, unintimidated, alone and self-reliant. The test of its success is whether it can face what is before it and respond to it without any of the innumerable subterfuges by which it ordinarily dodges the full development of experience. Suppressions and sublimations alike are devices by which we endeavour to avoid issues which might bewilder us. The essence of Tragedy is that it forces us to live for a moment without them. When we succeed we find, as usual, that there is no difficulty; the difficulty came from the suppressions and sublimations. The joy which is so strangely the heart of the experience is not an indication that 'all's right with the world' or that 'somewhere, somehow, there is Justice'; it is an indication that all is right here and now in the nervous system. Because Tragedy is the experience which most invites these subterfuges, it is the greatest and the rarest thing in literature, for the vast majority of works which pass by that name are of a different order. Tragedy is only possible to a mind which is for the moment agnostic or Manichean. The least touch of any theology which has a compensating Heaven to offer the tragic hero is fatal. That is why *Romeo and Juliet* is not a Tragedy in the sense in which *King Lear* is.

But there is more in Tragedy than unmitigated experience. Besides Terror there is Pity, and if there is substituted for either something a little different – Horror or Dread, say, for Terror; Regret or Shame for Pity; or that kind of Pity which yields the adjective 'Pitiable' in place of that which yields 'Piteous' – the whole effect is altered. It is the relation between the two sets of impulses, Pity and Terror, which gives its specific character to Tragedy, and from that relation the peculiar poise of the Tragic experience springs.

The metaphor of a balance or poise will bear consideration. For Pity and Terror are opposites in a sense in which Pity and Dread are not. Dread of Horror are nearer than Terror to Pity, for they contain attraction as well as repulsion. As in colour, tones just not in harmonic relation are peculiarly unmanageable and jarring, so it is with these more easily describable responses. The extraordinarily stable experience of Tragedy, which is capable of admitting almost any other impulses so long as the relation of the main components is exactly right, changes at once if these are altered. Even if it keeps its coherence it becomes at once a far narrower, more limited, and exclusive thing, a much more partial, restricted and specialized response. Tragedy is perhaps the most general, all-accepting, all-ordering experience known. It can take anything into its organization, modifying it so that it finds a place. It is invulnerable; there is nothing which does not present to the tragic attitude when fully developed a fitting aspect and only a fitting aspect. Its sole rivals in this respect are the attitudes of Falstaff and of the Voltaire of *Candide*. But pseudo-tragedy – the greater part of Greek Tragedy as well as almost all Elizabethan Tragedy outside Shakespeare's six masterpieces comes under this head – is one of the most fragile and precarious of attitudes. Parody easily overthrows it, the ironic addition paralyses it; even a mediocre joke may make it look lopsided and extravagant.

This balanced poise, stable through its power of inclusion, not through the force of its exclusions, is not peculiar to Tragedy. It is a general characteristic of all the most valuable experiences of the arts. It can be given by a carpet or a pot or by a gesture as unmistakably as by the Parthenon, it may come about through an epigram as clearly as though a Sonata. We must resist the temptation to analyse its cause into sets of opposed characters in the object. As a rule no such analysis can be made. The balance is not in the structure of the stimulating object, it is in the response. By remembering this we escape the danger of supposing that we have found a formula for Beauty.

Although for most people these experiences are infrequent apart from the arts, almost any occasion may give rise to them. The most important general condition is mental health, a high state of 'vigilance'; the next is the frequent occurrence of such experiences in the recent past. None of the effects of art is more transferable than this balance or equilibrium.

Despite all differences in the impulses concerned, a certain general similarity can be observed in all these cases of supremely fine and complete organization. It is this similarity which has led to the legends of the 'aesthetic state', the 'aesthetic emotion' and the single quality Beauty, the same in all its manifestations. We had occasion in Chapter Two to suggest that the characteristics by which aesthetic experience is usually defined – that impersonality, disinterestedness and detachment so much stressed and so little discussed by aestheticians – are really two sets of quite different characters. One set we have seen (Chapters Ten and Twenty-four) to be merely conditions of communication having nothing essentially to do with value, conditions involved in valueless and valuable communications alike. We have suggested above, however, that this kind of detachment and severance from ordinary circumstances and accidental personal interests may be of special service in these supremely valuable[1] communications, since it makes the breaking down of inhibitions more easy. This same facilitation of response is also, it should be added, the explanation of the peculiarly pernicious effect of bad but competent art.

We may now turn to consider that other set of characters which have been confused with these communicative conditions, and which may justifiably be taken as defining a special field for those interested in the values of experience. There are two ways in which impulses may be organized; by exclusion and by inclusion, by synthesis and by elimination. Although every coherent state of mind depends upon both, it is permissible to contrast experiences which win stability and order through a narrowing of the response with those which widen it. A very great deal of poetry and art is content with the full, ordered development of comparatively special and limited experiences, with a definite emotion, for example, Sorrow, Joy, Pride, or a definite attitude, Love, Indignation, Admiration, Hope or with a specific mood, Melancholy, Optimism or Longing. And such art has its own value and its place in human affairs. No one will quarrel with 'Break, break, break', or with the *Coronach* or with *Rose Aylmer* or with *Love's Philosophy*,[2] although clearly they are limited and exclusive. But they are not the greatest kind of poetry; we do not expect from them what we find in the *Ode to the Nightingale*, in *Proud Maisie*, in *Sir Patrick Spens*, in *The Definition of Love* or in the *Nocturnall upon S. Lucie's Day*.

The structures of these two kinds of experiences are different,

---

[1] It may perhaps be desirable to point out that this description of the effects of art follows from the theory of value outlined in Chapter Seven. They are the most valuable experiences because they are the least wasteful. Thus the place assigned to them is not a mere personal expression of preference.

[2] May I assume that references here will not distress the reader? Tennyson, Scott, Landor, Shelley, Keats, Scott, Anon; Marvell, Donne, Peacock. I am anxious to facilitate the actual detailed comparison of these poems.

and the difference is not one of subject but of the relations *inter se* of the several impulses active in the experience. A poem of the first group is built out of sets of impulses which run parallel, which have the same direction. In a poem of the second group the most obvious feature is the extraordinarily heterogeneity of the distinguishable impulses. But they are more than heterogeneous, they are opposed. They are such that in ordinary, non-poetic, non-imaginative experience, one or other set would be suppressed to give as it might appear freer development to the others.

The difference comes out clearly if we consider how comparatively unstable poems of the first kind are. They will not bear an ironical contemplation. We have only to read *The War Song of Dinas Vawr* in close conjunction with the *Coronach*, or to remember that unfortunate phrase 'Those lips, O slippery blisses'! from *Endymion*, while reading *Love's Philosophy*, to notice this. Irony in this sense consists in the bringing in of the opposite, the complementary impulses; that is why poetry which is exposed to it is not of the highest order, and why irony itself is so constantly a characteristic of poetry which is.

These opposed impulses from the resolution of which such experiences spring cannot usually be analysed. When, as is most often the case, they are aroused through formal means, it is evidently impossible to do so. But sometimes, as in the above cited cases, they can, and through this accident literary criticism is able to go a step further than the criticism of the other arts.

We can only conjecture dimly what difference holds between a balance and reconciliation of impulses and a mere rivalry or conflict. One difference is that a balance sustains one state of mind, but a conflict two alternating states. This, however, does not take us very far. The chief misconception which prevents progress here is the switchboard view of the mind. What conception should be put in its place is still doubtful, but we have already (Chapters Fourteen and Twenty) discussed the reasons which make a more adequate conception imperative. The rest of the difficulty is due merely to ignorance; we do not yet know enough about the central nervous system.

With this preliminary disavowal of undue certainty we may proceed. The equilibrium[1] of opposed impulses, which we suspect to be the ground-plan of the most valuable aesthetic responses, brings into play far more of our personality than is possible in experiences of a more defined emotion. We cease to be orientated in one definite direction; more facets of the mind are exposed and, what is the same thing, more aspects of things are able to affect us. To respond, not through one narrow channel of interest, but simultaneously and coherently through many, is to be *disinterested* in the only sense of the word which concerns us here. A state of mind which is not disinterested is one which sees things only from one standpoint or under one aspect. At the same time since more of our personality is engaged the independence and individuality of other things becomes greater. We seem to see 'all round' them, to see them as they really are; we see them apart from any one particular interest which they may have for us. Of course without some interest we should not see them at all, but the less any one particular interest is indispensable, the more *detached* our attitude becomes. And to say that we are *impersonal* is merely a curious way of saying that our personality is more *completely* involved.

These characters of aesthetic experiences can thus be shown to be very natural consequences of the diversity of their components. But that so many different impulses should enter in is only what may be expected in an experience whose ground-plan is a balance of opposites. For every impulse which does not complete itself in isolation tends to bring in allied systems. The state of irresolution shows this clearly. The difference between

---

[1] This topic is discussed from a slightly different angle in *The Foundations of Æsthetics* (Allen and Unwin, 1922).

any such welter of vacillating impulses and the states of composure we are considering may well be a matter of mediating relations between the supporting systems brought in from either side. One thing only perhaps is certain; what happens is the exact opposite to a deadlock, for compared to the experience of great poetry every other state of mind is one of bafflement.

The consciousness which arises in these moments of completed being lends itself inevitably to transcendental descriptions. 'This Exstasie doth unperplex', we seem to see things as they really are, and because we are freed from the bewilderment which our own maladjustment brings with it,

> The heavy and the weary weight
> Of all this unintelligible world
> Is lightened.

Wordsworth's Pantheistic interpretation of the imaginative experience in *Tintern Abbey*[1] is one which in varying forms has been given by many poets and critics. The reconciliation of it with the account here presented raises a point of extreme Importance, the demarcation of the two main uses of language.

[1] I will quote the familiar passage for the reader's convenience:

> I have felt
> A presence that disturbs me with the joy
> Of elevated thoughts: a sense sublime
> Of something far more deeply interfused,
> Whose dwelling is the light of setting suns,
> And the round ocean and the living air,
> And the blue sky, and in the mind of man:
> A motion and a spirit that impels
> All thinking things, all objects of all thought
> And rolls through all things.

Not itself an instance of imaginative utterance, although some instances *can* be found in the poem.

33

TRUTH AND REVELATION THEORIES

Oh never rudely will I blame his faith
In the might of stars and angels! 'Tis not merely
The human being's pride that peoples space
With life and mystical predominance;
Since likewise for the stricken heart of Love
This visible nature, and this common world
Is all too narrow . . .

Coleridge, *Piccolomini*

Knowledge, it is recognized, is good, and since the experiences which we have been discussing may readily be supposed to give knowledge, there is a strong tradition in criticism which seeks to derive their value from the worth of knowledge. But not all knowledge is equally valuable: the kind of information which we can acquire indefinitely by steady perusal of Whitaker or of an Encyclopaedia is of negligible value. Therefore a special kind of knowledge has been alleged.

The problem which ensues is for many people the most

interesting part of critical theory. That so many capital-letter words – such as Real, Ideal, Essential, Necessary, Ultimate, Absolute, Fundamental, Profound, and many others – tend to appear in Truth doctrines is evidence of the interest. This heavy artillery is more than anything else a mode of emphasis, analogous to italics, underlining and solemn tones of utterance. It serves to impress upon the reader that he would do well to become serious and attentive, and like all such devices it tends to lose its effect unless cunningly employed.

We may most conveniently begin by considering a range of representative doctrines chosen from the writings of famous critics with a view to illustrating chiefly their differences. Some, it is true, will hardly repay investigation. It is far too easy to write, with Carlyle 'All real art is the disimprisonment of the soul of fact'[1] or 'The infinite is made to blend itself with the finite; to stand visible, and, as it were, attainable there. Of this sort are all true works of art; in this (if we know a work of art from the daub of artifice) we discern eternity looking through time, the God-like rendered visible'.[2]

All the difficulty begins when this has been written, and what has been said is of no assistance towards its elucidation. Nor is Pater, for all his praise of clarity and accuracy, of much better quality. 'Truth! there can be no merit, no craft at all, without that. And, further, all beauty is in the long run only fineness of truth or what we call expression, the finer accommodation of speech to that vision within'.[3] It would perhaps be difficult, outside Croce,[4] to find a more unmistakable confusion between

---

[1] *Shooting Niagara.*

[2] *Sartor Resartus.*

[3] *Essay on Style.*

[4] A discussion of Croce's doctrines might seem advisable at some point. But all that is strictly necessary has already been said in *The Foundations of Æsthetics.* It may be repeated here in the vigorous terms of Giovanni Papini (*Four and Twenty*

value and communicative efficacy. But the *Essay* is a veritable museum of critical blunders.

The extracts which follow are arranged approximately in order of obscurity. They rise from the most matter of fact to the most mystical uses of truth-notions in criticism. All might be taken as glosses upon the phrase 'Truth to Nature'; they serve to show what different things may be meant by what is apparently simple language.

We may begin with Aristotle. He makes three remarks which bear upon the matter. The first is in connection with the antithesis between Tragedy and History.

> 'Poetry is a more philosophical and a more serious thing than History: for Poetry is chiefly conversant about general (universal) truth, History about particular. In what manner, for example, any person of a certain character would speak or act, probably or necessarily – this is universal; and this is the object

Minds): 'If you disregard critical trivialities and didactic accessories, the entire aesthetic system of Croce amounts merely to a hunt for pseudonyms of the word 'art', and may indeed be stated briefly and accurately in this formula: art = intuition = expression = feeling = imagination = fancy = lyricism = beauty. And you must be careful not to take these words with the shadings and distinctions which they have in ordinary or scientific language. Not a bit of it. Every word is merely a different series of syllables signifying absolutely and completely the same thing.' When you are not careful the amalgam of confusions and contradictions which ensues is very remarkable. It is interesting to notice that Croce's appeal has been exclusively to those unfamiliar with the subject, to the man of letters and the dilettante. He has been ignored by serious students of the mind. How many of those for example who have been impressed by his dicta as to expression and language have been aware of how the problem has been discussed before, or have ever heard of the 'imageless thought' controversy? Upon the ways in which Croce's strategy has inveigled the guileless into supposing him to be saying something, Papini is excellent. 'The Barabbas of art, the Thug of philosophy, the Apache of culture' – Papini so describes himself – has here rendered a notable service to those who have been depressed by the vogue of 'Expressionism'.

of Poetry. But what Alcibiades did, or what happened to him –
this is particular truth.' (*Poetics*, Nine.)

His second remark is made in connection with the requisites
of Tragic Character:

'The third requisite (in addition to goodness in a special sense,
appropriateness, and consistency) of Character is that it have
verisimilitude'.¹ (*Poetics*, Fifteen.)

Aristotle's third observation is in the same chapter:

'The poet when he imitates passionate or indolent men and
such, should preserve the type and yet ennoble it'.²

Wordsworth's interpretation carries us a definite stage nearer
to the mystical:

'Aristotle, I have been told, has said that poetry is the most
philosophic of all writing. It is so. Its object is truth – not
individual and local, but general and operative. Not standing
upon external testimony, but carried alive into the heart by passion: truth which is its own testimony, which gives competence
and confidence to the tribunal to which it appeals, and receives
them from the same tribunal'.³

¹ ὅμοιον. This word is variously translated 'resemblance' (Twining), and
'truth to life' (Butcher). Its usual meaning in the *Poetics* is 'the quality of *being like
ourselves*', '*average* humanity'.
² Cf. Eastlake, *Literature of the Fine Arts*.

'The elephant with his objectionable legs and inexpressive hide may
still be supposed to be a very normal specimen and may accordingly
be a fit object for artistic imitation.'

³ Preface to *Lyrical Ballads*.

Wordsworth remains still on the hither side of the gap, as does Goethe in suggesting that 'The beautiful is the manifestation of secret laws of nature which, but for this disclosure, had been for ever concealed from us'.[1] But Coleridge, from whom Wordsworth probably heard about Aristotle, takes the step into mysticism unhesitatingly:

> 'If the artist copies the mere nature, the *natura naturata*, what idle rivalry! – if he proceeds only from a given form which is supposed to answer to the notion of beauty – what an emptiness, what an unreality, there always is in his productions. Believe me, you must master the essence, the *natura naturans*, which presupposes a bond between nature in the higher sense and the soul of man.'[2]

But Coleridge held many mystical views, not always easy to reconcile with one another. In the same Essay he continues:

> 'In the objects of nature are presented as in a mirror all the possible elements, steps and processes of intellect antecedent to consciousness, and therefore to the full development of the intelligential act; and man's mind is the very focus of all the rays of intellect which are scattered throughout the images of nature. Now so to place these images, totalized and fitted to the limits of the human mind, as to elicit from and to superinduce upon the forms themselves the moral reflections to

---

[1] Compare Thomas Rymer, *A Short View of Tragedy*.

> 'A little preparation and forecast might do well now and then. For his Desdemona's Marriage, he might have helped out the probability by figuring how that some way or other a Blackamoor woman had been her nurse and suckled her; or that once upon a time some *Virtuoso* had transfused into her veins the Blood of a Black Sheep.' We may take it such are not the secret laws of nature to which Goethe was alluding.

[2] On *Poesy or Art*.

which they approximate, to make the external internal, the
internal external, to make nature thought and thought nature –
this is the mystery of genius in the Fine Arts.'

Even when Coleridge is most 'the God-intoxicated man' his
remarks to a careful reader suggest that if they could be decoded,
as it were, they would provide at least a basis for interesting
speculation. Many adumbrations of this mystical view might be
quoted. 'There is a communication between mystery and mystery, between the unknown soul and the unknown reality; at one
particular point in the texture of life the hidden truth seems to
break through the veil', writes Mr. Middleton Murry in an
Essay[1] which as an emotive utterance disguised to resemble an
argument is of interest. How this feeling of insight arises we
have seen in the foregoing chapter; the sense of immediate revelation of which he treats as 'the primary stuff out of which
literature is created' is certainly characteristic of the greater kinds
of art. And there must be few who have not by one arrangement
or another contrived from these visionary moments a philosophy which, for a time, has seemed to them unshakable
because for a time emotionally satisfying. But emotional satisfaction gained at the cost of intellectual bondage is unstable. When
it does not induce a partial stupor it breaks down. The freely
inquiring mind has a fatal way of overthrowing all immediate
and mystical intuitions which, instead of being duly subordinate, insist on giving it orders.

For the inquiring mind is simply the human being's way of
finding a place and function for all its experiences and activities,
a place and function compatible with the rest of its experience.
When the mystical insight is understood, and its claims fitly
directed, although it may seem to those who still misunderstand

---

[1] 'Literature and Religion' in The *Necessity of Art*, published by The Student
Christian Movement, p. 155.

it to have lost all the attributes for which they have sought to retain it, and to be no longer either mystical or an insight, it does not lose but gains in value. But this further adjustment is often very difficult to make.

These Revelation Doctrines, when we know what they are really about, come nearer, we shall see, to supplying an explanation of the value of the arts than any of the other traditional accounts. But the process of translation is no easy matter. They are not what they seem, these utterances apparently about Truth. In interpreting them we shall find ourselves forced to consider language from an angle and with a closeness which are not usual, and to do so, certain very powerful resistances and deeply ingrained habits of the mind have first to be broken down.

34

THE TWO USES OF LANGUAGE

> The intelligible forms of ancient poets
> The fair humanities of old religion . . .
> They live no longer in the faith of reason:
> But still the heart doth need a language, still
> Doth the old instinct bring back the old names.
>
> Coleridge, *Piccolomini*

There are two totally distinct uses of language. But because the theory of language is the most neglected of all studies they are in fact hardly ever distinguished. Yet both for the theory of poetry and for the narrower aim of understanding much which is said about poetry a clear comprehension of the differences between these uses is indispensable. For this we must look somewhat closely at the mental processes which accompany them.

It is unfortunate but not surprising that most of the psychological terms which we naturally employ tend to blur the distinction. 'Knowledge', 'belief', 'assertion', 'thought', and 'understanding', for example, as ordinarily used, are ambiguous in a fashion which disguises and obscures the point which must be brought out. They record distinctions which are oblique to the distinctions required, they are cross-cuts of analysis made in the wrong place and in the wrong direction, useful enough for some purposes no doubt, but for this present purpose very confusing. We shall do well to put them out of mind for a while if possible.

The chief departure made from current conceptions in the sketch of the mind given in Chapter Eleven lay in the substitution of the *causes*, the *characters* and the *consequences* of a mental event, for its aspects as *thought, feeling* and *will*. This treatment was introduced with a view to the analysis which now occupies us. Among the causes of most mental events, we urged, two sets may be distinguished. On the one hand there are the present stimuli reaching the mind through the sensory nerves, and, in co-operation with these, the effects of past stimuli associated with them. On the other hand is a set of quite different factors, the state of the organism, its needs, its readiness to respond to this or that kind of stimulus. The impulses which arise take their character and their course from the interaction of these two sets. We must keep them clearly distinguished.

The relative importance of the two sets of factors varies enormously. A sufficiently hungry man will eat almost anything which can be chewed or swallowed. The nature of the substance, within these limits, has very little effect upon his behaviour. A replete person, by contrast, will only eat such things as he expects will taste pleasant, or regards as possessing definite beneficial properties, for example, medicines. His behaviour, in other words, depends almost entirely upon the character of his optical or olfactory stimulation.

So far as an impulse owes its character to its stimulus (or to such effects of past accompanying or connected stimuli as are revived) so far is it a *reference*, to use the term which we introduced in Chapter Eleven, to stand for the property of mental events which we substitute for thought or cognition.[1] It is plain that the independent internal conditions of the organism usually intervene to distort reference in some degree. But very many of our needs can only be satisfied if the impulses are left undistorted. Bitter experience has taught us to leave some of them alone, to let them reflect or correspond with external states of affairs as much as they can, undisturbed as far as possible by internal states of affairs, our needs and desires.

In all our behaviour can be distinguished stimuli we receive, and the ways in which we use them. What we receive may be any kind of stimulus, but only when the reaction we make to it tallies with its nature and varies with it in quasi-independence of the uses we make of it does reference occur.

Those to whom visual images are of service in considering complex matters may find it convenient at this point to imagine a circle or sphere constantly bombarded by minute particles (stimuli). Within the sphere may be pictured complex mechanisms continually changing for reasons having nothing to do with the external stimuli. These mechanisms by opening little gateways select which of the stimuli shall be allowed to come in and take effect. So far as the subsequent convulsions are due to the nature of the impacts and to lingering effects of impacts which have accompanied similar impacts in the past, the convulsions are referential. So far as they are due to the independent motions of the internal mechanisms themselves, reference fails. This diagrammatic image may possibly be of convenience to some. By those who distrust such things it may with advantage be disregarded. It is not introduced as a contribution to neurology, and is in no way a ground for the author's view.

[1] The reader who is a psychologist will notice many points in this statement at which elaboration and qualifications are required. For example, when we are 'introspecting' factors normally belonging to the second set may enter the first. But he will be able, if he grasps the general theory, to supply these complications himself. I did not wish to burden the text with unnecessary intricacies.

The extent to which reference is interfered with by needs and desires is underestimated even by those who, not having yet forgotten the events of 1914–1918, are most sceptical as to the independence of opinions and desires. Even the most ordinary and familiar objects are perceived as it pleases us to perceive them rather than as they are, whenever error does not directly deprive us of advantages. It is almost impossible for anyone to secure a correct impression of his own personal appearance or of the features of anyone in whom he is personally interested. Nor is it perhaps often desirable that he should.

For the demarcation of the fields where impulse should be as completely as possible dependent upon and correspondent with external situation, those in which reference should take prior place from those in which it may be subordinated to appetencies with advantage, is not a simple matter. On many views of the good and of what should be, themselves results of subordinating reference to emotional satisfactions, there could be no question. Truth, it would be said, has claims prior to all other consider-ations. Love not grounded upon knowledge would be described as worthless. We ought not to admire what is not beautiful and if our mistress be not really beautiful when impartially considered we ought, so the doctrine runs, to admire her, if at all, for other reasons. The chief points of interest about such views are the confusions which make them plausible. Beauty as an internal quality of things is usually involved, as well as Good the unanalysable Idea. Both are special twists given to some of our impulses by habits deriving ultimately from desires. They linger in our minds because to think of a thing as Good or Beautiful gives more immediate emotional satisfaction than to refer to it as satisfying our impulses in one special fashion (cf. Chapter Seven) or another (cf. Chapter Thirty-two).

To think about Good or Beauty is not necessarily to refer to anything. For the term 'thinking' covers mental operations in which the impulses are so completely governed by internal factors and so out of control of stimulus that no reference occurs. Most 'thinking of' includes reference in some degree, of course, but not all, and similarly much reference would not commonly be described as thinking. When we drop something which is too hot to hold we would not usually be said to have done so through thinking. The two terms overlap, and their definitions, if there be a definition of 'thinking' as commonly used, are of different types. This is why 'Thought' was on an earlier page described as marking an oblique distinction.

To return, the claims of reference are by no means easy to adjust with other claims. An immense extension of our powers of referring has recently been made. With amazing swiftness Science has opened out field after field of possible reference. Science is simply the organization of references with a view solely to the convenience and facilitation of reference. It has advanced mainly because other claims, typically the claims of our religious desires, have been set aside. For it is no accident that Science and Religion conflict. They are different principles upon which impulses may be organized, and the more closely they are examined the more inevitable is the incompatibility seen to be. Any so-called reconciliation which is ever effected will involve bestowing the name Religion upon something utterly different from any of the systematizations of impulses which it now denotes, for the reason that the belief elements present would have a different character.

Many attempts have been made to reduce Science to a position of subjection to some instinct or emotion or desire, to curiosity for example. A special passion for knowledge for its own sake has even been invented. But in fact all the passions and all the instincts, all human needs and desires may *on occasion* supply the motive force for Science. There is no human activity which may not on occasion require undistorted reference. The essential point, however, is that Science is autonomous. The impulses developed in it are modified only by one another, with a view to the greatest possible completeness and systematization, and for the facilitation of further references. So far as other considerations distort them they are not yet Science or have fallen out of it.

To declare Science autonomous is very different from subordinating all our activities to it. It is merely to assert that so far as any body of references is undistorted it belongs to Science. It is not in the least to assert that no references may be distorted if advantage can thereby be gained. And just as there are innumerable human activities which require undistorted references if they are to be satisfied, so there are innumerable other human activities not less important which equally require distorted references or, more plainly, *fictions*.

The use of fictions, the imaginative use of them rather, is not a way of hoodwinking ourselves. It is not a process of pretending to ourselves that things are not as they are. It is perfectly compatible with the fullest and grimmest recognition of the exact state of affairs on all occasions. It is no make-believe. But so awkwardly have our references and our attitudes become entangled that such pathetic spectacles as Mr. Yeats trying desperately to believe in fairies or Mr. Lawrence impugning the validity of solar physics, are all too common. To be forced by desire into any unwarrantable belief is a calamity. The state which ensues is often extraordinarily damaging to the mind. But this common misuse of fictions should not blind us to their immense services provided we do not take them for what they are not, degrading the chief means by which our attitudes to actual life may be adjusted into the material of a long-drawn delirium.[1]

---

[1] Revelation Doctrines when once given a foothold tend to interfere everywhere. They serve as a kind of omnipotent major premise justifying any and every conclusion. A specimen: 'Since the function of Art is to pierce through to the Real World, then it follows that the artist cannot be too definite in his outlines, and that good drawing is the foundation of all good art.' – Charles Gardner, *Vision and Vesture*, p. 54.

If we knew enough it might be possible that all necessary attitudes could be obtained through scientific references alone. Since we do not know very much yet, we can leave this very remote possibility, once recognized, alone.

Fictions whether aroused by statements or by analogous things in other arts may be used in many ways. They may be used, for example, to deceive. But this is not a characteristic use in poetry. The distinction which needs to be kept clear does not set up fictions in opposition to verifiable truths in the scientific sense. A statement may be used for the sake of the *reference*, true or false, which it causes. This is the *scientific* use of language. But it may also be used for the sake of the effects in emotion and attitude produced by the reference it occasions. This is the *emotive* use of language. The distinction once clearly grasped is simple. We may either use words for the sake of the references they promote, or we may use them for the sake of the attitudes and emotions which ensue. Many arrangements of words evoke attitudes without any reference being required *en route*. They operate like musical phrases. But usually references are involved as *conditions* for, or *stages in*, the ensuing development of attitudes, yet it is still the attitudes not the references which are important. It matters not at all in such cases whether the references are true or false. Their sole function is to bring about and support the attitudes which are the further response. The questioning, verificatory way of handling them is irrelevant, and in a competent reader it is not allowed to interfere. 'Better a plausible impossibility than an improbable possibility' said Aristotle very wisely; there is less danger of an inappropriate reaction.

The differences between the mental processes involved in the two cases are very great, though easily overlooked. Consider what failure for each use amounts to. For scientific language a difference in the references is itself failure: the end has not been attained. But for emotive language the widest differences in reference are of no importance if the further effects in attitude and emotion are of the required kind.

Further, in the scientific use of language not only must the references be correct for success, but the connections and relations of references to one another must be of the kind which we call logical. They must not get in one another's way, and must be so organized as not to impede further reference. But for emotive purposes logical arrangement is not necessary. It may be and often is an obstacle. For what matters is that the series of attitudes due to the references should have their own proper organization, their own emotional interconnection, and this often has no dependence upon the logical relations of such references as may be concerned in bringing the attitudes into being.

A few notes of the chief uses of the word 'Truth' in Criticism may help to prevent misunderstanding:

1. The scientific sense that, namely, in which references, and derivatively statements symbolizing references, are true, need not delay us. A reference is true when the things to which it refers are actually together in the way in which it refers to them Otherwise it is false. This sense is one very little involved by any of the arts. For the avoidance of confusions it would be well if the term 'true' could be reserved for this use. In purely scientific discourse it could and should be, but such discourse is uncommon. In point of fact the emotive power which attaches to the word is far too great for it to be abandoned in general discussion; the temptation to a speaker who needs to stir certain emotions and evoke certain attitudes of approval and acceptance is overwhelming. No matter how various the senses in which it may be used, and even when it is being used in no sense whatever, its effects in promoting attitudes will still make it indispensable; people will still continue to use the word with the same promiscuity as ever.

2. The most usual other sense is that of acceptability. The 'Truth' of *Robinson Crusoe* is the acceptability of the things we are

told, their acceptability in the interests of the effects of the narrative, not their correspondence with any actual facts involving Alexander Selkirk or another. Similarly the falsity of happy endings to *Lear* or to *Don Quixote*, is their failure to be acceptable to those who have fully responded to the rest of the work. It is in this sense that 'Truth' is equivalent to 'internal necessity' or rightness. That is 'true' or 'internally necessary' which completes or accords with the rest of the experience, which co-operates to arouse our ordered response, whether the response of Beauty or another. 'What the Imagination seizes as Beauty must be Truth', said Keats, using this sense of 'Truth', though not without confusion. Sometimes it is held that whatever is redundant or otiose, whatever is not required, although not obstructive or disruptive, is also false. 'Surplusage!' said Pater, 'the artist will dread that, as the runner on his muscles'[1] himself perhaps in this instance sweating his sentence down too finely. But this is to make excessive demands upon the artist. It is to apply the axe of retrenchment in the wrong place. Superabundance is a common characteristic of great art, much less dangerous than the preciousness that too contrived an economy tends to produce. The essential point is whether what is unnecessary interferes or not with the rest of the response. If it does not, the whole thing is all the better probably for the extra solidity which it thereby gains.

This internal acceptability or 'convincingness' needs to be contrasted with other acceptabilities. Thomas Rymer, for example, refused to accept Iago for external reasons: 'To entertain the audience with something new and surprising against common sense and nature, he would pass upon us a close, dissembling rascal, instead of all open-hearted, frank, plain-dealing Souldier, a character constantly born by them for some thousands of years

[1] *Essay on Style*, p. 19.

in the World.' 'The truth is,' he observes, 'this author's head was full of villainous, unnatural images'.[1]

He is remembering no doubt Aristotle's remark that 'the artist must preserve the type and yet ennoble it', but interpreting it in his own way. For him the type is fixed simply by convention and his acceptances take no note of internal necessities but are governed merely by accordance with external canons. His is an extreme case, but to avoid his error in subtler matters is in fact sometimes the hardest part of the critic's undertaking. But whether our conception of the type is derived in some such absurd way, or taken, for example, as from a handbook of zoology, is of slight consequence. It is the taking of any *external* canon which is critically dangerous. When in the same connection Rymer objects that there never was a Moorish General in the service of the Venetian Republic, he is applying another external canon, that of historic fact. This mistake is less insidious, but Ruskin used to be particularly fond of the analogous mistake in connection with the 'truth' of drawing.

3 Truth may be equivalent to Sincerity. This character of the artist's work we have already touched upon briefly in connection with Tolstoy's theory of communication (Chapter Twenty-three). It may perhaps be most easily defined from the critic's point of view negatively, as the absence of any apparent attempt on the part of the artist to work effects upon the reader which do not work for himself. Too simple definitions must be avoided. It is well known that Burns in writing '*Ae fond kiss?* was only too anxious to escape *Nancy's* (Mrs. Maclehose's) attentions, and similar instances could be multiplied indefinitely. Absurdly naïve views upon the matter[2] exemplified by the opinion that Bottomley must have believed himself to be inspired or he would not have moved his audiences, are far too common. At the

[1] *A Short View of Tragedy.*
[2] Cf. A. Clutton-Brock, *The Times,* 11th July 1922, p. 13.

level at which Bottomley harangued any kind of exaltation in the orator, whether due to pride or to champagne, would make his stuff effective. But at Burns's level a very different situation arises. Here his probity and sincerity *as an artist* are involved; external circumstances are irrelevant, but there is perhaps internal evidence in the poem of a flaw in its creating impulse. Compare as a closely similar poem in which there is no flaw, Byron's '*When we two parted*'.

35

POETRY AND BELIEFS

What I see very well is the wide-spread, infinite harm of putting fancy for knowledge (to speak like Socrates), or rather of living by choice in a twilight of the mind where fancy and knowledge are indiscernible.

Euripides the Rationalist

It is evident that the bulk of poetry consists of statements which only the very foolish would think of attempting to verify. They are not the kind of things which can be verified. If we recall what was said in Chapter Sixteen as to the natural generality or vagueness of reference we shall see another reason why references as they occur in poetry are rarely susceptible of scientific truth or falsity. Only references which are brought into certain highly complex and very special combinations, so as to correspond to the ways in which things actually hang together, can be either true or false, and most references in poetry are not knit together in this way.

But even when they are, on examination, frankly false, this is no defect. Unless, indeed, the obviousness of the falsity forces the reader to reactions which are incongruent or disturbing to the poem. And equally, a point more often misunderstood, their truth, when they are true, is no merit.[1] The people who say 'How True!' at intervals while reading Shakespeare are misusing his work, and, comparatively speaking, wasting their time. For all that matters in either case is acceptance, that is to say, the initiation and development of the further response.

Poetry affords the clearest examples of this subordination of reference to attitude. It is the supreme form of *emotive* language. But there can be no doubt that originally all language was emotive; its scientific use is a later development, and most language is still emotive. Yet the late development has come to seem the natural and the normal use, largely because the only people who have reflected upon language were at the moment of reflection using it scientifically.

The emotions and attitudes resulting from a statement used emotively need not be directed towards anything to which the statement refers. This is clearly evident in dramatic poetry, but much more poetry than is usually supposed is dramatic in structure. As a rule a statement in poetry arouses attitudes much more wide and general in direction than the references of the statement. Neglect of this fact makes most verbal analysis of poetry irrelevant. And the same is true of those critical but emotive utterances about poetry which gave rise to this discussion. No

[1] No merit, that is, in *this connection*. There may be some exceptions to this, cases in which the explicit recognition of the truth of a statement as opposed to the simple acceptance of it, is *necessary* to the full development of the further response. But I believe that such cases will on careful examination be found to be very rare with competent readers, Individual differences, corresponding to the different degrees to which individuals have their belief feelings, their references, and their attitudes entangled, are to be expected. There are, of course, an immense number of scientific beliefs present among the conditions of every attitude. But since acceptances would do equally well in their place they are not *necessary* to it.

one, it is plain, can read poetry successfully without, consciously or unconsciously, observing the distinction between the two uses of words. That does not need to be insisted upon. But further no one can understand such utterances about poetry as that quoted from Dr. Mackail in our third chapter, or Dr. Bradley's cry that 'Poetry is a spirit', or Shelley's that 'A poem is the very image of life expressed in its eternal truth', or the passages quoted above from Coleridge, without distinguishing the making of a statement from the incitement or expression of an attitude. But too much inferior poetry has been poured out as criticism, too much sack and too little bread; confusion between the two activities, on the part of writers and readers alike, is what is primarily responsible for the backwardness of critical studies. What other stultifications of human endeavour it is also responsible for we need not linger here to point out. The separation of prose from poetry, if we may so paraphrase the distinction, is no mere academic activity. There is hardly a problem outside mathematics which is not complicated by its neglect, and hardly any emotional response which is not crippled by irrelevant intrusions. No revolution in human affairs would be greater than that which a widespread observance of this distinction would bring about.

One perversion in especial needs to be noticed. It is constantly present in critical discussion, and is in fact responsible for Revelation Doctrines. Many attitudes, which arise without dependence upon any reference, merely by the interplay and resolution of impulses otherwise awakened, can be momentarily encouraged by suitable beliefs held as scientific beliefs are held. So far as this encouragement is concerned, the truth or falsity of these beliefs does not matter, the immediate effect is the same in either case. When the attitude is important, the temptation to base it upon some reference which is treated as established scientific truths are treated is very great, and the poet thus easily comes to invite the destruction of his work; Wordsworth put forward his

Pantheism, and other people doctrines of Inspiration, Idealism and Revelation.

The effect is twofold; an appearance of security and stability is given to the attitude, which thus seems to be justified; and at the same time it is no longer so necessary to sustain this attitude by the more difficult means peculiar to the arts, or to pay full attention to form. The reader can be relied upon to do more than his share. That neither effect is desirable is easily seen. The attitude for the sake of which the belief is introduced is thereby made not more but less stable. Remove the belief, once it has affected the attitude; the attitude collapses. It may later be restored by more appropriate means, but that is another matter. And all such beliefs are very likely to be removed; their logical connections with other beliefs scientifically entertained are, to say the least, shaky. In the second place these attitudes, produced not by the appropriate means but, as it were by a short cut, through beliefs, are rarely so healthy, so vigorous and full of life as the others. Unlike attitudes normally produced they usually require an increased stimulus every time that they are reinstated. The belief has to grow more and more fervent, more and more convinced, in order to produce the same attitude. The believer has to pass from one paroxysm of conviction to another, enduring each time a greater strain.

This substitution of an intellectual formula for the poem or work of art is of course most easily observed in the case of religion, where the temptation is greatest. In place of an experience, which is a direct response to a certain selection of the possibilities of stimulation, we have a highly indirect response, made, not to the actual influences of the world upon us, but to a special kind of belief as to some particular state of affairs.[1] There

[1] In view of a possible misunderstanding at this point, compare Chapter Ten, especially the final paragraph. If a belief in Retributive Justice, for example, is fatal to *Prometheus Unbound*, so in another way is the belief that the Millennium is at hand. To steer an unperplexed path between these opposite dangers is

is a suppressed conditional clause implicit in all poetry. If things were such and such then. . . and so the response develops. The amplitude and fineness of the response, its sanction and authority, in other words, depend upon this freedom from actual assertion in all cases in which the belief is questionable on any ground whatsoever. For any such assertion involves suppressions, of indefinite extent, which may be fatal to the wholeness, the integrity of the experience. And the assertion is almost always unnecessary; if we look closely we find that the greatest poets, as poets, though frequently not as critics, refrain from assertion. But it is easy, by what seems only a slight change of approach, to make the initial step an act of faith, and to make the whole response dependent upon a belief as to a matter of fact. Even when the belief is true, the damage done to the whole experience may be great, in the case of a person whose reasons for this belief are inadequate, for example, and the increased temporary vivacity which is the cause of perversion is no sufficient compensation. As a convenient example it may be permisible to refer to the Poet Laureate's anthology, *The Spirit of Man*, and I have the less hesitation since the passages there gathered together are chosen with such unerring taste and discrimination. But to turn them into a statement of a philosophy is very noticeably to degrade them and to restrict and diminish their value. The use of verse quotations as chapter headings is open to the same objection. The experiences which ensue may seem very similar to the experiences of free reading; they feel similar; but all the signs which can be most trusted, after-effects for example, show them to be different. The vast differences in the means by which they are brought about is also good ground for supposing them to be dissimilar, but this difference is obscured through the ambiguities of the term 'belief'.

extremely difficult. The distinctions required are perhaps better left to the reader's reflection than laboured further in the faulty terminology which alone at present is available.

There are few terms which are more troublesome in psychology than belief, formidable though this charge may seem. The sense in which we believe a scientific proposition is not the sense in which we believe emotive utterances, whether they are political 'We will not sheathe the sword', or critical 'The progress of poetry is immortal', or poetic. Both senses of belief are complicated and difficult to define. Yet we commonly appear to assume that they are the same or that they differ only in the kind and degree of evidence available. Scientific belief we may perhaps define as readiness to act as though the reference symbolized by the proposition which is believed were true. Readiness to act in *all* circumstances and in *all* connections into which it can enter. This rough definition would, of course, need elaborating to be complete, but for our present purposes it may suffice. The other element usually included in a definition of belief, namely a feeling or emotion of acceptance, the 'This is sooth, accept it!' feeling, is often absent in scientific belief and is not essential.

Emotive belief is very different. Readiness to act as though some references were true is often involved, but the connections and circumstances in which this readiness remains are narrowly restricted. Similarly the extent of the action is ordinarily limited. Consider the acceptances involved in the understanding of a play, for example. They form a system any element of which is believed while the rest are believed and so long as the acceptance of the whole growing system leads to successful response. Some, however, are of the form 'Given this then that would follow', general beliefs, that is to say, of the kind which led Aristotle, in the passage quoted above, to describe Poetry as a more philosophical thing than history because chiefly conversant of universal truth. But if we look closely into most instances of such beliefs we see that they are entertained only in the special circumstances of the poetic experience. They are held as conditions for further effects, our attitudes and emotional responses, and not as we hold beliefs in laws of nature, which we expect to find verified on all occasions. If dramatic necessities were actually scientific laws we should know much more psychology than any reasonable person pretends that we do. That these beliefs as to 'how any person of a certain character would speak or act, probably or necessarily', upon which so much drama seems to depend, are not scientific, but are held only for the sake of their dramatic effect, is shown clearly by thc ease with which we abandon them if the advantage lies the other way. The medical impossibility of Desdemona's last speech is perhaps as good an example as any.

The bulk of the beliefs involved in the arts are of this kind, provisional acceptances, holding only in special circumstances (in the state of mind which is the poem or work of art) acceptances made for the sake of the 'imaginative experience' which they make possible. The difference between these emotive beliefs and scientific beliefs is not one of degree but of kind. As feelings they are very similar, but as attitudes their difference in structure has widespread consequences.

There remains to be discussed another set of emotive effects which may also be called beliefs. Instead of occurring part way in, or at the beginning of a response, they come as a rule at the end, and thus are less likely to be confused with scientific beliefs. Very often the whole state of mind in which we are left by a poem, or by music, or, more rarely perhaps, by other forms of art, is of a kind which it is natural to describe as a belief. When all provisional acceptances have lapsed, when the single references and their connections which may have led up to the final response are forgotten, we may still have an attitude and an emotion which has to introspection all the characters of a belief. This belief, which is a consequence not a cause of the experience, is the chief source of the confusion upon which Revelation Doctrines depend.

If we ask what in such cases it is which is believed, we are likely to receive, and to offer, answers both varied and vague. For strong belief-feelings, as is well known and as is shown by certain doses of alcohol or hashish, and pre-eminently of nitrous oxide, will readily attach themselves to almost any reference, distorting it to suit their purpose. Few people without experience of the nitrous-oxide revelation have any conception of their capacity for believing or of the extent to which belief-feelings and attitudes are parasitic. Thus when, through reading *Adonais*, for example, we are left in a strong emotional attitude which feels like belief, it is only too easy to think that we are believing in immortality or survival, or in something else capable of statement, and fatally easy also to attribute the value of the poem to the alleged effect, or conversely to regret that it should depend upon such a scientifically doubtful conclusion. Scientific beliefs, as opposed to these emotive beliefs, are beliefs '*that* so and so'. They can be stated with greater or less precision, as the case may be, but always in some form. It is for some people difficult to admit beliefs which are objectless, which are not about anything or in anything; beliefs which cannot be stated. Yet most of the beliefs of children and primitive peoples, and of the unscientific generally seem to be of this kind. Their parasitic nature helps to confuse the issue. What we have to distinguish are beliefs which are grounded in fact, i.e., are due to reference, and beliefs which are due to other causes, and merely attach themselves to such references as will support them.

That an objectless belief is a ridiculous or an incomplete thing is a prejudice deriving only from confusion. Such beliefs have, of course, no place in science, but in themselves they are often of the utmost value. Provided always that they do not furnish themselves with illicit objects. It is the objectless belief which is masquerading as a belief in this or that, which is ridiculous; more often than not it is also a serious nuisance. When they are kept from tampering with the development of reference such emotional attitudes may be, as revelation doctrines in such strange forms maintain, among the most important and valuable effects which the arts can produce.

It is often held that recent generations suffer more from nervous strain than some at least of their predecessors, and many reasons for this have been suggested. Certainly the types of nervous disease most prevalent seem to have changed. An explanation not sufficiently noticed perhaps is the break-down of traditional accounts of the universe, and the strain imposed by the vain attempt to orient the mind by belief of the scientific kind alone. In the pre-scientific era, the devout adherent to the Catholic account of the world, for example, found a sufficient basis for nearly all his main attitudes in what he took to be scientific truth. It would be fairer to say that the difference between ascertained fact and acceptable fiction did not obtrude itself for him. Today this is changed, and if he believes such an account, he does not do so, if intelligent, without considerable difficulty or without a fairly persistent strain. The complete sceptic, of course, is a new phenomenon, dissenters in the past having commonly disbelieved only because they held a different belief of the same kind. These topics have, it is true, been touched upon by psycho-analysts, but not with a very clear understanding of the situation. The Vienna School would merely have us away with antiquated lumber; the Zurich School would hand us a new outfit of superstitions. Actually what is needed is a habit of mind which allows both reference and the development of attitudes their proper independence. This habit of mind is not to be attained at once, or for most people with ease. We try desperately to support our attitudes with beliefs as to facts, verified or accepted as scientifically established, and by so doing we weaken our own emotional backbone. For the justification of any attitude *per se* is its success for the needs of the being. It is not justified by the soundness of the views which may seem to be, and in pathological cases are, its ground and causes. The source of our attitudes should be in experience itself; compare

Whitman's praise of the cow which does not worry about its soul. Opinion as to matters of fact, knowledge, belief, are not necessarily involved in any of our attitudes to the world in general, or to particular phases of it. If we bring them in, if, by a psychological perversion only too easy to fall into, we make them the basis of our adjustment, we run extreme risks of later disorganization elsewhere.

Many people find great difficulty in accepting or even in understanding this position. They are so accustomed to regarding 'recognized facts' as the natural basis of attitudes, that they cannot conceive how anyone can be otherwise organized. The hard-headed positivist and the convinced adherent of a religion from opposite sides encounter the same difficulty. The first at the best suffers from an insufficient material for the development of his attitudes; the second from intellectual bondage and unconscious insincerity. The one starves himself; the other is like the little pig in the fable who chose to have his house built of cabbages and ate it, and so the grim wolf with privy paw devoured him. For clear and impartial awareness of the nature of the world in which we live and the development of attitudes which will enable us to live in it finely are both necessities, and neither can be subordinated to the other. They are almost independent, such connections as exist in well-organized individuals being adventitious. Those who find this a hard saying may be invited to consider the effect upon them of those works of art which most unmistakably attune them to existence. The central experience of Tragedy and its chief value is an attitude indispensable for a fully developed life. But in the reading of King Lear what facts verifiable by science, or accepted and believed in as we accept and believe in ascertained facts, are relevant? None whatever. Still more clearly in the experiences of some music, of some architecture and of some abstract design, attitudes are evoked and developed which are unquestionably independent of all beliefs as to fact, and these are exceptional only in being protected by accident from the most insidious perversion to which the mind is liable. For the intermingling of knowledge and belief is indeed a perversion, through which both activities suffer degradation.

These objectless beliefs, which though merely attitudes seem to be knowledge, are not difficult to explain. Some system of impulses not ordinarily in adjustment within itself or adjusted to the world finds something which orders it or gives it fit exercise. Then follows the peculiar sense of ease, of restfulness, of free, unimpeded activity, and the feeling of acceptance, of something more positive than acquiescence. This feeling is the reason why such states may be called beliefs. They share this feeling with, for example, the state which follows the conclusive answering of a question. Most attitude-adjustments which are successful possess it in some degree, but those which are very regular and familiar, such as sitting down to meat or stretching out in bed, naturally tend to lose it. But when the required attitude has been long needed, where its coming is unforeseen and the manner in which it is brought about complicated and inexplicable, where we know no more than that formerly we were unready and that now we are ready for life in some particular phase, the feeling which results may be intense. Such are the occasions upon which the arts seem to lift away the burden of existence, and we seem ourselves to be looking into the heart of things. To be seeing whatever it is as it really is, to be cleared in vision and to be recpients of a revelation.

We have considered already the detail of these states of consciousness and their conjectural impulse basis. We can now take this feeling of a revealed significance, this attitude of readiness, acceptance and understanding, which has led to so many Revelation Doctrines, not as actually implying knowledge, but for what it is – the conscious accompaniment of our successful adjustment to life. But it is, we must admit, no certain sign by itself that our adjustment is adequate or admirable. Even the most firm adherents to Revelation Doctrines admit that there are bogus revelations, and on our account it is equally important to distinguish between 'feelings of significance' which indicate that all is well and those which do not. In a sense all indicate that *something* is going well, otherwise there would be no acceptance, no belief but rejection. The real question is 'What is it?' Thus after the queer reshuffling of inhibitions and releases which follows the taking of a dose of alcohol, for example, the sense of revelation is apt to occur with unusual authority. Doubtless this feeling of significance is a sign that as the organism is for the moment, its affairs are for the moment thriving. But when the momentary special condition of the system has given place to the more usual, more stable and more generally advantageous adjustment, the authority of the vision falls away from it; we find that what we were doing is by no means so wonderful or so desirable as we thought and that our belief-was nonsensical. So it is less noticeably with many moments in which the world seems to be showing its real face to us.

The chief difficulty of all Revelation Doctrines has always been to discover what it is which is revealed. If these states of mind are knowledge it should be possible to state what it is that they know. It is often easy enough to find something which we can suppose to be what we know. Belief feelings, we have seen, are *parasitic*, and will attach themselves to all kinds of hosts. In literature it is especially easy to find hosts. But in music, in the non-representative arts of design, in architecture or ceramics, for example, the task of finding something to believe, or to believe in, is not so easy. Yet the 'feeling of significance' is as common[1]

---

[1] Cf. Gurney, *The Power of Sound*, p. 126. 'A splendid melodic phrase seems continually not like an object of sense, but like an *affirmation*; not so much prompting admiring ejaculation as compelling passionate assent.' His explanation, through association with speech, seems to me inadequate. He adds that the use of terms such as '*expressiveness and significance*, as opposed to

in these other arts as in literature. Denial of this is usually proof only of an interest limited to literature.

The difficulty has usually been met by asserting that the alleged knowledge given in the revelation is non-intellectual. It refuses to be rationalized, it is said. Well and good; but if so why call it knowledge? Either it is capable of corroborating or of conflicting with the other things we usually call knowledge, such as the laws of thermo-dynamics, capable of being stated and brought into connection with what else we know; or it is not knowledge, not capable of being stated. We cannot have it both ways, and no sneers at the limitations of logic, the commonest of the resources of the confused, amend the dilemma. In fact it resembles knowledge only in being an attitude and a feeling very similar to some attitudes and feelings which may and often do accompany knowledge. But 'Knowledge' is an immensely potent emotive word engendering reverence towards any state of mind to which it is applied. And these 'feelings of significance' are those among our states of mind which most deserve to be revered. That they should be so obstinately described as knowledge even by those who most carefully remove from them all the characteristics of knowledge is not surprising.

Traditionally what is said to be known thus mystically through the arts is Beauty, a remote and divine entity not otherwise to be apprehended, one of the Eternal Absolute Values. And this is doubtless emotively a way of talking which is effective for a while. When its power abates, as the power of such utterances will, there are several developments which may easily be used to revive it. 'Beauty is eternal, and we may say that it is already manifest as a heavenly thing – the beauty of Nature is indeed an

meaninglessness and triviality, may be allowed, without the implication of any reference to transcendental views which one may fail to understand, or theories of interpretation which one may entirely repudiate.'

earnest to us of the ultimate goodness which lies behind the apparent cruelty and moral confusion of organic life. . . . Yet we feel that these three are ultimately one, and human speech bears constant witness to the universal conviction that Goodness is beautiful, that Beauty is good, that Truth is Beauty. We can hardly avoid the use of the word 'trinity', and if we are theists at all we cannot but say that they are one, because they are the manifestation of one God. If we are not theists there is no explanation.'[1]

Human speech is indeed the witness, and to what else does it not witness? It would be strange if in a matter of such moment as this the greatest of all emotive words did not come into play. 'In religion we believe that God is Beauty and Life, that God is Truth and Light, that God is Goodness and Love, and that because he is all these they are all one, and the Trinity in Unity and Unity in Trinity is to be worshipped.'[2] No one who can interpret emotive language, who can avoid the temptation to illicit belief so constantly presented by it need find such utterances 'meaningless'. But the wrong approach is easy and far too often pressingly invited by the speakers, labouring themselves under misconceptions. To excite a serious and reverent attitude is one thing. To set forth an explanation is another. To confuse the two and mistake the incitement of an attitude for a statement of fact is a practice which should be discouraged. For intellectual dishonesty is an evil which is the more dangerous the more it is hedged about with emotional sanctities. And after all there is another explanation, which would long ago have been quietly established to the world's great good had men been less ready to sacrifice the integrity of their thought and feeling for the sake of a local and limited advantage.

*

[1] Percy Dearmer, *The Necessity of Art*, p. 180.
[2] A W. Pollard, *ibidem*, p. 135.

The last movement of this machine to think with is now completed. I am too well acquainted with it, and have spent too many hours putting it together to suppose that it can be worked equally well by every reader. Half these hours have in fact been spent in simplifying its structure, in taking out reservations and qualifications, references to other views, controversial matter, and supernumerary distinctions. From one point of view, it would be a better book with these left in, but I wished to make it manageable by those who had not spent a quite disproportionate amount of energy in reflection upon abstract matters. And if to some readers parts of it appear unnecessary – either *irrelevant*, in the one case; or *over-obvious* in the other – I have nothing to add which would make them change their opinion. The first I can only ask to look again, with the hope that a connection which has been missed will be noticed. The second, I would remind that I write in an age when, in the majority of social circles, to be seriously interested in art is to be thought an oddity.

APPENDIX A

On value

A friendly reviewer, Mr. Conrad Aiken, complains that my theory of value is not sufficiently relativistic, that it inevitably involves the surreptitious re-entrance of the 'absolute' value which we had been at such pains to exclude. Except for the word 'surreptitious' and the suggestion that the 'absolute' value we arrive at is the same thing as the ultimate idea discussed in Chapter Six, I agree to this. The purpose of the theory is just to enable us to compare different experiences in respect of their value; and their value, I suggest, is a quantitative matter. To put it briefly the best life is that in which as much as possible of our possible personality is engaged. And of two personalities that one is the better in which there is more which can be engaged without confusion. We all know people of unusually wide and varied possibilities who pay for their width in disorder, and we know others who pay for their order by narrowness. What the theory attempts to provide is a system of measurement by which we can compare not only different experiences belonging to the same personality but different personalities. We do not yet know how to make the measurements required. We have to use the roughest kinds of estimates and very indirect indications. But to know at least what would have to be measured if we were to reach precision and how to make the comparison is a step towards the goal. The parallel, though I am not fond of it, between the new absolutism which Relativity has reached and this quantitative way of comparing the experiences and preferences of individuals may perhaps be helpful. But whereas the physicist has measurements to work from, the psychologist as yet has none. And further, it is likely that modes of mental organization which are at present impossible or dangerously unstable may become possible and even easy in the future with changes in social structure and material conditions. This last consideration might give any critic a nightmare. Nothing less than our whole sense of man's history and destiny is involved in our final decision as to value.

APPENDIX B

The poetry of T. S. Eliot

We too readily forget that, unless something is very wrong with our civiization, we should be producing three equal poets at least for every poet of high rank in our great-great-grandfathers' day. Something must indeed be wrong; and since Mr. Eliot is one of the very few poets that current conditions have not overcome, the difficulties which he has faced, and the cognate difficulties which his readers encounter, repay study.

Mr. Eliot's poetry has occasioned an unusual amount of irritated or enthusiastic bewilderment. The bewilderment has several sources. The most formidable is the unobtrusiveness, in some cases the absence, of any coherent intellectual thread upon which the items of the poem are strung. A reader of 'Gerontion', of 'Preludes', or of 'The Waste Land', may, if he will, after repeated readings, introduce such a thread. Another reader after much effort may fail to contrive one. But in either case energy will have been misapplied. For the items are united by the accord, contrast, and interaction of their emotional effects, not by an intellectual scheme that analysis must work out. The value lies in the unified response which this interaction creates in the right reader. The only intellectual activity required takes place in the realization of the separate items. We can, of course, make a 'rationalization' of the whole experience, as we can of any experience. If we do, we are adding something which does not belong to the poem Such a logical scheme is, at best, a scaffolding that vanishes when the poem is constructed. But we have so built into our nervous system a demand for intellectual coherence, even in poetry, that we find a difficulty in doing without it.

This point may be misunderstood for the charge most usually brought against Mr. Elliot's poetry is that it is over-intellectualized. One reason for this is his use of allusion. A reader who in one short poem picks up allusions to *The Aspern Papers*, *Othello*, 'A Toccata of Galuppis', Marston, *The Phoenix and the Turtle*, *Antony and Cleopatra* (twice), 'The Extasie', *Macbeth*, *The Merchant of Venice*, and Ruskin, feels that his wits are being unusually well exercised. He may easily leap to the conclusion that the basis of the poem is in wit also. But this would be a mistake. These things come in, not that the reader may be ingenious or admire the writer's erudition (this last accusation has tempted several critics to disgrace themselves), but for the sake of the emotional aura which they bring and the attitudes they incite. Allusion in Mr. Eliot's hands is a technical device for compression. 'The Waste Land' is the equivalent in content to an epic. Without this device twelve books would have been needed. But these allusions and the notes in which some of them are elucidated have made many a petulant reader turn down his thumb at once. Such a reader has not begun to understand what it is all about.

This objection is connected with another, that of obscurity. To quote a recent pronouncement upon 'The Waste Land' from Mr. Middleton Murry: 'The reader is compelled, in the mere effort to understand, to adopt an attitude of intellectual suspicion, which makes impossible the communication of feeling. The work offends against the most elementary canon of good writing: that the immediate effect should be unambiguous.' Consider first this 'canon'. What would happen, if we pressed it, to Shakespeare's greatest sonnets or to Hamlet? The truth is that very much of the best poetry is necessarily ambiguous in its immediate effect. Even the most careful and responsive reader must read and do hard work before the poem forms itself clearly and unambiguously in his mind. An original poem, as much as a new branch of mathematics, compels the mind which receives it to grow, and this takes time. Anyone who upon reflection asserts the contrary for his own case must be either a demigod or dishonest; probably Mr. Murry was in haste. His remarks show that he has failed in his attempt to read the poem, and they reveal, in part, the reason for his failure – namely, his own over-intellectual approach. To read it successfully he would have to discontinue his present self-mystifications.

The critical question in all cases is whether the poem is worth the trouble it entails. For 'The Waste Land' this is considerable. There is Miss Weston's From Ritual to Romance to read, and its 'astral' trimmings to be discarded – they have nothing to do with Mr. Eliot's poem. There is Canto Twenty-six of the Purgatorio to be studied – the relevance of the close of that canto to the whole of Mr. Eliot's work must be insisted upon. It illuminates his persistent concern with sex, the problem of our generation, as religion was the problem of the last. There is the central position of Tiresias in the poem to be puzzled out – the cryptic form of the note which Mr. Eliot writes on this point is just a little tiresome. It is a way of underlining the fact that the poem is concerned with many aspects of the one fact of sex, a hint that is perhaps neither indispensable nor entirely successful.

When all this has been done by the reader, when the materials with which the words are to clothe themselves have been collected, the poem still remains to be read. And it is easy to fail in this undertaking. An 'attitude of intellectual suspicion' must certainly be abandoned. But this is not difficult to those who still know how to give their feelings precedence to their thoughts, who can accept and unify an experience without trying to catch it in an intellectual net or to squeeze out a doctrine. One form of this attempt must be mentioned. Some, misled no doubt by its origin in a Mystery, have endeavoured to give the poem a symbolical reading. But its symbols are not mystical, but emotional. They stand, that is, not for ineffable objects, but for normal human experience. The poem, in fact, is radically naturalistic; only its compression makes it appear otherwise. And in this it probably comes nearer to the original Mystery which it perpetuates than transcendentalism does.

If it were desired to label in three words the most characteristic feature of Mr. Eliot's technique, this might be done by calling his poetry a 'music of ideas'. The ideas are of all kinds, abstract and concrete, general and particular, and, like the musician's phrases, they are arranged, not that they may tell us something, but that their effects in us may combine into a coherent whole of feeling and attitude and produce a peculiar liberation of the will. They are there to be responded to, not to be pondered or worked out. This is, of course, a method used intermittently in very much poetry, and only an accentuation and isolation of one of its normal resources. The peculiarity of Mr. Eliot's later, more puzzling, work is his deliberate and almost exclusive employment of it. In the earlier poems this logical freedom appears only occasionally. In 'The Love Song of J. Alfred Prufrock', for example, there is a patch at the beginning and another at the end, but the rest of the poem is quite straightforward. In 'Gerontion', the first long poem in this manner, the air of monologue, of a stream of associations, is a kind of disguise, and the last two lines,

> Tenants of the house,
> Thoughts of a dry brain in a dry season,

are almost an excuse. The close of 'A Cooking Egg' is perhaps the passage in which the technique shows itself most clearly. The reader who appreciates the emotional relevance of the title has the key to the later poems in his hand. I take Pipit to be the retired nurse of the hero of the poem, and *Views of the Oxford Colleges* to be the, still treasured, present which he sent her when he went up to the University. The middle section of the poem I read as a specimen of the rather withered pleasantry in which contemporary culture has culminated and beyond which it finds much difficulty in passing. The final section gives the contrast which is pressed home by the title. Even the most mature egg was new laid once. The only other tide of equal significance that I can recall is Mrs. Wharton's *The Age of Innocence*, which might well be studied in this connection. 'The Waste Land' and 'The Hollow Men' (the most beautiful of Mr. Eliot's poems, and in the last section a new development) are purely a 'music of ideas', and the pretence of a continuous thread of associations is dropped.

How this technique lends itself to misunderstandings we have seen. But many readers who have failed in the end to escape bewilderment have begun by finding on almost every line that Mr. Eliot has written – if we except certain youthful poems on American topics – that personal stamp which is the hardest thing for the craftsman to imitate and perhaps the most certain sign that the experience, good or bad, rendered in the poem is authentic. Only those unfortunate persons who are incapable of reading poetry can resist Mr. Eliot's rhythms. The poem as a whole may elude us while every fragment, as a fragment, comes victoriously home. It is difficult to believe that this is Mr. Eliot's fault rather than his reader's, because a parallel case of a poet who so constantly achieves the hardest part of his task and yet fails in the easier is not to be found. It is much more likely that we have been trying to put the fragments together on a wrong principle.

Another doubt has been expressed. Mr. Eliot repeats himself in two ways. The nightingale, Cleopatra's barge, the rats, and the smoky candle-end, recur and recur. Is this a sign of a poverty of inspiration? A more plausible explanation is that this repetition is in part a consequence of the technique above described, and in part something which many writers who are not accused of poverty also show. Shelley, with his rivers, towers, and stars, Conrad, Hardy, Walt Whitman, and Dostoevski spring to mind. When a writer has found a theme or image which fixes a point of relative stability in the drift of experience, it is not to be expected that he will avoid it. Such themes are a means of orientation. And it is quite true that the central process in all Mr. Eliot's best poems is the same; the conjunction of feelings which, though superficially opposed – as squalor, for example, is opposed to grandeur – yet tend as they develop to change places and even to unite. If they do not develop far enough the intention of the poet is missed. Mr. Eliot is neither sighing after vanished glories nor holding contemporary experience up to scorn.

Both bitterness and desolation are superficial aspects of his poetry. There are those who think that he merely takes his readers into the Waste Land and leaves them there, that in his last poem he confesses his impotence to release the healing waters. The reply is that some readers find in his poetry not only a clearer, fuller realization of their plight, the plight of a whole generation, than they find elsewhere, but also through the very energies set free in that realization a return of the saving passion.

INDEX

Routledge Classics
Get inside a great mind

Romantic Image
with a new epilogue by the author
Frank Kermode

'In this extremely important book of speculative and scholarly criticism Mr Kermode is setting out to redefine the notion of the Romantic tradition, especially in relation to English poetry and criticism ... a rich, packed, suggestive book.'
Times Literary Supplement

One of our most brilliant and accomplished critics, Frank Kermode here redefines our conception of the Romantic movement, questioning both society's harsh perception of the artist as well as poking fun at the artist's occasionally inflated self-image. Written with characteristic wit and style, this ingeniously argued and hugely enjoyable book is a classic of its kind.

Hb: 0–415–26186–4   Pb: 0–415–26817–2

Totem and Taboo
Some Points of Agreement between the Mental Lives of Savages and Neurotics
Sigmund Freud

'With *Totem and Taboo* Freud invented evolutionary psychology.'
Oliver James

Widely acknowledged to be one of Freud's greatest cultural works, when *Totem and Taboo* was first published in 1913, it caused outrage. Thorough and thought-provoking, *Totem and Taboo* remains the fullest exploration of Freud's most famous themes. Family, society, religion are all put on the couch here. Freud's theories have influenced every facet of modern life, from film and literature to medicine and art.

Pb: 0–415–25387–X

For these and other classic titles from Routledge, visit
www.routledgeclassics.com

Some titles not available in North America

Routledge Classics
Get inside a great mind

Leonardo da Vinci
A Memory of his Childhood
Sigmund Freud

'Freud's *Leonardo* changed the art of biography forever. Henceforth none would be complete without a rummage through the subject's childhood origins.'
Oliver James

The ultimate prodigy, Leonardo da Vinci was an artist of great originality and power, a scientist, and a powerful thinker. According to Sigmund Freud, he was also a flawed, repressed homosexual. The only biography the great psychoanalyst wrote, it remained Freud's favourite composition. The text includes the first full emergence of the concept of narcissism and develops Freud's theories of homosexuality. While based on controversial research, the book offers a fascinating insight into two men – the subject and the author.

Pb: 0–415–25386–1

The Wheel of Fire
Interpretations of Shakespearian Tragedy
G. Wilson Knight

'I confess that reading his essays seems to me to have enlarged my understanding of the Shakespearean pattern, which, after all, is quite the main thing.'
T. S. Eliot

Originally published in 1930, this classic of modern Shakespeare criticism proves both enlightening and innovative. Standing head and shoulders over all other Shakespearian interpretations, *The Wheel of Fire* is the masterwork of the brilliant English scholar G. Wilson Knight. Founding a new and influential school of Shakespearian criticism, *The Wheel of Fire* was Knight's first venture in the field – his writing sparkles with insight and wit, and his analyses are key to contemporary understandings of Shakespeare.

Hb: 0–415–25561–9   Pb: 0–415–25395–0

For these and other classic titles from Routledge, visit

www.routledgeclassics.com

Routledge Classics

Get inside a great mind

The Pursuit of Signs
Semiotics, literature, deconstruction with a new preface by the author
Jonathan Culler

'Twenty years ago, if you wanted to know where literary theory was at, I'd say
"semiotics", and Culler's *Pursuit of Signs* was the best way to see the links.
Today? Same answer. Overview, criticism, problems and solutions: Culler
offers them all in each chapter, on key topics and questions of the
humanities.'
Mieke Bal, Professor of Theory of Literature, University of Amsterdam

Dancing through semiotics, reader-response criticism, the value of the
apostrophe and much more, Jonathan Culler opens up for every reader the
closed world of literary criticism. To gain a deeper understanding of the
literary movement that has dominated recent Anglo-American literary
criticism, *The Pursuit of Signs* is a must.

Hb: 0–415–25536–8   Pb: 0–415–25382–9

Writing and Difference
Jacques Derrida

'Almost from the moment deconstruction emerged as a glittering force on
the academic scene, its many detractors have been saying that it is "dead".
And yet the term deconstruction has penetrated almost every aspect of
culture.'
New York Times

In the 1960s a radical concept emerged from the great French thinker
Jacques Derrida. He called the new process 'deconstruction'. The academic
community was rocked on a scale hitherto unknown, with *Writing and
Difference* attracting both accolades and derision. Read the book that
changed the way we think; read *Writing and Difference*, the classic
introduction.

Hb: 0–415–25537–6   Pb: 0–415–25383–7

For these and other classic titles from Routledge, visit
www.routledgeclassics.com